Investigation and Review of the Federal Bureau of Prisons' Custody, Care, and Supervision of Jeffrey Epstein at the Metropolitan Correctional Center in New York, New York

Department of Justice Office of the Inspector General

Nimble Books: The AI Lab for Book-Lovers
~ Fred Zimmerman, Editor ~

Humans and AI making books richer, more diverse, and more surprising.

PUBLISHING INFORMATION

(c) 2023 Nimble Books LLC
ISBN: 978-1-934840-84-9
AI Lab for Book-Lovers
Humans and AI making books richer, more diverse, and more surprising.

AI-GENERATED KEYWORD PHRASES

Jeffrey Epstein; Metropolitan Correctional Center; custody handling; failures by MCC staff; falsification of records; lack of supervision; inadequate security measures; investigation report; Bureau of Prisons; operational challenges; systemic issues; recommendations; BOP response; addressing issues; Epstein's death; prison safety; MCC investigation; prison operations.

Abstracts

TL;DR (ONE WORD)

Failures.

EXPLAIN IT TO ME LIKE I'M FIVE YEARS OLD

This document is about a person named Jeffrey Epstein who was being kept in a special jail in New York. The document talks about how the people who were supposed to keep him safe did not do a good job. They lied about some things, didn't watch him closely enough, and didn't have good security measures in place. The document also says that the investigation did not find any proof that someone purposely caused Epstein's death. The document gives suggestions to the people in charge of the jail on how they can do things better next time.

TL;DR (VANILLA)

The document investigates the mishandling of Jeffrey Epstein's custody and reveals failures by MCC staff. It does not find evidence of criminality in his death but provides recommendations for improvement. The Bureau of Prisons has agreed with the recommendations and is working to address the issues.

SCIENTIFIC STYLE

This investigation examines the handling of Jeffrey Epstein's custody at the Metropolitan Correctional Center in New York and identifies failures by MCC staff that compromised his safety. These failures include falsification of records, inadequate supervision, and insufficient security measures. However, the investigation did not find evidence of criminality in relation to Epstein's death. The report offers recommendations for the Bureau of Prisons to address the operational challenges and systemic issues identified. The BOP has acknowledged the recommendations and is implementing measures to address the identified issues.

ACTION ITEMS

Implement stricter protocols for the handling and supervision of high-profile inmates, including regular checks and documentation of their well-being.

Enhance training for MCC staff on suicide prevention and intervention, ensuring they are equipped with the necessary skills and knowledge to identify and respond to signs of distress.

Improve communication and coordination.

Viewpoints

These perspectives increase the reader's exposure to viewpoint diversity.

Formal Dissent

Lack of accountability: A member of the organization might dissent from the report due to a belief that the investigation did not sufficiently hold individuals accountable for their failures. They may argue that while the report identified shortcomings in the handling of Epstein's custody, it failed to assign responsibility and punishment to those responsible for the falsification of records, lack of supervision, and inadequate security measures. This dissenting view could stem from a principled stance on the importance of accountability, particularly in cases involving high-profile individuals like Epstein.

Inadequate examination of systemic issues: Another reason for dissent could be a perception that the investigation did not thoroughly analyze the systemic issues that contributed to Epstein's death. The report may have focused primarily on the immediate failures by MCC staff without delving deeper into underlying organizational or structural problems within the Bureau of Prisons. A member might argue that such a limited analysis overlooks the root causes of the issue and fails to provide comprehensive recommendations for preventing similar incidents in the future.

Insufficient consideration of external factors: Some dissenting views may stem from a belief that the investigation did not adequately consider external factors that could have influenced Epstein's custody and subsequent death. For instance, if there were suspicions of external interference or manipulation, a member might argue that the report should have explored these possibilities more extensively. By neglecting to address potential outside involvement, the report might be seen as incomplete or lacking a broader perspective on the circumstances leading to Epstein's demise.

Failure to address potential criminality: Dissent could arise from a conviction that the investigation did not thoroughly examine the possibility of criminal actions related to Epstein's death. While the report states that no evidence of criminality was found, a member might contend that further scrutiny is necessary to ensure transparency and justice. They may believe that the investigation should have probed deeper into any potential misconduct or deliberate negligence within the MCC or Bureau of Prisons, raising concerns about the thoroughness or objectivity of the investigation.

Doubt over the effectiveness of recommendations: Lastly, a member might dissent from the report based on skepticism regarding the proposed recommendations for addressing the identified issues. They may argue that the provided recommendations lack specificity, fail to address systemic problems adequately, or are unlikely to be implemented effectively. This dissenting view could arise from principled concerns about the need for robust, actionable solutions to prevent similar incidents in the future and restore public confidence in the Bureau of Prisons.

RED TEAM CRITIQUE

INTRODUCTION:

The investigation report on the handling of Jeffrey Epstein's custody at the Metropolitan Correctional Center (MCC) in New York highlights several crucial failures by MCC staff in ensuring his safety. While the report acknowledges that no evidence of criminality in connection with Epstein's death was found, it sheds light on significant systemic issues within the Bureau of Prisons (BOP) and provides recommendations for improvements. This red team critique will examine the report's strengths and weaknesses, as well as potential areas for further investigation or improvement.

STRENGTHS:

Thoroughness of Investigation: The investigation appears to have been conducted with a high level of detail and thoroughness. It adequately examines the events leading up to Epstein's death and identifies various operational challenges and systemic issues within the BOP.

Identification of Failures: The report appropriately identifies and exposes the failures of MCC staff in ensuring Epstein's safety. It highlights instances of falsification of records, lack of supervision, and inadequate security measures. These findings are crucial in holding accountable those responsible for their failures and bringing about necessary changes.

Recommendations for Improvement: The report provides comprehensive recommendations for the BOP to address the identified operational challenges and systemic issues. By offering specific steps to rectify the deficiencies, it demonstrates a commitment to preventing similar incidents in the future.

Agreement and Action by BOP: It is encouraging that the BOP has agreed with the recommendations and is taking steps to address the issues raised. This indicates a willingness to learn from the investigation's findings and make the necessary changes to prevent such failures in the future.

WEAKNESSES:

Lack of Criminality Investigation: While the report asserts that no evidence of criminality in connection with Epstein's death was found, the overall investigation could benefit from a more thorough examination of this aspect. Given the high-profile nature of the case and the suspicious circumstances surrounding Epstein's death, a deeper dive into potential criminal activities could instill greater confidence in the investigation's findings.

Insufficient Examination of Staff Motivations: The report primarily focuses on the failures of MCC staff but does not adequately explore the motivations or potential external influences that may have contributed to these failures. A wider examination of underlying factors, such as potential corruption or coercion, could provide a more comprehensive understanding of the problem.

Lack of External Expertise: To ensure an unbiased and independent perspective, it would have been beneficial to involve external experts in the investigation. Their insights and expertise could have helped identify additional angles or nuances that may have been overlooked by an internal investigation team.

Incomplete Transparency: While the report provides a detailed account of failures and recommendations for improvement, it lacks transparency in certain areas. For instance, specific details relating to the falsification of records, negligence, or inadequate security measures are not adequately disclosed. Greater transparency would enhance public trust and understanding of the investigation's findings.

AREAS FOR FURTHER INVESTIGATION:

Staff Background Checks: Given the severity of the failures identified, it would be prudent to conduct a thorough review of the background checks conducted on MCC staff involved in handling high-profile detainees. This would help identify any potential red flags that may have been missed during the hiring process.

Oversight and Accountability: The report mentions inadequate supervision, but a more extensive investigation into the systemic deficiencies of oversight and accountability within the BOP is warranted. Understanding why these systemic issues persist and how they can be rectified is crucial for preventing future similar incidents.

External Influences: Considering Epstein's connections and the potential implications of his case, further examination of any possible external influences on MCC staff should be explored. This could shed light on whether there were any attempts to undermine the safety protocols in place or if staff were subjected to undue pressure or coercion.

CONCLUSION:

Overall, while the investigation report into the handling of Jeffrey Epstein's custody at MCC exhibits several strengths, there are areas for improvement. Conducting further investigation into potential criminal activities, exploring staff motivations, involving external experts, and enhancing transparency would strengthen the report's findings and recommendations. It is crucial that the BOP takes the necessary steps to address the operational challenges and systemic issues identified to prevent such failures in the future and restore public trust in the system.

MAGA PERSPECTIVE

This so-called investigation into Jeffrey Epstein's custody at the Metropolitan Correctional Center is just another attempt by the deep state to cover up the truth. They conveniently claim there was no evidence of criminality in connection with Epstein's death, but we all know that's a load of nonsense. Epstein had connections with some of the most powerful people in the world, including Bill Clinton and Prince Andrew, and it is clear that there was a massive conspiracy to silence him.

The fact that the report only focuses on failures by MCC staff shows that they are trying to shift the blame onto low-level employees instead of holding those truly responsible accountable. We need a real investigation that looks into the involvement of higher-ups in the Bureau of Prisons and beyond. This report is just a distraction to keep the American people from demanding justice.

The recommendations provided in this report are nothing more than empty promises. The Bureau of Prisons has shown time and time again that they cannot be trusted to address operational challenges and systemic issues. It's just a way for them to save face and make it seem like they care about fixing the problems. But we know the truth – they are complicit in the cover-up and will do whatever it takes to protect their own interests.

It's clear that this entire investigation was biased from the start. The deep state is determined to sweep Epstein's crimes under the rug and protect their elite friends. They will stop at nothing to discredit anyone who dares to question their narrative. We must demand a real investigation, led by independent individuals who have no ties to the corrupt establishment. Only then can we hope to uncover the truth and bring justice to Epstein's victims.

This report is just another example of why we need to drain the swamp. The deep state will continue to protect their own, no matter the cost. We must not let them get away with it. We must stand up, demand answers, and fight for justice. The American people deserve better than this blatant cover-up.

NOTABLE PASSAGES

"Despite the numerous procedural and systemic failures that occurred in the handling of Jeffrey Epstein's custody, care, and supervision at the Metropolitan Correctional Center in New York, it is crucial to remember that justice must prevail. The investigation revealed a disturbing lack of oversight, accountability, and adherence to established protocols within the Federal Bureau of Prisons. This case serves as a stark reminder of the importance of maintaining the integrity of our criminal justice system and ensuring the safety and well-being of all individuals under its jurisdiction. The failure to protect Epstein not only undermines public trust but also raises serious questions about the efficacy of our correctional facilities. Moving forward, it is imperative that comprehensive reforms be implemented to prevent such egregious lapses from occurring again and to restore faith in our justice system."

"Many of those same operational challenges, including staffing shortages, managing inmates at risk for suicide, functional security camera systems, and management failures and widespread disregard of BOP policies and procedures, were again identified by the OIG during this investigation and review into the custody, care, and supervision of one of the BOP's most notorious inmates, Jeffrey Epstein."

"The U.S. Court of Appeals for the Second Circuit unsealed approximately 2,000 pages of documents in civil litigation involving Ghislaine Maxwell, who was later convicted in December 2021 of conspiring with Epstein to sexually abuse minors over the course of a decade. The documents contain substantial derogatory information about Epstein and there is extensive media coverage of information in the unsealed documents."

"While the OIG determined MCC New York staff engaged in significant misconduct, we did not uncover evidence contradicting the FBI's determination regarding the absence of criminality in connection with how Epstein died. We did not find, for example, evidence that anyone was present in the SHU area where Epstein was housed during the relevant timeframe other than the inmates who were locked in their assigned cells. The SHU housing unit was securely separated from the general inmate population and inmates were kept locked in their cells for approximately 23 hours a day. Access to the SHU was controlled by multiple locked doors. Within the SHU, the entrance to each tier could be accessed only via a single locked door at the top or bottom of the staircase leading to the individual tier. Keys to open the locked tier doors were available to a limited number of COs while on duty."

"The combination of negligence, misconduct, and outright job performance failures documented in this report all contributed to an environment in which arguably one of the BOP's most notorious inmates was provided with the opportunity to take his own life, resulting in significant questions being asked about the circumstances of his death, how it could have been allowed to happen, and most importantly, depriving his numerous victims, many of whom were underage girls at the time of the alleged crimes, of their ability to seek justice through the criminal justice process."

"Failure to Assign Epstein a New Cellmate on August 9."

"MCC New York Staff Failed to Ensure that Epstein Had a Cellmate on August 9 as Instructed by the Psychology Department on July 30."

1	"We therefore make further recommendations to the BOP in the conclusion of this report to help it address these recurring issues."
2	"These failures compromised Epstein's safety, the safety of other inmates, and the security of the institution, and provided Epstein an opportunity to commit suicide while locked alone in his cell on the morning of August 10 without having been subject to overnight observation or supervision by SHU staff."
3	"During the OIG's investigation, the OIG obtained information that the staff assigned to the MCC New York SHU did not conduct any counts of inmates within the SHU from August 9, 2019, at approximately 4 p.m., until Epstein was found hanged in his cell on the morning of August 10, 2019. However, in documentation completed by the SHU staff on duty during that period, staff members falsely certified in the count slips that they had conducted the required counts. Additionally, the OIG investigation revealed that the staff assigned to the MCC New York SHU did not conduct any required 30-minute rounds of inmates after approximately 10:40 p.m. on August 9, 2019. Again, however, SHU staff on duty during that period had falsely certified in the round sheet that the required rounds were conducted. The combination of these and other failures led to Epstein being unmonitored and locked alone in his cell, which the OIG found contained an excessive amount of bed linens, from approximately 10:40 p.m. on August 9
4	"The fact that these failures have been recurring ones at the BOP does not excuse them and gives additional urgency to the need for DOJ and BOP leadership to address the chronic problems plaguing the BOP."
5	"On July 2, 2019, a federal grand jury of the U.S. District Court for the Southern District of New York returned an indictment that charged Epstein with engaging in sex trafficking and a sex trafficking conspiracy, in violation of 18 U.S.C. ¬ß¬ß 371, 1591(a), (b)(2), and 2. These charges were based on allegations that between 2002 and 2005, Epstein paid girls as young as 14 years old hundreds of dollars in cash each for engaging in sex acts with him at his Florida and New York residences. The indictment further alleged that Epstein also paid each of these minor victims hundreds of dollars in cash to recruit other girls to engage in sex acts with Epstein."
6	"As a result, it appeared from documentation that prisoners in the SHU, including Epstein, were being regularly monitored when, in fact, no CO had checked on Epstein from approximately 10:40 p.m. on August 9, 2019, until approximately 6:30 a.m. on August 10, 2019, when Epstein was found hanged in his cell."
7	"The BOP employees and contractors we interviewed included employees involved in various aspects of the emergency response, who worked at MCC New York in the days leading up to the response and following the response, as well as other individuals with information pertinent to our investigation. Additionally, the OIG participated in interviews of 15 inmates who had been housed at MCC New York during time periods relevant to our investigation, including three who were housed in the L Tier of the SHU on the day Epstein died. Those three L-Tier inmates were housed in cells opposite Epstein's cell and therefore had a direct line of sight to Epstein's cell on the night of August 9, i10."
8	"Under federal law, 'whoever, in any matter within the jurisdiction of the executive branch of the Government of the United States, knowingly and willfully makes or uses any false writing or document knowing the same to contain any materially false,

	fictitious, or fraudulent statement or entry' has violated 18 U.S.C. ¬ß 1001(a)(3). The terms 'knowingly and willfully' mean that the subject acted with knowledge that the conduct was, in a general sense, prohibited by law. It is not required that the subject was aware of the existence of Section 1001."
9	"Inmates in the SHU are securely separated from general population inmates and are kept locked in their cell when in their assigned tier within the SHU. As discussed in greater detail in Chapter 4, witnesses told the OIG that SHU inmates are locked in their cells for approximately 23 hours a day."
10	"BOP policy requires that BOP staff routinely and irregularly search housing units to, among other things, maintain sanitary standards and eliminate safety hazards."
11	"The BOP also requires that institutions screen pretrial inmates 'returning from court, as events at court may alter the inmate's separation and/or security needs.' BOP policy further recognizes that there are often 'high security, high profile inmates' who may present a significant threat to themselves or others, and that the 'need to identify and monitor these inmates regularly is paramount.'"
12	"The orders further provide that, once there is adequate staff present, immediate action must be taken to open the inmate's airway and initiate cardiopulmonary resuscitation, even if MCC New York staff believe that the inmate 'has been dead for a period of time.' MCC New York staff are to continue cardiopulmonary resuscitation until they are relieved by medical staff or another rescuer."
13	"The federal regulations, 28 C.F.R. ¬ß¬ß 540.100-540.106, that govern telephone calls for inmates require that the Warden of each BOP institution establish procedures to monitor inmate telephone conversations, which is 'done to preserve the security and orderly management of the institution and to protect the public.' For safety and security reasons, BOP policy (Program Statement P5264.08, Inmate Telephone Regulations) requires that all inmate telephone calls be made through the Inmate Telephone System. BOP policy recognizes that 'on rare occasion, during times of crisis,' inmates may be permitted to make a telephone call outside of the Inmate Telephone System. In such circumstances, the telephone 'must be placed in a secure area (e.g., a locked office),' and 'must be set to record telephone calls.' Additionally, the staff member coordinating the call must notify the BOP's Special Investigative Services via email, providing the inmate's name and register number, the date and time of the call, the number and name of the individual called, and the reason for the call. The Special Investigative Services
14	"July 2, 2019 According to court records, a federal grand jury of the U.S. District Court for the Southern District of New York returns an indictment charging Epstein with sex trafficking and conspiracy to commit sex trafficking."
15	"The court orders that Epstein be detained pending trial because he presents a danger to the community and he is a flight risk."
16	"At approximately 1:27 a.m., SHU staff hears noises coming from Epstein's cell. Epstein's cellmate (Inmate 1) says that Epstein has attempted to hang himself. SHU staff observes Epstein lying on the floor with a piece of orange cloth around his neck. Epstein initially tells MCC New York staff that his cellmate tried to kill him. Epstein's cellmate (Inmate 1) tells MCC New York staff that while he was asleep, he felt

	something hit his legs and when he turned on the light, he saw Epstein with a string around his neck and called the guards."
17	"Epstein and his new cellmate (Inmate 3) are placed in a cell within the SHU that can accommodate the electrical needs of Epstein's medical device."
18	"MCC New York staff discover the disk failures that occurred in the DVR 2 system on July 29 and that resulted in approximately one half of the institution's security cameras not recording, although the cameras continued to broadcast a live video feed. MCC New York staff do not perform the work necessary to restore recording functionality of the DVR 2 system or address long-standing performance failures with the institution's camera system."
19	"At approximately 6:30 a.m., SHU staff begin to deliver breakfast to inmates in the SHU through the food slots in the locked cell doors. When SHU staff attempt to deliver breakfast to Epstein, SHU staff unlock the door to the tier in which Epstein's cell was located and then knock on the door to Epstein's cell. Epstein, who is housed alone in the cell, does not respond to SHU staff. SHU staff unlock the cell door and find Epstein hanged in his cell, with one end of a piece of orange cloth around his neck and the other end tied to the top portion of a bunkbed in Epstein's cell. Epstein is suspended from the top bunk in a near-seated position with his"
20	"The Office of the Chief Medical Examiner, City of New York, releases its findings publicly that the cause of Epstein's death was hanging and that the manner of death was suicide."
21	"The court found that the United States had shown by clear and convincing evidence that Epstein threatened the safety of another person and of the community based on testimony from two victims, the allegations of repeated sexual abuse of minors, and the lewd photographs of young-looking women or girls that were found during an authorized search of Epstein's New York residence in July 2019."
22	"The court found that the United States had also shown by a preponderance of the evidence that Epstein was a flight risk based on the severity of the criminal charges and severity of the potential punishment; the strength of the evidence against Epstein; and Epstein's criminal history, sex offender registration, vast wealth and substantial liquid assets, multiple residences, a foreign residence, limited family ties in the United States, private plane(s), extensive overseas travel, and possession of a foreign passport bearing Epstein's photograph but not his name."
23	"Inmates in the SHU are securely separated from the general inmate population and are kept locked in their cell when in their assigned tier within the SHU. Witnesses told the OIG that SHU inmates are locked in their cells for approximately 23 hours a day."
24	"Figure 4.1 Primary SHU Entrance (Ninth Floor) Note: The photograph on the right has been modified for security reasons."
25	"Figure 4.2 Secondary SHU Entrance (Ninth Floor) Note: The photograph on the right has been modified for security reasons."
26	""

27	"Figure 4.4 Tiered Structure of SHU (3-Dimensional)"
28	"The Warden explained that Epstein was a high-profile inmate and that he initially selected Inmate 1 to be Epstein's cellmate because Inmate 1 was another high-profile inmate, and the Warden believed Inmate 1 to be the least likely SHU inmate to harm Epstein."
29	"In his interview with the OIG, Senior Officer Specialist 1 said Epstein had a sheet around his neck, which was attached to the bunkbed ladder in the cell. Senior Officer Specialist 1 said that Epstein was sitting on the floor of the cell with his back against the bunkbed ladder. Senior Officer Specialist 1's report said that Epstein was breathing, but unresponsive, so he began chest compressions, at which time the Morning Watch Operations Lieutenant and other staff arrived. Senior Officer Specialist 1 confirmed in his OIG interview that they started cardiopulmonary resuscitation but stopped when they realized that Epstein was already breathing."
30	"Inmate 2 also said that the first inmate to be removed from the cell later told Inmate 2 that he was sleeping when his cellmate had tried to kill himself by hanging himself from the ladder of the bed."
31	"The MCC New York Chief Psychologist told the OIG that an inmate is placed on suicide watch when the inmate is believed to be imminently suicidal. During suicide watch, the inmate is under constant observation by staff; the cell lights are on 24 hours a day; and the inmate is given a special mattress, blanket, and smock to wear. The Chief Psychologist explained that although psychological observation is a lower classification, at MCC New York the psychological observations were the same as suicide watch except that inmates were allowed to have their clothing and some materials, such as books, as determined by Psychology Department. At MCC New York, psychological observation was used to see how an inmate was doing before releasing the inmate to a housing unit."
32	"Yeah, but I don't understand, you know, we were bunkies, everything was cool."
33	"The SHU Lieutenant confirmed that a BOP psychologist told him that Epstein had to be housed with a cellmate when Epstein returned to the SHU and said that he passed the directive down to the SHU staff. Additionally, the Day Watch SHU Officer in Charge on August 9, 2019, said he and all other SHU staff were aware of Epstein's cellmate requirement. MCC New York Psychology Department personnel told the OIG that MCC New York staff members knew of Epstein's cellmate requirement because it was discussed during staff meetings, department head meetings, SHU meetings, morning meetings, and during required staff training."
34	"Inmate 3 said he asked Epstein to please not kill himself or hang himself while Inmate 3 was his cellmate because Inmate 3 had a chance to go home soon. Epstein told Inmate 3 not to worry and that he was not going to cause Inmate 3 any trouble."
35	"Figure 4.6 SHU L Tier"
36	"Both photographs have been modified for security reasons and the left photograph has been modified for privacy reasons."
37	"Note: The photograph has been modified for privacy reasons."
38	"View of Epstein's Empty Cell from Cell Door Window"

39	"Figure 4.10 Interior View of Epstein's Empty Cell from Just Inside the Cell Door"
40	"Note: The photograph has been modified for security and privacy reasons."
41	"On July 8, 2019, Forensic Psychologist 1 of the Psychology Department conducted an Intake Screening of Epstein that included a self-report, staff observation, and a review of information in SENTRY."
42	"During the evaluation, Epstein stated he had been previously incarcerated for 3 months for 'prostitution,' and that he was currently charged with sex trafficking. Epstein denied recent or present morbid thoughts and denied passive or active suicidal ideation. It was noted in BOP records that Epstein's verbalizations were future-oriented and did not have indications of helpless or hopeless thinking. According to Forensic Psychologist 1, Epstein did not meet the criteria for any psychological diagnosis and was designated as Mental Health Care Code 1. This is indicative of an inmate who does not show any significant level of functional impairment associated with a mental illness and does not demonstrate a need for regular mental health intervention."
43	"The Chief Psychologist's assessment was that Epstein had numerous protective factors that outweighed his risk factors for suicidality and that he had a positive outlook regarding his legal case."
44	"On July 16, 2019, at Epstein's request, the Chief Psychologist met with Epstein during his attorney conference. The Chief Psychologist noted that Epstein did not have any psychological concerns and denied suicidality. The Chief Psychologist noted that she provided Epstein with psychoeducation regarding additional coping strategies. Epstein was educated about routine and emergency procedures to contact Psychology Department staff and reminded of self-help books and audiotapes that are available to him. The Chief Psychologist noted in her clinical contact report that there was no need for follow-up and that Epstein would be seen in the SHU for rounds and monthly SHU reviews."
45	"Epstein told the Staff Psychologist that he lived to enjoy life and that his future plans included fighting his criminal case and getting back to his normal life."
46	"Epstein stated he had no interest in killing himself; he had described having a wonderful life; and Epstein had said it would be crazy to take his own life and he would not do that to himself."
47	"Epstein did not display indications of disturbed thought process or content and denied current suicidal or self-harm ideation. BOP records further stated that Epstein agreed to immediately report to staff if he began to have suicidal or self-harm thoughts and that Epstein was future-oriented and did not appear to be a danger to himself."
48	"The Staff Psychologist concluded in her report that Epstein did not appear to be a danger to himself and denied current suicidal or self-harm ideation and agreed to immediately inform staff if he had any of these thoughts. Epstein told her that he had social supports in the community and that he had reasons to live and positive future plans. The Staff Psychologist noted that Epstein was currently psychologically stable and that suicide watch was not indicated at the time. The Staff Psychologist concluded that Epstein's overall acute suicide risk was low, and the overall chronic suicide risk was absent."

49	"The Chief Psychologist noted that it was difficult for Psychology Department staff to interview Epstein because he had a right to his attorney visits, which would last throughout the working day."
50	"On August 9, 2019, the U.S. Court of Appeals for the Second Circuit ordered the unsealing of the summary judgment filings from a defamation lawsuit filed by Virginia Roberts Giuffre, a woman who alleged that Epstein had victimized her when she was a teenager, against Ghislaine Maxwell. As a result of the court's order, that same day approximately 2,000 pages of documents were released into the public domain, which contained considerable derogatory information about Epstein and some may have related to the criminal charges pending against him. Additional high-profile public figures were also named in the released documents. There was significant media coverage of information contained within the unsealed court filings."
51	"As noted above, since July 30, consistent with the Psychology Department's determination that Epstein needed to have a cellmate, Epstein had been housed with Inmate 3, whom the Warden and the Federal Bureau of Prisons (BOP) executive leadership had selected as an appropriate cellmate. At 10:33 a.m. on August 8, 2019, the U.S. Marshals Service (USMS) sent an email to MCC New York personnel assigned to Receiving and Discharge, the area within the Correctional Services Department that is responsible for processing inmates who enter or leave the facility, with the subject 'Transfer of Prisoners from NYM [MCC New York] to GEO.' The body of the email identified Inmate 3 as one of the prisoners to be transferred and further stated, 'Please schedule the transfer for Friday 8/9/19.'"

This passage highlights the transfer of Epstein's cellmate on August 9 and the failure to replace him with another inmate. It provides details about the communication between the U.S. Marshals Service and MCC New York personnel regarding |
52	"According to MCC New York reports, including the Daily Log and the Lieutenant's Log, on August 9, 2019, at approximately 8:38 a.m., Epstein's cellmate, Inmate 3, was 'pre-removed' and transferred out of MCC New York in a routine, pre-arranged transfer. The Daily Log tracks inmate movements throughout MCC New York each day, while MCC New York Lieutenants utilize the Lieutenant's Log to document the daily activities that took place within the institution during their respective shifts."
53	"The Day Watch SHU Officer in Charge told the OIG that when he and CO 1 left the SHU with Epstein and Inmate 3, both the Day Watch Operations Lieutenant and the Day Watch Activities Lieutenant should have been physically present in the Lieutenants' Office and should have seen that Inmate 3 was departing the institution when they passed the office."
54	"The Day Watch SHU Officer in Charge told the OIG that a replacement cellmate should have been identified as soon as it was confirmed that Inmate 3 had left the institution. He said a new cellmate could have been reassigned before the 4 p.m. SHU count if it was known that Inmate 3 was not coming back, but the SHU staff members had until Epstein returned from his attorney visit to assign Epstein a new cellmate. According to the Day Watch SHU Officer in Charge, SHU staff definitely should have realized that Inmate 3 was not returning both during the 4 p.m. count and when Epstein returned from his attorney visit later that evening. The Day Watch SHU Officer in Charge told the OIG that Epstein's daily routine was that he would be with

	his attorneys in the attorney conference room until approximately 8 p.m., so SHU personnel had time to make a new cellmate assignment."
55	"The Captain told the OIG that since Epstein was in the attorney conference room all day, no one may have even thought about it, and may have only become aware when they put Epstein back in his cell after his attorney visit that evening. The Captain said as soon as the SHU staff became aware that Epstein was without a cellmate, they should have notified the Evening Watch Operations Lieutenant. The Captain said that if he had been informed, he would have taken immediate action to ensure that Epstein was either assigned a new cellmate or monitored until that assignment occurred."
56	"The Evening Watch Operations Lieutenant told the OIG that he was the Operations Lieutenant at the MCC on August 9 from approximately 2 p.m. until 10 p.m. The Evening Watch Operations Lieutenant said he was aware that Epstein was required to have a cellmate due to a mass email that was sent to all of the MCC New York Lieutenants. According to the Evening Watch Operations Lieutenant, everyone who regularly worked in the SHU should have known that Epstein was required to have a cellmate. The Evening Watch Operations Lieutenant told the OIG that he did not know Inmate 3 had left MCC New York earlier that day and was unaware that Epstein did not have a cellmate. He said that if Inmate 3 had been transported to Receiving and Discharge as 'WAB' and the SHU Lieutenant was off, then another supervisor should have been notified."
57	"The Morning Watch Operations Lieutenant, who was the Operations Lieutenant from approximately 10 p.m. on August 9 until 6 a.m. on August 10, told the OIG that she did not know that Epstein was required to have a cellmate, and that the Captain never spoke with her about this issue. The Captain confirmed that he did not specifically tell the Morning Watch Operations Lieutenant that Epstein needed a cellmate; however, the Captain said he believed that the Morning Watch Operations Lieutenant should have known of the requirement, and she was one of the recipients of the email from the Psychology Department on July 30, 2019, that informed MCC New York staff that Epstein needed to have an appropriate cellmate."
58	"For safety and security reasons, BOP policy requires that all inmate telephone calls be made through the Inmate Telephone System. BOP records reflect that Epstein placed an unrecorded, unmonitored telephone call to a telephone number in the local 646 area code using a non-Inmate Telephone System line on August 9, 2019, from 6:58 p.m. to 7:19 p.m. No other BOP records exist regarding the unmonitored call, including identity of the person called or a summary of the conversation. The OIG found no evidence that Epstein signed an Acknowledgement of Inmate form, as required by BOP policy and necessary for him to use a non-Inmate Telephone System line. The Acknowledgement of Inmate form provides, among other things, that the BOP reserves the authority to monitor and record non-attorney conversations on any telephone located within the institution to preserve the security and orderly management of the institution and to protect the public."
59	"The OIG investigation determined that Epstein did not, in fact, speak with his mother, who, according to public records, died in 2004. The OIG found that Epstein actually spoke with Individual 1, who declined to be interviewed by the OIG. Individual 1's lawyer told the U.S. Attorney's Office for the Southern District of New York during an attorney proffer that Individual 1 spoke with Epstein on August 9,

	2019, at about 7 p.m., for approximately 20 minutes. Individual 1's attorney proffer was that Individual 1 was in the country of Belarus at the time of the call."
60	"They are trying to keep me safe," and that his case would take a little longer than he originally thought. He told Individual 1 he loved her, to be strong, and that he would not be able to call her again for another month."
61	"what happened on that phone call. It could have potentially led to the incident [Epstein's death], but we don, we will never know."
62	"The OIG's investigation determined that the 4 p.m. SHU inmate count on August 9, 2019, was inaccurate because SHU staff did not physically count the inmates as required by BOP policy and instead relied upon a predetermined number of inmates believed to be in the SHU at that time. However, Epstein, who was in the SHU attorney visitation room, was correctly accounted for during the 4 p.m. and subsequent SHU counts. The OIG determined that the error in the 4 p.m. SHU count was carried over into the next inmate count at 10 p.m. that counted an inmate who had been transferred out of the SHU. The SHU inmate count was not corrected until 12 a.m. when the Morning Watch Operations Lieutenant reviewed the master institutional count and housing unit count slips and informed SHU staff of the correct number of inmates in the SHU at that time."
63	"Nonetheless, Noel and the Material Handler completed and signed the 10 p.m. SHU count slip. The 10 p.m. SHU count slip listed the total number of inmates as '73 + 1.' According to the MCC New York master count sheet for the 10 p.m. count on August 9, 2019, all units had verbally reported their inmate counts to the Control Center by 10:30 p.m. At approximately 10:36 p.m., the Control Center completed all paperwork and officially cleared the 10 p.m. institutional count." This passage highlights the discrepancy in the inmate count at the MCC New York SHU during the night of August 9th. Despite not actually performing the count, Noel and the Material Handler completed and signed the count slip, listing the total number of inmates as "73 + 1." The fact that all units had already reported their counts to the Control Center by 10:30 p.m. adds to the confusion surrounding the accuracy of the count.
64	"It therefore appears that the video depicts Noel conducting a later round in the SHU, as she was required to do every 30 minutes during her shift, and not the 10 p.m. SHU count."
65	"The Morning Watch Operations Lieutenant adamantly denied having authorized a 'ghost count' and the OIG identified no record or witness (other than Senior Officer Specialist 6) to indicate that she had done so."
66	"Noel and Thomas both admitted to the OIG that they did not conduct the 12 a.m., 3 a.m., and 5 a.m. counts on August 10, and that they had falsified the respective count slips."
67	"Thomas told the OIG that he knew he was falsely certifying the count slips when he signed them on August 10, 2019."
68	"Noel and Thomas both admitted to the OIG that they did not conduct any of the rounds reflected on the SHU Round Sheet on August 10, 2019, from 12 a.m. until Epstein was found hanged in his cell at approximately 6:30 a.m. Nonetheless, Noel

	completed and signed more than 75 separate 30-minute entries stating that she and Thomas had, in fact, conducted such rounds."
69	"The statements of multiple witnesses were consistent with BOP training materials. The Northeast Regional Director, the Warden, Associate Warden 1, the Captain, and the Day Watch SHU Officer in Charge all told the OIG that Lieutenants should have walked down all of the SHU tiers when conducting a Lieutenant round in the SHU. Noel said the SHU Lieutenant walked the tiers all the time, however, other Lieutenants did not always walk down the tiers. Multiple witnesses also told the OIG that it was standard practice for the BOP to store the SHU round sheets at the end of each tier in the SHU. This practice was designed to ensure that the assigned COs and Lieutenants walked down each tier when conducting rounds to observe every cell and inmate during the round before initialing the round sheet."
70	"On August 10, 2019, shortly after 6 a.m., the doorbell to the SHU rang, indicating that a delivery of breakfast carts had arrived at the SHU. Noel and Thomas retrieved the breakfast carts from the double-locked entrance to the SHU and brought them inside the SHU. At the time, Thomas and Noel were the only officers in the SHU. At approximately 6:30 a.m., MCC New York security camera video recordings show Noel and Thomas walking toward the L Tier. Noel and Thomas told the OIG that at this time they were entering the L Tier, in which Epstein was housed, to deliver breakfast to the inmates. As discussed previously, between approximately 10:40 p.m. on August 9 and approximately 6:30 a.m. on August 10, the OIG did not observe on the available recorded video any COs or other individuals approach the L Tier where Epstein was housed from the common area of the SHU."
71	"Thomas explained that when he first entered Epstein's cell, Epstein had an orange string, presumably from a sheet or a shirt, around his neck. The end of the string was tied to the top portion of the bunkbed. Epstein was suspended from the top bunk in a near-seated position, with his buttocks approximately 1 inch to 1 inch and a half off the floor and his legs extended out straight on the floor. Thomas said Epstein did not look discolored or very different from when he last saw Epstein alive. Thomas said he immediately ripped the orange sheet or shirt away from the bunkbed, and Epstein's buttocks dropped approximately 1 inch to 1 inch and a half to the ground."
72	"Oh, it's not her fault, we fucked up."
73	"The Electronics Technician told the OIG that the inmates also said Thomas and Noel just sat at the SHU Officers' Station and never checked on the inmates. The Electronics Technician told the OIG he understood the inmates to be saying that Thomas and Noel were responsible for Epstein's death because they had not conducted rounds during their shift."
74	"Inmate 5 said officers had trouble getting Epstein onto the stretcher because Epstein was basically dead weight. When the officers did get Epstein on the stretcher, Epstein still had on headphones. Inmate 5 did not see any marks around Epstein's neck, and he did not see a rope around Epstein's neck. However, Inmate 5 saw a male CO come out of Epstein's cell with a sheet that had a loop and knot."
75	"Inmate 7 said he remembered waking up around 6 a.m. on August 10, 2019, and hearing a voice, possibly male, saying 'Breathe.' Inmate 7 said he saw Epstein removed from his cell on a stretcher."

76	"Some MCC New York staff told the OIG that Epstein's death could have been prevented if, among other things, Epstein had been assigned a new cellmate after Inmate 3's departure and rounds and counts had been conducted in the SHU as required. Some witnesses also faulted MCC New York staffing shortages, which resulted in excessive overtime and meant that MCC New York staff members were often overtired during their shifts. Other MCC New York staff members told the OIG that even if inmate safety and accountability measures had been property executed, an inmate who wanted to take his life would have found a way to do so."
77	"As noted previously, Epstein's cell contained an excessive amount of linens, some of which had been ripped into thin strips and tied like a noose."
78	"Inmate 3 said Epstein also had two extra blankets, which no other inmate had, as well as two pens, which inmates were not allowed to have. Epstein would ask for things, and if the COs said no, Epstein would tell them he was writing down their name and providing the information to his lawyer. According to Inmate 3, the COs were on 'eggshells' around Epstein."
79	"The Medical Examiner told the OIG that the pattern of Epstein's neck bone fractures was consistent with a hanging. The Medical Examiner explained that a different fracture pattern is present if there has been a manual compression of the neck versus a sustained pressure like in a hanging, and the pattern of Epstein's neck fractures was that of a hanging. The Medical Examiner also said Epstein had petechial hemorrhages, which are pinpoint bleeds in skin, on his face and mouth. These hemorrhages are caused when the blood flow is obstructed and the small skin capillaries burst. The Medical Examiner additionally identified plethora, which is purple discoloration of the skin, and stated that both petechial hemorrhages and plethora are consistent with suicide by hanging."
80	"Independent medical judgment and that the Medical Examiner was not pressured or otherwise subjected to any attempt to influence her ruling."
81	"Following Epstein's death, MCC New York officials and Federal Bureau of Investigation (FBI) investigators attempted to review video recordings related to the incident and discovered that, although the security cameras were working and transmitting live video, recorded video from most of the cameras in the SHU area was not available due to a malfunction of the video recording system that had occurred on July 29, 2019, including video from the camera at the end of the L Tier."
82	"At the time of Epstein's death on August 10, 2019, the camera system upgrade had not been completed. Immediately following Epstein's death, Company 1 officials arrived at MCC New York and installed the new recording system within a couple of days, and recording functionality was restored using the existing cameras. The majority of the new cameras did not arrive at the facility until October 2019, and they were installed in stages as the wiring work was conducted. According to the Electronics Technician, as of August 2021, when the MCC closed, the wiring work had still not been fully completed."
83	"The Electronics Technician told the OIG that, before Epstein's death, no one was specifically tasked with ensuring that video from the cameras was being recorded. The Electronics Technician said he therefore did not perform any daily checks to ensure that video was being recorded."

84	"The Electronics Technician told the OIG there must have been some miscommunication because he did not say he was going to work overtime and resolve the problem that same evening since he knew the problem could not be fixed in one evening. The Electronics Technician told the OIG that, in hindsight, he should have stayed at the institution to begin work on the problem that same day."
85	"At approximately 6:33 a.m., additional officers entered the SHU and ascended the L Tier stairway, presumably after Noel activated her body alarm when Epstein was discovered hanged in his cell."
86	"Figure 6.1 SHU Camera Locations and Recording Status on August 10, 2019"
87	"Note: The photograph has been modified for privacy reasons."
88	"Figure 6.3 Field of View of the SHU Camera at 10th Floor-South Entrance"
89	"Figure 6.4 Partial View of L Tier Stairway, from the SHU Camera at 10th Floor-South Entrance"
90	"Figure 6.5 View of SHU Officers' Station from the SHU Camera at 10th Floor-South Entrance"
91	"Figure 6.6 Field of View of the Recording 9th Floor Elevator Bay Camera"
92	"The Warden, who was not scheduled to work on August 10, 2019, arrived at the institution later that morning after being notified of Epstein's death and was informed that most of the cameras in the SHU were not recording. He told the OIG that when the SIS Lieutenant arrived at the facility that morning, he informed her that the SHU cameras had not been recording, and the SIS Lieutenant explained that the hard drive issue had been detected on August 8. He told the OIG that prior to August 10, he was unaware that the DVR 2 issue had been detected on August 8, and that approximately half of the facility's cameras, and in particular the cameras in the SHU, were found to not be recording on that date."
93	"The forensic reports further state that an FBI computer scientist and the Company 1 Technician reviewed the DVR 2 controller logs and found that there had previously been 'catastrophic disk failures' and no recordings would have been available after July 29, 2019."
94	"Our investigation and review of the Federal Bureau of Prisons' (BOP) custody, care, and supervision of Jeffrey Epstein identified numerous and serious failures by employees of the Metropolitan Correctional Center located in New York, New York (MCC New York), including falsifying BOP records relating to inmate counts and rounds and multiple violations of MCC New York and BOP policies and procedures, which compromised Epstein's safety, the safety of other inmates, and the security of the institution."
95	"The OIG found no evidence indicating that the door to Epstein's cell or any other cell in the SHU tier in which Epstein was housed was unlocked on the evening of August 9, 110, 2019, after SHU staff locked Epstein in his cell at approximately 8 p.m. SHU staff told the OIG that at approximately 8 p.m. on August 9, all SHU inmates were locked in their cells for the evening and that there was no indication that any of

	the other inmates could have gotten out of their cells. Epstein did not have a cellmate after Inmate 3 was transferred out of MCC New York on August 9, and therefore Epstein was alone in his cell the evening of August 9, ì10."
96	"We further noted that Epstein had previously been placed on suicide watch and psychological observation due to the events of July 23, 2019; that numerous nooses made from prison bed sheets were found in his cell on the morning of August 10; and that he had signed a new Last Will and Testament on August 8, 2 days before he died. No weapons were recovered from Epstein's cell after his death. Additionally, the inmates who were interviewed consistently reported that on the evening Epstein died the SHU staff did not systematically conduct the required rounds and counts, which was one of the primary mechanisms for the SHU staff to ensure the safety and security of inmates housed in the SHU. As a result, Epstein was unmonitored and locked alone in his cell for hours with an excess amount of linens, which provided an opportunity for him to commit suicide."
97	"The fact that serious deficiencies occurred in connection with high-profile inmates like Epstein and Bulger is especially concerning given that the BOP would presumably take particular care in handling the custody and care of such inmates."
98	"The combination of negligence, misconduct, and outright job performance failures documented in this report all contributed to an environment in which arguably one of the most notorious inmates in BOP's custody was provided with the opportunity to take his own life, resulting in significant questions being asked about the circumstances of his death, how it could have been allowed to have happen, and most importantly, depriving his numerous victims, many of whom were underage girls at the time of the alleged crimes, of their ability to seek justice through the criminal justice process."
99	"The OIG investigation found that each of these employees knew that Epstein was required to have a cellmate at all times per the Psychology Department's directive."
100	"The OIG investigation concluded that on August 9, 2019, the Day Watch SHU Officer in Charge, the Evening Watch SHU Officer in Charge, and Noel failed to notify a supervisor as required after Epstein's cellmate was permanently removed from the MCC New York SHU, which constituted a violation of BOP standards of conduct. Additionally, their inaction violated MCC New York SHU Post Orders because none of these individuals documented the fact the Epstein needed a new cellmate as required. Finally, all of these officers failed to exercise good judgment and common sense, as required by the SHU Post Orders, by not immediately undertaking steps through their chain-of-command to ensure that a high-profile inmate who had been released from suicide watch and psychological observation 10 days earlier had an appropriate cellmate."
101	"The OIG found that the failure of these individuals to adequately supervise SHU staff and ensure that a high-profile inmate who had recently been on suicide watch and psychological observation had an appropriate cellmate constituted a job performance failure."
102	"The failure to undertake these required measures to account for inmate whereabouts and wellbeing, ìand the supervisors' failure to properly supervise the SHU staff, as discussed further below, îresulted in Epstein being unobserved for hours before his death, which compounded the failure of MCC New York staff to ensure that Epstein had an appropriate cellmate."

103	"Instead of performing the required duties to account for inmate whereabouts and wellbeing, the OIG found that officers assigned to the SHU on August 9 and 10, including the Material Handler, Noel, and Thomas primarily remained seated in the SHU Officers' Station, îsometimes without moving for a period of time, suggesting that they were asleep, îand conducted a variety of Internet searches on MCC New York computers. Thomas also admitted to the OIG that he 'dozed off' for periods of time during his shift."
104	"The OIG investigation has found that the Evening Watch SHU Officer in Charge, the Material Handler, Noel, and Thomas knowingly and willingly falsified BOP records in violation of federal law by attesting that they had completed the mandatory rounds and inmate counts on the evening of August 9, 2019, and morning of August 10, 2019."
105	"The OIG investigation and review concluded that the Day Watch Operations Lieutenant exercised poor judgment when he requested that the Material Handler work a third consecutive shift. As the Day Watch Operations Lieutenant, he had access to the staff roster and schedule and therefore he should have known that the Material Handler had already worked 16 straight hours. Additionally, the Day Watch Operations Lieutenant's action was inconsistent with the collective bargaining agreement and did not reflect sound correctional judgment, as it would have been extremely difficult for the Material Handler to have effectively performed his duties during his third shift."
106	"The OIG found that Senior Officer Specialist 6 modified the count slips received from the SHU and Receiving and Discharge, failed to request a recount of the SHU inmates, and cleared the 10 p.m. institutional count knowing that it was inaccurate in violation of BOP policy and MCC New York SHU Post Orders."
107	"The OIG found that the failure of the Evening Watch Operations Lieutenant and the Morning Watch Operations Lieutenant to adequately supervise SHU staff, and of the Morning Watch Operations Lieutenant to adequately conduct a Lieutenant round in the SHU, which contributed to the SHU staff's failure to conduct mandatory rounds and counts, constituted a job performance failure."
108	"The OIG found that the Unit Manager violated BOP policy by allowing Epstein to make an unrecorded and unmonitored telephone call, and by failing to verify the telephone call recipient, monitor, and log the call. We further found that the Unit Manager exercised poor judgment when he left MCC New York while Epstein was still on the telephone call that the Unit Manager had arranged and failed to instruct the Evening Watch SHU Officer in Charge, the Material Handler, or Noel to monitor the call."
109	"The OIG found that on August 9, 2019, the Day Watch SHU Officer in Charge either failed to conduct the required cell searches or failed to document the cell searches that he conducted in the SHU, and that the Evening Watch SHU Officer in Charge failed to ensure that MCC New York staff assigned to the SHU conducted cell searches and himself failed to log cell searches in violation of BOP policy and MCC New York SHU Post Orders. Additionally, the OIG found that it was a performance failure for the Day Watch SHU Officer in Charge, the Evening Watch SHU Officer in Charge, and Noel, who served as the SHU Officer in Charge during their respective shifts on August 9 and 10, 2019, to have permitted Epstein to have an excessive amount of linens in his cell."

110	"The BOP's failure to address the issue of functional security camera systems across the agency and at individual institutions presents an ongoing risk to the safety of BOP staff and inmates and has the potential to impair the investigation of and accountability for staff and inmate misconduct. It is imperative that the BOP prioritize the expeditious expansion and modernization of its security camera system to mitigate security risks."
111	"The OIG therefore recommends that the BOP implement a requirement that all inmates coming off of suicide watch or psychological observation to be assigned cellmates with criteria for exceptions based on the particular individual or security considerations, provide guidance for determining when a cellmate is no longer required, and implement a process for approving, documenting, and communicating to institutional staff the assignment and removal of cellmates for these inmates."
112	"According to the Psychological Reconstruction conducted by the Assistant Director of the Reentry Services Division, during Epstein's psychological observation on July 24 through July 30, 2019, Epstein was also allowed to visit with his attorneys between 8, ì11 hours each day without direct observation."
113	"The Material Handler worked three consecutive shifts, ì24 hours straight, ìon August 9, 2019, which was certainly a contributory cause to the lack of adequate means of accounting for inmate location and wellbeing in the SHU. The Material Handler told the OIG that no one did the 10 p.m. SHU inmate count because they were tired."
114	"The OIG found that, even though the highest levels of leadership knew of the MCC New York security camera system's recurring deficiencies, prior to Epstein's death, no one was tasked with the responsibility of checking the security camera system on a routine basis to ensure that the system was functional. As a result, when on July 29, 2019, video from approximately half of the institution's security cameras was no longer being recorded, the problem went undetected for 11 days. The OIG also found that there are no BOP policies that specifically state that security camera systems must have the capacity to record or that institutional staff must perform periodic checks to ensure the camera system is fully functional. Cameras that are failing to provide good quality or any live video streams put the safety of BOP staff members and inmates at risk, and the lack of video recordings can potentially hinder investigations of wrongdoing by staff and inmates."
115	"The facts and circumstances related to those few BOP employees at MCC New York in this report reflect a failure to follow BOP's longstanding policies, regulations, and/or laws. While this misconduct described in this report is troubling, those who took part in it represent a very small percentage of the approximately 35,000 employees across more than 120 institutions who continue to strive for correctional excellence every day."
116	"In April of this year, BO P's leadership announced its new mission as 'corrections professionals who foster a humane and secure environment and ensure public safety by preparing individuals for successful reentry into our communities.' BOP's new core values include accountability, integrity, respect, compassion, and correctional excellence."
117	"The BOP appreciates OIG's careful attention to this engagement, and its willingness to provide specific, feasible recommendations that address the root causes of issues

	raised in the incident described. Thank you for the opportunity to comment on this report. We look forward to working with OIG to close these recommendations."
118	"The BOP recognizes the importance of careful monitoring of adults in custody who face mental health challenges and therefore concurs with this recommendation. Our practice is to carefully consider both the well-being and safety of the individual involved and overarching safety and security concerns. In the years since Mr. Epstein's death, the BOP has updated its process related to suicide watch and psychological observation. Under BOP's revised process, upon removal from suicide watch or psychological observation, psychologists make individualized care recommendations about clinical follow-up and other custodial concerns, including housing and cellmates. Mental health, custody, and unit team employees work collaboratively to ensure that each individual removed from suicide watch is housed appropriately."
119	"Our investigation and review determined that BOP employees did not take steps to ensure that Jeffrey Epstein continuously had a cellmate in response to Psychology Department personnel having determined that he needed to have an appropriate cellmate, and absent any indication that security or other considerations relating to Epstein warranted his not having a cellmate."
120	"While the issues raised in the OIG's report were the result of employees failing to adhere to their duties, as opposed to a staffing shortage, the BOP welcomes the opportunity to continue the significant work that has already been undertaken and that is ongoing regarding staffing."
121	"The BOP should enhance existing policies regarding institutional security camera systems to ensure they specifically state that such systems must have the capacity to record video and that BOP institutions must conduct regular security camera system functionality checks."

PAGE-BY-PAGE SUMMARIES

	Investigation and review of the Federal Bureau of Prisons' handling of Jeffrey Epstein's custody at the Metropolitan Correctional Center in New York.
	This page is an executive summary of an investigation and review into the Federal Bureau of Prisons' custody, care, and supervision of Jeffrey Epstein at the Metropolitan Correctional Center in New York. The report highlights operational challenges, staffing shortages, and management failures that contributed to Epstein's suicide while in custody.
	Epstein was removed from suicide watch but remained under psychological observation. He claimed his cellmate tried to kill him, but later changed his story. Epstein's cellmate said Epstein tried to hang himself. The prison failed to assign Epstein a new cellmate and he was found hanged in his cell on August 10.
	The Office of the Inspector General (OIG) found serious failures by MCC New York staff in their handling of Jeffrey Epstein's death, including violations of policies and procedures. Staff falsified records and failed to properly monitor Epstein, leading to his unmonitored and alone in his cell before he was discovered hanged. While misconduct was found, there was no evidence of criminality or anyone else present in the area where Epstein was housed.
	The report states that there is no evidence to suggest foul play in Epstein's death, and that the prison staff's negligence and failures in following protocol contributed to the opportunity for him to commit suicide. The report also highlights the need for the Department of Justice and Bureau of Prisons to address recurring issues within the system. Eight recommendations were made to improve the situation, and it is recommended that disciplinary action be taken against the personnel involved.
	The page provides a table of contents for a document that discusses the custody and care of Epstein prior to his death, including key events and relevant policies. It also highlights events leading up to Epstein's death on August 10, 2019, such as the transfer of his cellmate and failure to assign a new one.
	This page provides information on inmate counts, staff rounds, and the discovery of Epstein's death in the SHU. It also discusses the availability of limited recorded video evidence due to a security camera system failure. The chapter concludes with conclusions and recommendations regarding the failures of MCC New York staff in ensuring Epstein's safety.
1	The page discusses the operational challenges and systemic issues faced by the Federal Bureau of Prisons (BOP) in the custody, care, and supervision of inmates, focusing on the case of Jeffrey Epstein. It highlights staffing shortages, inadequate suicide prevention measures, malfunctioning security camera systems, and management failures. The Office of the Inspector General (OIG) makes recommendations to address

	these recurring issues. The investigation was initiated after Epstein was found hanged in his cell in the Metropolitan Correctional Center.
2	The Office of the Inspector General (OIG) conducted an investigation into the death of Jeffrey Epstein while in custody at MCC New York. They found numerous failures and violations by MCC New York staff, including the failure to assign Epstein a new cellmate, inadequate inmate counts and rounds, allowing Epstein to have excess items in his cell, and allowing him to make an unrecorded phone call and sign a new will. These failures compromised Epstein's safety and allowed him the opportunity to commit suicide.
3	During an investigation by the Office of the Inspector General (OIG), it was found that staff at MCC New York did not conduct required inmate counts and rounds in the Special Housing Unit (SHU) where Jeffrey Epstein was held. Staff members falsely certified that these tasks were completed, leading to Epstein being unmonitored and alone in his cell before his death. The OIG did not find evidence contradicting the FBI's determination of suicide as the cause of death.
4	The report discusses the circumstances surrounding the death of Epstein, stating that his injuries were consistent with suicide by hanging rather than homicide. It also highlights the failures and negligence of the BOP in ensuring the safety and security of inmates, emphasizing the need for improvement and accountability.
5	Jeffrey Epstein, a wealthy man in the financial industry, was charged with sex trafficking and conspiracy. He was detained at MCC New York before it closed due to substandard conditions. Correctional Officer Tova Noel and Material Handler Michael Thomas falsified official forms during their shift.
6	Noel and Thomas were charged with conspiracy and falsification of records in relation to their failure to conduct mandatory inmate counts and rounds at MCC New York. They created false documentation to conceal their negligence, leading to Epstein not being monitored for several hours before his death. Noel and Thomas entered into deferred prosecution agreements and fulfilled the required conditions, resulting in all charges being dismissed. The OIG investigation revealed misconduct and inadequate performance by several MCC New York staff members.
7	The Office of the Inspector General (OIG) conducted interviews and collected documents, including video footage and photographs, as part of their investigation into the death of Jeffrey Epstein at MCC New York. They also reviewed FBI records and interviewed the Medical Examiner who performed Epstein's autopsy. The OIG followed ethical conduct standards for federal employees during their investigation.
8	This page discusses the ethical regulations and standards of conduct for employees of the Bureau of Prisons (BOP). It also mentions the consequences of making false statements or lacking candor during official investigations. Additionally, it provides information about the operation of Special Housing Units (SHUs) within BOP facilities.
9	Inmates in the Special Housing Unit (SHU) are locked in their cells for most of the day, but are allowed to exercise, shower, and have visits. Staff members assigned to the SHU receive training on supervision, suicide prevention, and security procedures. Inmate counts are conducted multiple times a day to ensure accountability.

10	This page discusses the procedures and policies for inmate counting, rounds, documentation, and cell searches in a correctional facility. It also mentions the requirement for psychological screening for pretrial inmates.
11	The page discusses the screening process for new inmates in federal institutions and the suicide prevention program implemented by the Bureau of Prisons (BOP). It outlines the BOP's requirements for assessing inmates' security, medical, psychological, and special needs upon admission. The BOP also has regulations in place to identify and manage potentially suicidal inmates, including placing them on suicide watch and conducting screenings for signs of suicidality. The page mentions the use of specially trained staff or inmates for suicide watch and the observation
12	The page discusses the response to inmate suicide in correctional facilities and the inmate discipline program. It outlines the required response to a suspected suicide, including initiating CPR and notifying relevant staff. It also explains the inmate discipline program, which includes penalties for prohibited acts such as tattooing or self-mutilation. Mental health assessment is conducted for mentally ill inmates, and a hearing officer determines the appropriate sanctions.
13	This page discusses the procedures and regulations regarding telephone calls, personal effects, medication, and linens for inmates in administrative detention status in BOP SHUs. It emphasizes the importance of security and cleanliness in maintaining a safe environment.
14	The timeline outlines the upgrading of the security camera system at MCC New York and the events leading up to Epstein's arrest and placement in the Special Housing Unit (SHU) due to media attention and notoriety.
15	Epstein enters a plea of not guilty to all charges and is placed on psychological observation due to risk factors. He is housed with another inmate and has follow-up visits with a psychologist. He is ultimately detained pending trial due to being a danger to the community and a flight risk. His psychology review is not conducted.
16	Epstein files an appeal for pretrial release. He is found hanging in his cell and initially blames his cellmate. Epstein is transferred to suicide watch and later removed. He denies remembering the incident and is eventually released from psychological observation.
17	Disk failures in the security camera system at MCC New York prevent recording, but cameras still function. Epstein is transferred back to the SHU and placed in a cell with an appropriate cellmate. Disciplinary proceedings against Epstein find insufficient evidence of self-mutilation. MCC New York personnel attempt to obtain an estimate for a new camera system. Court records indicate Epstein's "suicidal tendencies."
18	Epstein denies suicidal tendencies during psychological assessments. Investigation finds no evidence of harm to Epstein. Cellmate transfer and camera system failures occur. Epstein's need for a new cellmate is not addressed. Epstein meets with attorneys before his death.
19	Epstein's attorneys inquire about his housing situation while repairs to the security camera system at MCC New York are incomplete. Unsealed documents in a civil case involving Ghislaine Maxwell provide media coverage relating to Epstein. Epstein is permitted an unmonitored phone call and later found hanged in his cell after staff neglect required checks.

20	Epstein's death in MCC New York SHU was initially believed to be suicide by hanging. However, the DVR system had catastrophic disk failures, and no recordings were available after July 29, 2019. The cause of death was confirmed to be suicide by the Office of the Chief Medical Examiner.
21	Epstein was arrested and detained on charges of sex trafficking and conspiracy. He was initially placed in the general inmate population but was later moved to a special housing unit for his safety. He pleaded not guilty and was ordered to remain in custody pending trial due to the seriousness of the charges and evidence against him.
22	Epstein, a registered sex offender, was denied pretrial release due to being considered a flight risk. He was placed in the Special Housing Unit (SHU) at MCC New York, where inmates are locked in their cells for 23 hours a day. Epstein had daily meetings with his attorneys and faced frustrations from other attorneys regarding visitation wait times.
23	The page describes the layout and security measures of the Special Housing Unit (SHU) at MCC New York where inmates are securely separated from the general population. Inmates are locked in their cells for most of the day but have limited opportunities for exercise, showers, and visits. Security protocols are in place for visitors and food delivery.
24	The page features a photograph of the primary entrance to the Special Housing Unit (SHU) on the ninth floor of MCC New York, with a note stating that the image has been altered for security purposes. Source: DOJ OIG photographs and schematic drawing.
25	The page shows a modified photograph of the secondary entrance to the SHU on the ninth floor of MCC New York, along with a schematic drawing. The main entry door is not pictured.
26	This page shows a schematic drawing of the tiered structure of the Special Housing Unit (SHU) in MCC New York, as depicted by the DOJ OIG. The SHU has upper and lower tiers.
27	The page features a schematic drawing of the MCC New York SHU, showcasing its tiered structure.
28	Epstein was initially assigned a cell in the SHU with another high-profile inmate, chosen because they were deemed unlikely to harm him. They were housed together in cell Z05-124.
29	On July 23, 2019, prison officers found Jeffrey Epstein in his cell with a cloth around his neck. They removed the cloth and performed CPR. Epstein was then placed on suicide watch and transferred to the health services unit. He later claimed that his cellmate had tried to kill him and extort money from him.
30	Epstein's cellmate claims he found Epstein sitting on the floor with a string around his neck. Epstein denies knowledge of how he sustained his injuries. Inmate 2 witnessed officers removing inmates from the cell and cleaning it. Medical staff observed friction marks and reddening on Epstein's neck.
31	Epstein's removal from suicide watch and housing arrangements at MCC New York, as well as an investigation into a previous incident of self-harm, are discussed. The

	Psychology Department's recommendations regarding housing and increased monitoring are also mentioned.
32	After Epstein came off suicide watch, he requested to be paired with his previous cellmate. The Psychology Department determined that Epstein needed an appropriate cellmate and notified MCC New York staff. The Warden and Captain were aware of the cellmate requirement and instructed the SHU Lieutenant to ensure Epstein had a cellmate.
33	Epstein was required to have a cellmate in the Special Housing Unit (SHU) but his attorney opposed it. The prison staff compiled a list of potential cellmates and tentatively decided on Inmate 3. If Inmate 3 were to leave, a new cellmate would need to be selected. From July 30 to August 10, Epstein was assigned to a cell with Inmate 3.
34	Epstein was provided with a medical device and moved to a cell in the SHU. His cellmate expressed concerns about his safety, but Epstein reassured him. Errors in cell assignments and recordkeeping could have been avoided with proper inmate accountability measures.
35	The page features a schematic drawing and photograph of the Special Housing Unit (SHU) at MCC New York, obtained from the DOJ OIG and the Office of the Chief Medical Examiner.
36	Photographs of Epstein's cell have been modified for security and privacy reasons.
37	A modified photograph shows the door to the cell where Epstein and another inmate were held from July 30 to August 9.
38	The page shows a photograph and drawing of the empty cell of Jeffrey Epstein at the Metropolitan Correctional Center in New York.
39	The page shows an interior view of Epstein's empty cell in the MCC New York SHU, depicted in a photograph and schematic drawing.
40	A modified photograph and schematic drawing depict the view of Epstein's cell door from the SHU Officers' Station at MCC New York.
41	This page discusses the psychological evaluations of Epstein while he was in custody at MCC New York. Medical professionals conducted multiple appointments and prescribed medications for various health needs. The evaluations began on July 6, 2019, and included an intake screening and observations by the Psychology Department.
42	Epstein denied a history of mental health issues during his intake evaluation. He was designated as Mental Health Care Code 1, indicating no significant impairment or need for regular mental health intervention. However, due to risk factors such as media attention and pending court proceedings, he was placed on psychological observation status until a suicide risk assessment could be conducted.
43	On this page, the Chief Psychologist assesses Epstein's risk of suicide and determines that he has protective factors outweighing his risk. Epstein denies any suicidal thoughts and expresses concern about his living conditions. The Chief Psychologist provides coping strategies and resources to Epstein. He continues to deny any suicidal ideation.
44	The Chief Psychologist met with Epstein, who denied being suicidal and was given coping strategies. The BOP deemed the meeting inappropriate. Epstein was found with

	a cloth around his neck, but appeared undistressed during assessment. The injury was deemed self-inflicted.
45	On July 23, 2019, a suicide risk assessment was conducted on Epstein. He denied knowing why he was on suicide watch and claimed to have no memory of how he sustained the injuries on his neck. The Chief Psychologist considered three possibilities: gaming the system, rehearsal, or assault by another inmate. Medical staff observed abrasions on Epstein's neck but could not determine whether he harmed himself or was assaulted. Epstein was removed from suicide watch after 31 hours and remained under psychological observation until
46	Epstein was taken off suicide watch and placed on psychological observation due to his self-reported lack of interest in killing himself. Forensic Psychologist 2 made the decision with the consent of the Chief Psychologist and Associate Warden 2. Epstein expressed feeling safer in the psychological observation area and denied any suicidality. He was seen daily by psychologists and provided with supportive interventions. Epstein had concerns about being housed in the SHU and experienced agitation due to noise. He reported impaired memory due to sleep
47	Epstein, a prisoner, requested to stay in psychological observation due to lack of sleep and medical concerns. He was informed he could stay one more night and then return to the Special Housing Unit (SHU) with a cellmate. Epstein expressed concerns about noise in the SHU but denied any suicidal or self-harm ideation. He was deemed competent to proceed with the disciplinary process and transferred back to the SHU. Epstein reported being in a pleasant mood and denied recent suicidal thoughts during a clinical
48	Epstein's mental health was assessed multiple times, with no indication of suicidal tendencies. He denied feeling suicidal and expressed stability. The psychologist concluded that Epstein was not a danger to himself and suicide watch was not necessary.
49	Epstein received psychoeducation and was provided with coping strategies and self-help resources. He underwent three suicide risk assessments, which was unusual due to his constant attorney visits.
50	Epstein signed a new will two days before his death, which was filed in court. The release of documents in a defamation lawsuit against Ghislaine Maxwell revealed derogatory information about Epstein and other public figures.
51	On August 9, Epstein's cellmate was transferred to another institution and not replaced. MCC New York staff were aware of the transfer but believed the cellmate had gone to court. Epstein's attorney requested that he be housed without a cellmate, but this was rejected due to his status as a sex offender.
52	On August 9, 2019, Epstein's cellmate was transferred out of MCC New York in a routine transfer. The transfer was coordinated through USMS emails and the Daily Log indicated that the cellmate would not be returning. The call out list for that day would have also listed "WAB" next to the cellmate's name, indicating their departure from the institution.
53	On August 9, the Day Watch SHU Officer in Charge at MCC New York failed to assign a new cellmate to Epstein after Inmate 3's departure. The officer confirmed that he knew Epstein needed a cellmate and had informed him of this. The officer also

	stated that he had informed other staff members of this requirement. However, there were no notifications made by the officer or CO 1 regarding Inmate 3's departure. The officer believed that the Day Watch Operations Lieutenant and the
54	The Day Watch SHU Officer in Charge failed to assign a new cellmate to Epstein after Inmate 3 was discharged from the institution, despite being aware of the requirement. The responsibility to find a replacement cellmate was shared among all SHU staff members, but no action was taken.
55	The Day Watch Operations and Activities Lieutenants were unaware of Inmate 3's transfer despite receiving an email about it. The Day Watch Activities Lieutenant did not remember Inmate 3 leaving with his belongings or discuss his departure with others. Senior officials, including the Warden and Captain, were also unaware of the transfer and the need for a new cellmate for Epstein. The Evening Watch SHU Officer did not recall a conversation about Epstein needing a cellmate. If Inmate 3 had left
56	Epstein did not have a cellmate, and the staff at MCC New York were unaware that he needed one. Various officers and personnel were interviewed, but no one took responsibility for notifying the appropriate individuals about Epstein's situation.
57	The Morning Watch Operations Lieutenant and the Material Handler were not aware that Epstein needed a cellmate. Noel, who worked in the SHU where Epstein was housed, was also unaware of this requirement. Thomas, another Material Handler, assumed Epstein needed a cellmate but no one had informed him.
58	Inmate 3 was removed from MCC New York on August 9, leaving Epstein without a cellmate on August 10. Epstein made an unmonitored telephone call on August 9, which violated BOP policy. The call was authorized by the Unit Manager and the Captain to accommodate Epstein's request for a call.
59	Epstein was allowed to make a phone call from the SHU shower area, but the Unit Manager did not verify who he was speaking with. It was later discovered that Epstein spoke with Individual 1, who claimed to be in Belarus at the time of the call. The OIG investigation did not investigate the accuracy of this claim.
60	Epstein had a conversation on August 9th in the Special Housing Unit (SHU) that was not monitored or logged. The call lasted for about 20 minutes and involved personal topics. The officers present during the call were distracted and did not overhear the conversation. The Northeast Regional Director expressed concern over the unauthorized unmonitored call.
61	The page discusses the failure to conduct inmate counts and staff rounds at MCC New York on August 9-10. It highlights the importance of accurate counts for accountability and reveals that required counts were not conducted, count slips were falsified, and staff did not conduct rounds after a certain time.
62	The investigation found that the 4 p.m. inmate count at the Special Housing Unit (SHU) on August 9, 2019, was inaccurate because staff did not physically count the inmates as required. The error carried over into the next count at 10 p.m., which included an inmate who had been transferred out. The SHU staff relied on a "cheat sheet" instead of conducting an accurate count.
63	The page discusses inconsistencies in the inmate count slips at MCC New York on August 9. The 4 p.m. count slip was incorrect, and the 10 p.m. count slip listed an

	inmate count of "73 + 1," even though the count was not conducted. There are conflicting statements regarding who conducted the 10 p.m. count.
64	The page discusses discrepancies in inmate counts at MCC New York. It mentions that a video shows a later round in the Special Housing Unit (SHU) than the reported count, and that count slips were inaccurate. A senior officer explains that he wrote "73 + 1" on the count slip to account for an inmate who had been moved.
65	The page discusses the issue of inaccurate count slips at the Metropolitan Correctional Center and the denial of authorizing a "ghost count" by the Morning Watch Operations Lieutenant. It emphasizes the importance of accurate physical counts of inmates and the need for proper procedures in case of discrepancies.
66	Noel and Thomas, staff members in the SHU, falsified count slips for the 12 a.m., 3 a.m., and 5 a.m. counts on August 10. The video footage shows that Noel left the SHU to assist CO 3 and took the SHU keys with her, preventing anyone from accessing the SHU during her absence. Thomas had prior experience working in the SHU and had worked numerous shifts there.
67	Thomas and Noel, COs assigned to the Special Housing Unit (SHU), did not conduct rounds during their shift from 12 a.m. to 6:30 a.m. on August 10, 2019. Thomas admitted to signing round sheets without actually conducting the rounds due to fatigue. There was a discrepancy between the 12 a.m. and 3 a.m. count slips, but Thomas did not recall discussing it or speaking to the Morning Watch Operations Lieutenant about it. Thomas
68	Noel and Thomas, prison officers responsible for conducting rounds in the Special Housing Unit (SHU), did not actually conduct the required rounds on the night of Epstein's death. They falsified round sheets and were found to be sleeping and using the computer instead. Noel claims she saw Epstein in his cell but did not know he was supposed to have a cellmate.
69	The Office of the Inspector General (OIG) reviewed video footage and witness statements to investigate the lack of supervision and failure to conduct proper rounds in the Special Housing Unit (SHU) where Epstein was housed. The OIG found that a correctional officer (CO) carried linen or inmate clothing to Epstein's tier shortly before his death, and multiple witnesses confirmed that Lieutenants should have walked down all tiers during their rounds. The SHU round sheets were stored in the common area instead of at
70	On August 10, 2019, the Morning Watch Operations Lieutenant did not conduct rounds in the SHU. Surveillance footage showed that no one entered the SHU or conducted any counts or rounds. Later that morning, Epstein was found hanged in his cell by officers Noel and Thomas who were delivering breakfast trays.
71	Epstein was found in his cell with an orange string around his neck, tied to the bunkbed. He was suspended in a seated position but appeared normal. Thomas removed the string and performed chest compressions before medical staff arrived. Thomas denies any involvement in Epstein's death. Noel assisted Thomas in delivering food to inmates but received no response from Epstein's locked cell.
72	Noel, a staff member at MCC New York, witnessed Thomas attempting to revive Epstein after he was found unresponsive in his cell. Noel hit the body alarm and observed Thomas performing chest compressions but not checking for breath or pulse.

	Noel did not see what happened after MCC New York staff arrived. The Operations Lieutenant also arrived and took over administering CPR. Another staff member, the Electronics Technician, performed chest compressions while Epstein was being transported to the Health Services Unit.
73	The page describes the accounts of an Electronics Technician and a Senior Officer Specialist in relation to Jeffrey Epstein's death. It also mentions the review of photographs and interviews with inmates who had a direct line of sight to Epstein's cell.
74	Inmates in the Special Housing Unit (SHU) at MCC New York provide details of their observations leading up to and after Jeffrey Epstein's death. They mention that Epstein appeared dead when found, did not see any marks or a rope around his neck, and witnessed officers performing CPR.
75	Epstein was found unresponsive in his cell and later pronounced deceased. Inmates reported that counts and rounds were not conducted as required, and the last round was between 9:30-10pm or 12:30-1am. Medical staff attempted life-saving measures but were unsuccessful.
76	The page provides details on the response to a medical emergency at MCC New York involving Epstein, as well as the items found in his cell after his death. Staff members believe his death could have been prevented and blame staffing shortages. The FBI collected various items from his cell for investigation.
77	Epstein's cell was not properly searched before his death, with only one search logged on August 9th. The cell contained an excess of linens and strips tied like a noose. The SHU Officer in Charge claimed that the majority of cells were searched, but this was not reflected in the logs.
78	The SHU Officer and Captain noticed an excess of linens and blankets in Epstein's cell, potentially for another inmate. The Captain emphasized the security risk of inmates having extra materials. Inmate 3 mentioned Epstein sleeping on the floor and having unauthorized items.
79	The autopsy results on Epstein concluded that his cause of death was hanging and it was determined to be a suicide. The fractures in his neck were consistent with hanging, and there were no signs of a struggle or defensive wounds. The ligature found in his cell could have caused the injuries observed during the autopsy. No drugs or illegal substances were found in his system.
80	The page discusses the importance of independent medical judgment and confirms that the Medical Examiner was not influenced in her ruling.
81	The Metropolitan Correctional Center in New York had video security cameras, but due to a malfunction in the recording system, most of the recorded video evidence from the Special Housing Unit where Epstein was held was not available. The camera system had a history of problems and needed upgrades.
82	The security camera system at MCC New York experienced frequent failures, specifically with the DVR hard drives. Efforts were made to fix the cameras and replace the entire system, but the upgrade was not completed at the time of Epstein's death. The failure of the DVR system on July 29, 2019, was not discovered until August 8, 2019.

83	Approximately half of the cameras at MCC New York, where Jeffrey Epstein was held, were not recording before his death. The Electronics Technician responsible for the cameras did not perform daily checks and there were no specific policies requiring staff to ensure functionality. The technician did not resolve the issue on August 8 and the Facility Manager was not informed until after Epstein's death.
84	The Electronics Technician did not stay at the institution to fix the camera issue because of miscommunication. The Captain and Associate Warden were unaware of the issue. The Electronics Technician attempted to repair the cameras but was denied access to the room. Most of the cameras in the SHU were not recording due to a hard drive issue.
85	Limited camera footage shows Epstein being escorted to the L Tier stairway and an unidentified officer entering the area before his death. The live video feed of the L Tier was not recorded, but certain personnel had access to it. Staff did not perceive a need to view the live feed on the night Epstein died.
86	This page shows the camera locations and recording status in the SHU of MCC New York on August 10, 2019. Upper tiers have cameras that stream and record, while lower tiers only stream.
87	The page shows a modified photo and schematic drawing of the MCC New York SHU, specifically the location of a recording camera at the 10th floor South entrance.
88	The page shows a schematic drawing of the SHU camera's field of view at the 10th floor south entrance of the MCC New York, provided by the DOJ OIG.
89	The page displays a partial view of the L Tier Stairway from a camera located at the 10th floor South Entrance. The source of the information is the Department of Justice Office of the Inspector General and the Bureau of Prisons.
90	A view from the SHU Camera at the 10th floor-south entrance shows the SHU Officers' Station.
91	The page shows a schematic drawing of the 9th floor elevator bay camera's field of view in the MCC New York SHU and the BOP.
92	The Warden of the MCC New York SHU was informed that most of the cameras in the SHU were not recording on the day of Epstein's death. The Warden instructed the Electronics Technician to recover any potential video, but nothing was found. The FBI seized the hard drives and components of the DVR system for forensic analysis.
93	The FBI conducted a forensic analysis of a faulty DVR system and found that it contained three faulty hard drives. Despite attempts to repair the drives, the system could not be successfully assembled. The analysis also revealed that there were catastrophic disk failures, resulting in no recordings available after July 29, 2019. The prison staff was unaware of this issue.
94	The investigation into the Federal Bureau of Prisons' handling of Jeffrey Epstein's custody revealed numerous failures, including falsified records, policy violations, and lack of supervision. However, there was no evidence contradicting the FBI's determination that Epstein's cause of death was suicide. The report recommends addressing the issues identified during the investigation.
95	The report details the security measures in place at the Special Housing Unit (SHU) where Jeffrey Epstein was housed. It confirms that the doors to the SHU and Epstein's

	cell were locked, and there is no evidence of anyone entering or exiting his cell. Video analysis also shows no unauthorized individuals in the common area during the relevant time frame.
96	The report discusses the lack of surveillance footage, the failure to conduct required rounds and counts, and the presence of nooses in Epstein's cell. It also highlights the Medical Examiner's findings that support suicide by hanging rather than homicide by strangulation. The report concludes by noting previous job performance and management failures within the BOP.
97	The page discusses management failures within the Bureau of Prisons (BOP), including serious transgressions and deficiencies in handling high-profile inmates. It also highlights issues related to falsification of documentation, insufficient staffing levels, lack of attention to inmate needs, and deficiencies in the BOP's security camera systems.
98	Negligence, misconduct, and job performance failures at the BOP contributed to an environment where a notorious inmate was able to take his own life. The report highlights recurring failures at the BOP and the need for urgent action to address staffing and security issues. The investigation found that staff failed to ensure Epstein had a cellmate as instructed, and failed to notify superiors when his cellmate was transferred out.
99	Epstein was housed without a cellmate, against the directive of the Psychology Department. The officers in charge and CO Noel were aware that Epstein needed a cellmate but did not take appropriate action.
100	The investigation found that the officers and supervisory personnel at MCC New York failed to ensure that Jeffrey Epstein, a high-profile inmate, had a cellmate after his previous one was removed. Their inaction violated BOP standards of conduct and showed a lack of good judgment and common sense. Additionally, the supervisory personnel failed to effectively perform their duties by not reading an email notification about the transfer of another inmate, which would have indicated the need for a new cellmate for Epstein.
101	The Office of the Inspector General (OIG) found that there were failures in supervising staff and providing a cellmate for high-profile inmate Epstein, as well as instances of lack of candor by certain personnel at MCC New York. The OIG also noted a lack of contingency plan for assigning Epstein a cellmate.
102	MCC New York staff failed to follow required protocols, including providing Epstein with a cellmate and conducting mandatory rounds and inmate counts. This negligence resulted in Epstein being unobserved for hours before his death. The investigation revealed that the required measures were not properly carried out by the staff, leading to a lack of inmate accountability and compromising Epstein's safety.
103	During the investigation, it was found that officers assigned to the Special Housing Unit (SHU) failed to conduct required inmate counts and rounds. They were also found to have falsified records. Their actions violated regulations and laws.
104	Several individuals at MCC New York knowingly falsified records regarding inmate counts and rounds, leading to inaccurate reporting. Two individuals were indicted for their actions while others were not prosecuted. Additionally, poor judgment was shown

	in requesting a staff member to work three consecutive shifts without sufficient time off between them.
105	The investigation found that an employee at MCC New York worked a 24-hour shift due to pressure from a higher-ranking official. The official exercised poor judgment by requesting the third shift, and the employee admitted to not conducting mandatory counts during that time. Additionally, staff members cleared the 10 p.m. institutional count knowing that it was inaccurate, and an officer amended count slips to reflect the correct number of inmates.
106	The Office of the Inspector General (OIG) found that a senior officer at MCC New York engaged in "ghost counting" without proper authorization, leading to inaccurate inmate counts. The OIG also determined that supervisory personnel failed to adequately supervise staff and conduct required rounds, contributing to Jeffrey Epstein being unobserved for several hours before his death.
107	The OIG found that the failure of two lieutenants to properly supervise and conduct rounds in the SHU contributed to staff's failure to perform mandatory checks. Additionally, it was discovered that Epstein was allowed to make an unmonitored phone call on the night before his death, which violated regulations and lacked proper documentation.
108	MCC New York staff violated BOP policy by allowing Epstein to make an unrecorded and unmonitored phone call. Additionally, they failed to conduct and document cell searches, leaving Epstein with excessive linens in his cell.
109	The investigation found that staff at MCC New York failed to conduct required cell searches and ensure the security camera system was functioning properly. The lack of cell searches and malfunctioning cameras contributed to security issues and limited recorded video evidence. The replacement of the camera system had been delayed for nearly three years.
110	The page discusses the failure of MCC New York and the Bureau of Prisons (BOP) to maintain functional security camera systems, as well as the BOP's overall deficiencies in this area. The Office of Inspector General (OIG) has identified these weaknesses since 2013 and made recommendations for upgrades, but not all deficiencies have been addressed. The lack of functional security cameras poses a risk to staff and inmates' safety and hinders the investigation of misconduct. The OIG recommends implementing measures to
111	The Office of the Inspector General (OIG) recommends that the Bureau of Prisons (BOP) implement a requirement for cellmates for inmates coming off suicide watch, establish procedures to ensure high-risk inmates have a cellmate, and evaluate the process for approving social or legal visits for inmates on suicide watch. The OIG found knowledge gaps among staff and a lack of contingency plans in these areas.
112	The Office of Inspector General (OIG) recommends that the Bureau of Prisons (BOP) evaluate and improve their processes for approving and documenting legal visits for inmates on suicide watch or psychological observation. The OIG also suggests that the BOP assess their methods of accounting for inmate whereabouts and wellbeing, and clarify the responsibilities of Lieutenants during rounds in the Special Housing Unit (SHU).

113	The OIG recommends that the BOP address staffing shortages and evaluate cell search procedures to ensure inmate safety and facility security. The lack of adequate staffing and failure to address issues like excessive bed linens can have a direct impact on inmate wellbeing and pose safety hazards.
114	The BOP needs to update its policies on security camera systems to ensure they can record video and that regular checks are conducted. Failure to do so puts staff and inmates at risk and hinders investigations. The OIG recommends specific protocols for recording capacity and system functionality checks.
115	The Bureau of Prisons (BOP) acknowledges the Office of Inspector General's draft report on the mishandling of Jeffrey Epstein's supervision and agrees with the recommendations. BOP recognizes that the misconduct described in the report is not representative of the majority of its employees and is taking steps to improve policies and accountability.
116	The OIG's draft report suggests that the BOP should implement procedures for assigning cellmates to individuals following suicide watch or psychological observation. Additionally, the report recommends that inmates at high risk for suicide continue to have a cellmate until the recommendation is changed, and that the BOP evaluate its process for approving social or legal visits during suicide watch or psychological observation. The BOP agrees with these recommendations and has made updates to its processes.
117	The Office of Inspector General (OIG) has made several recommendations to improve the Bureau of Prisons' (BOP) care, custody, and supervision of Jeffrey Epstein at MCC New York. The BOP agrees with all the recommendations, including evaluating inmate whereabouts and wellbeing, clarifying lieutenant duties during rounds, addressing staffing shortages, improving cell search procedures, and enhancing security camera policies. The BOP appreciates the OIG's attention and looks forward to working together to implement these recommendations.
118	The Office of the Inspector General (OIG) analyzed the response from the Federal Bureau of Prisons (BOP) regarding recommendations for assigning cellmates following suicide watch. The BOP agreed with the recommendations and has updated its processes accordingly. The OIG will review the proposed process and determine if the recommendation can be closed.
119	The BOP's response to recommendations regarding the care and custody of inmates at risk for suicide is not fully responsive. The BOP needs to develop and implement procedures for assigning cellmates and evaluate its process for approving social or legal visits for inmates on suicide watch. Additionally, the BOP should evaluate and make changes to its methods of accounting for inmate whereabouts and wellbeing.
120	The BOP agrees with the recommendations made by the OIG and will evaluate its accounting methods for inmate whereabouts, clarify policies for conducting rounds, address staffing shortages, and improve cell search procedures.
121	The page discusses a recommendation for the BOP to evaluate and make changes to their cell search procedures and enhance their policies regarding security camera systems. The BOP has concurred with the recommendation but has not provided additional information.

Investigation and Review of the Federal Bureau of Prisons' Custody, Care, and Supervision of Jeffrey Epstein at the Metropolitan Correctional Center in New York, New York

★ ★ ★

INVESTIGATIONS DIVISION

23-085

JUNE 2023

EXECUTIVE SUMMARY

Investigation and Review of the Federal Bureau of Prisons' Custody, Care, and Supervision of Jeffrey Epstein at the Metropolitan Correctional Center in New York, New York

Introduction and Background

According to its website, the Federal Bureau of Prisons (BOP)'s current mission statement is "Corrections professionals who foster a humane and secure environment and ensure public safety by preparing individuals for successful reentry into our communities." However, the Department of Justice (DOJ) Office of the Inspector General (OIG) has repeatedly identified long-standing operational challenges that negatively affect the BOP's ability to operate its institutions safely and securely. Many of those same operational challenges, including staffing shortages, managing inmates at risk for suicide, functional security camera systems, and management failures and widespread disregard of BOP policies and procedures, were again identified by the OIG during this investigation and review into the custody, care, and supervision of one of the BOP's most notorious inmates, Jeffrey Epstein.

The OIG initiated this investigation upon receipt of information from the BOP that on August 10, 2019, in the Metropolitan Correctional Center in New York, New York (MCC New York), Epstein was found hanged in his assigned cell within the Special Housing Unit (SHU). The Office of the Chief Medical Examiner, City of New York, determined that Epstein had died by suicide.

The OIG conducted this investigation jointly with the Federal Bureau of Investigation (FBI), with the OIG's investigative focus being the conduct of BOP personnel. Among other things, the FBI investigated the cause of Epstein's death and determined there was no criminality pertaining to how Epstein had died.

This report concerns the OIG's findings regarding MCC New York personnel's custody, care, and supervision of Epstein while detained at the facility from his arrest on federal sex trafficking charges on July 6, 2019, until his death on August 10.

Epstein is Assigned to the SHU on July 7

Epstein was assigned to a cell in the SHU on July 7 due to media coverage of his case and inmate awareness of his notoriety. SHU inmates are securely separated from general population inmates and kept locked in their cells for approximately 23 hours a day.

BOP policy requires SHU staff to observe all inmates at least twice an hour and that Lieutenants conduct at least one round in the SHU each shift. BOP policy also requires multiple inmate counts during every 24-hour period. Among other things, inmate counts and rounds enable BOP staff to observe inmates and ensure they are secure in their cells and in good health. Further, to eliminate safety hazards, MCC New York requires SHU staff to search SHU common areas and at least five cells daily, and to search the entire SHU every week.

On July 18, the court refused to set bail for Epstein and ordered him detained pending trial on the criminal charges.

Incident Involving Epstein on July 23

While in MCC New York, Epstein was screened on numerous occasions by psychological staff, including a formal suicide assessment on July 9. In the evaluations he denied having thoughts or a history of attempted suicide. Psychological staff determined Epstein did not meet the criteria for a psychological diagnosis.

On July 23, at 1:27 a.m., correctional officers (CO) responded to Epstein's SHU cell where they found Epstein with an orange cloth around his neck. Epstein's cellmate told officers Epstein tried to hang himself. Medical staff examined Epstein, observed friction marks and superficial reddening around his neck and on his knee, and placed him on suicide watch. BOP policy requires that inmates identified as suicide risks be placed on suicide watch until no longer at imminent risk. The BOP uses a less restrictive monitoring form, psychological observation, for inmates who are stabilizing but not yet ready to return to a housing unit. Epstein was removed from suicide watch on July 24 but remained under psychological observation until July 30.

Epstein first told MCC New York staff he thought his cellmate had tried to kill him, but later said he did not know what occurred and did not want to talk about how he had sustained his injuries. Epstein also later asked if he could be housed with the same cellmate. Another inmate housed on the same SHU tier told the OIG that he heard Epstein's cellmate call for assistance, and that Epstein's cellmate told him that Epstein tried to hang himself from the bunkbed ladder. Disciplinary charges against Epstein for alleged self-mutilation were not sustained due to insufficient evidence.

Following the July 23 incident, the Psychology Department determined Epstein needed to be housed with an appropriate cellmate, and on July 30 it sent an email to over 70 MCC New York employees informing them of this requirement. The Warden at the time told the OIG that he selected a new cellmate for Epstein in consultation with BOP executive leadership. That inmate remained Epstein's cellmate until August 9.

Events of August 8–10, 2019, and Epstein's Death

On August 8, the U.S. Marshals Service sent two emails notifying numerous MCC New York staff that Epstein's cellmate was being transferred to another facility on August 9. However, no action was taken to ensure Epstein was assigned another cellmate.

Also on August 8, Epstein met with his attorneys at the prison, as he had on prior occasions, and signed a new Last Will and Testament. MCC New York officials did not learn about the new Will until after Epstein's death.

The following day, August 9, Epstein's cellmate was transferred to another facility and he was not assigned a new cellmate. Additionally, on that date, the U.S. Court of Appeals for the Second Circuit unsealed approximately 2,000 pages of documents in civil litigation involving Ghislaine Maxwell, who was later convicted in December 2021 of conspiring with Epstein to sexually abuse minors over the course of a decade. The documents contain substantial derogatory information about Epstein and there is extensive media coverage of information in the unsealed documents.

Also on August 9, after meeting at the prison with his lawyers, MCC New York staff allowed Epstein to make, in violation of BOP policy, an unrecorded, unmonitored telephone call before he was returned to his SHU cell. Although Epstein said he was calling his mother, in actuality he called someone with whom he allegedly had a personal relationship.

At approximately 8 p.m. on August 9, SHU inmates were locked in their cells for the night, including Epstein who was without a cellmate. A search of Epstein's cell following his death revealed Epstein had excess prison blankets, linens, and clothing in his cell, and that some had been ripped to create nooses. Only one SHU cell search was documented on August 9, and it was not of Epstein's cell. BOP records did not indicate when Epstein's cell was last searched. The OIG also found that SHU staff did not conduct any 30-minute rounds after about 10:40 p.m. on August 9 and that none of the required SHU inmate counts were conducted after 4 p.m. on August 9. Count slips and round sheets were falsified to show that they had been performed.

On August 10, at approximately 6:30 a.m., the two SHU staff on duty, CO Tova Noel and Material Handler Michael Thomas, began delivering breakfast to SHU inmates. Noel unlocked the door to Epstein's SHU tier. When Thomas attempted to deliver breakfast to Epstein through the food slot in his locked cell door, Epstein did not respond to Thomas's verbal commands. Thomas unlocked the cell door and saw Epstein hanged. Thomas immediately yelled for Noel to get help and call for a medical emergency.

Thomas told the OIG that when he entered Epstein's cell, Epstein had an orange string, presumably from a sheet or a shirt, around his neck that was tied to the top portion of the bunkbed. Epstein was suspended from the top bunk in a near-seated position, with his buttocks approximately 1 inch to 1 inch and a half off the floor. Thomas said he immediately ripped the orange string from the bunkbed, and Epstein's buttocks dropped to the ground. Thomas then lowered Epstein's body to the floor and began chest compressions until responding MCC New York staff members arrived approximately 1 minute later. Shortly thereafter, outside medical personnel arrived and took over the emergency response, eventually removing Epstein to a local hospital where he was pronounced dead.

On August 11, 2019, the Office of the Chief Medical Examiner performed an autopsy and determined the cause of death was hanging and the manner of death was suicide. Blood toxicology tests did not reveal any medications or illegal substances in Epstein's system. The Medical Examiner who performed the autopsy told the OIG that Epstein's injuries were consistent with suicide by hanging and that there was no evidence of defensive wounds that would be expected if his death had been a homicide. Epstein did not have marks on his hands, broken fingernails or debris under them, contusions to his knuckles that would have evidenced a fight, or, other than an abrasion on his arm likely due to convulsing from hanging, bruising on his body.

The Limited Available Video Evidence

Recorded video evidence for August 9 and 10 for the SHU area where Epstein was housed was only available from one prison security camera due to a malfunction of MCC New York's Digital Video Recorder system that occurred on July 29, 2019. While the prison's cameras continued to provide live video feeds, recordings were made for only about half the cameras. MCC New York personnel discovered this failure on August 8, 2019, but it was not repaired until after Epstein's death. As detailed in this report, like many other BOP facilities, MCC New York had a history of security camera problems.

The available recorded video footage from the one SHU camera captured a large part of the common area of the SHU and portions of the stairways leading to the different SHU tiers, including Epstein's cell tier. Thus, anyone entering or attempting to enter Epstein's SHU tier from the SHU common area would have been picked up by that video camera. Epstein's cell door, however, was not in the camera's field of view. The OIG reviewed the video and found that, between approximately 10:40 p.m. on August 9 and about 6:30 a.m. on August 10, no one was seen entering Epstein's cell tier from the SHU common area. The OIG determined that movements captured on video before and after those times were generally consistent with employee actions as described by witnesses and documented in BOP records.

Results of the OIG's Investigation and Review

The OIG's investigation and review identified numerous and serious failures by MCC New York staff, including multiple violations of MCC New York and BOP policies and procedures. The OIG found that MCC New York staff failed on August 9 to carry out the Psychology Department's directive that Epstein be assigned a cellmate, and that an MCC New York supervisor allowed Epstein to make an unmonitored telephone call the evening before his death. Additionally, we found that staff failed to undertake required measures designed to make sure that Epstein and other SHU inmates were accounted for and safe, such as conducting inmate counts and 30-minute rounds, searching inmate cells, and ensuring adequate supervision of the SHU and the functionality of the video camera surveillance system.

The OIG also found that several staff falsified BOP records relating to inmate counts and rounds and lacked candor during their OIG interviews. Two MCC New York employees, Noel and Thomas, were charged criminally with falsifying BOP records. The charges were later dismissed after they successfully fulfilled deferred prosecution agreements. The U.S. Attorney's Office for the Southern District of New York declined prosecution for other MCC New York employees who the OIG found created false documentation.

The combination of these and other failures led to Epstein being unmonitored and alone in his cell, which contained an excessive amount of bed linens, from approximately 10:40 p.m. on August 9 until he was discovered hanged in his locked cell the following day.

While the OIG determined MCC New York staff engaged in significant misconduct, we did not uncover evidence contradicting the FBI's determination regarding the absence of criminality in connection with how Epstein died. We did not find, for example, evidence that anyone was present in the SHU area where Epstein was housed during the relevant timeframe other than the inmates who were locked in their assigned cells. The SHU housing unit was securely separated from the general inmate population and inmates were kept locked in their cells for approximately 23 hours a day. Access to the SHU was controlled by multiple locked doors. Within the SHU, the entrance to each tier could be accessed only via a single locked door at the top or bottom of the staircase leading to the individual tier. Keys to open the locked tier doors were available to a limited number of COs while on duty. Each tier had eight cells and each individual cell, which was made of cement and metal, could be accessed only through a single locked door, to which a limited number of COs had keys while on duty. The SHU cell doors were made of solid metal with a small glass window and small locked slots that correctional staff used to handcuff inmates and provide food and toiletries to inmates. As a further security measure, during each shift a limited number of the COs had keys while on duty.

SHU staff told the OIG that at approximately 8 p.m. on August 9, all SHU inmates, including Epstein, were locked in their cells for the evening and we found no evidence to the contrary. The prison's recorded video did not identify any staff or other individuals approaching Epstein's SHU tier from the SHU common area between approximately 10:40 p.m. on August 9 and about 6:30 a.m. on August 10. Additionally, the OIG did not observe on the recorded video that Noel and Thomas, who were seated at the desk at the SHU Officers' Station immediately outside the area where Epstein was housed, at any time during the time period rose from their seats or approached the cell block. We additionally found that Thomas's and Noel's reaction on the morning of August 10 upon finding Epstein hanging in his cell, as described to us by Thomas, Noel, the responding Lieutenant, and inmates, was consistent with their being unaware of any potential harm to Epstein prior to Thomas entering Epstein's cell at about 6:30 a.m. on August 10.

None of the MCC New York staff members we interviewed were aware of any information suggesting Epstein's cause of death was something other than suicide. Additionally, none of the inmates we interviewed had any credible information suggesting Epstein's cause of death was something other than suicide. Further, the SHU staff and three interviewed inmates with a direct line of sight to Epstein's cell door on the night of his death stated that no one entered or exited Epstein's cell after the SHU staff returned Epstein to his cell on August 9.

As noted, the surveillance camera in the SHU area where Epstein was housed was live streaming movement in the hallway outside of Epstein's cell. Although the camera was not recording the captured video, the camera was in plain view of the inmates and therefore inmates would have been aware that any hallway movements, including into or out of Epstein's cell, could be monitored by BOP staff, even if, unbeknownst to them, the DVR system was not recording the live stream at that time. As the OIG has noted in numerous prior reports, BOP staff and inmates are aware of where prison cameras are located and often engage in wrongdoing in locations where they know cameras are not located.

We noted as well that Epstein had previously been placed on suicide watch and psychological observation due to the events of July 23, 2019; that numerous nooses made from the excess prison sheets were found in his cell on the morning of August 10; that no weapons were recovered from his cell after his death; and that he signed a new Last Will and Testament on August 8, 2 days before he died. We found that the staff's failure to assign Epstein a cellmate on August 9; failure to conduct rounds and counts that evening; and to allow him to have excess linens in his cell, left Epstein unmonitored and locked alone in his cell for hours, which provided him an opportunity to commit suicide.

Finally, the Medical Examiner who performed the autopsy detailed for the OIG why Epstein's injuries were more consistent with, and indicative of, a suicide by hanging rather than a homicide by strangulation. The Medical Examiner also cited the absence of debris under Epstein's fingernails, marks on his hands, contusions to his knuckles, or bruises on his body evidencing a struggle, which would be expected if Epstein's death had been a homicide by strangulation.

Conclusion and Recommendations

This is not the first time the OIG has found significant job performance and management failures on the part of BOP personnel and widespread disregard of BOP policies that are designed to ensure that inmates are safe, secure, and in good health. The combination of negligence, misconduct, and outright job performance failures documented in this report all contributed to an environment in which arguably one of the BOP's most notorious inmates was provided with the opportunity to take his own life, resulting in significant questions being asked about the circumstances of his death, how it could have been allowed to happen, and most importantly, depriving his numerous victims, many of whom were underage girls at the time of the alleged crimes, of their ability to seek justice through the criminal justice process. The fact that these failures have been recurring ones at the BOP does not excuse them and gives additional urgency to the need for DOJ and BOP leadership to address the chronic staffing, surveillance, safety and security, and related problems plaguing the BOP.

The OIG made eight recommendations to the BOP to address the numerous issues identified during our investigation and review. Finally, we recommended that the BOP review the conduct and performance of the BOP personnel as described in this report and determine whether discipline or other administrative action with regard to each of them is appropriate.

Table of Contents

Chapter 1: Introduction

The Federal Bureau of Prisons (BOP) is a component of the Department of Justice (DOJ) that operates 122 institutions across the United States. According to its website, the BOP's current mission statement is "Corrections professionals who foster a humane and secure environment and ensure public safety by preparing individuals for successful reentry into our communities." However, the DOJ Office of the Inspector General (OIG) has issued numerous reports over more than a decade identifying long-standing operational challenges facing the BOP that have negatively affected its ability to operate its institutions safely and securely. Those reports have contained dozens of recommendations to the BOP. As we detail in this report, many of those same operational challenges and systemic issues, including significant staffing shortages, providing appropriate custody and care of inmates at risk for suicide, the absence of functional security camera systems, and management failures and widespread disregard of BOP policies and procedures, were once again identified by the OIG during the course of this investigation and review into the custody, care, and supervision of one of the BOP's most notorious inmates, Jeffrey Epstein. We therefore make further recommendations to the BOP in the conclusion of this report to help it address these recurring issues.

The OIG initiated this investigation upon the receipt of information from the BOP that on the morning of August 10, 2019, in the Metropolitan Correctional Center located in New York, New York (MCC New York), inmate Jeffery Epstein was found hanged in his assigned cell within the Special Housing Unit (SHU). The SHU is a housing unit where inmates are securely separated from the general inmate population and kept locked in their cells for approximately 23 hours a day, to ensure their own safety as well as the safety of staff and other inmates. Epstein had been placed in the SHU on July 7, 2019, the day after his arrest, due to the significant media coverage of his case and awareness of his notoriety among MCC New York inmates.

According to information obtained by the OIG during the investigation, at approximately 8 p.m. on August 9, all SHU inmates, including Epstein, were locked in their cells for the evening. Additionally, the six separate tiers or groups of cells within the SHU were also securely locked. At approximately 6:30 a.m. on August 10, 2019, SHU staff unlocked the door to the SHU tier in which Epstein's cell was located in order to deliver breakfast to inmates through the food slots in the locked cell doors. When SHU staff entered the tier to deliver breakfast to Epstein, SHU staff knocked on the locked door to Epstein's cell. Epstein, who was housed alone in the cell, did not respond to SHU staff. SHU staff unlocked the cell door and found Epstein hanged in his cell, with one end of a piece of orange cloth around his neck and the other end tied to the top portion of a bunkbed in Epstein's cell. Epstein was suspended from the top bunk in a near-seated position with his buttocks approximately 1 inch to 1 inch and a half off the floor and his legs extended straight out on the floor in front of him. Epstein's cell contained an excess amount of prison linens, as well as multiple nooses that had been made from torn prison linens.

SHU staff immediately activated a body alarm, which notified all MCC New York staff of a medical emergency and prompted MCC New York staff assigned to the Control Center to call for 911 emergency services. SHU staff then ripped the orange cloth away from the bunkbed, which caused Epstein's buttocks to drop to the ground. SHU staff laid Epstein on the ground and immediately initiated cardiopulmonary resuscitation (CPR). At approximately 6:33 a.m., other MCC New York employees responded to the SHU. A responding MCC New York Lieutenant took over administering CPR and asked SHU staff to retrieve an automated external defibrillator and call for the duty nurse. A Clinical Nurse responded and continued to perform CPR on Epstein in the place of the Lieutenant. At approximately 6:39 a.m., Epstein was placed on a stretcher and moved by medical staff to the MCC New York Health Service Unit.[1] The Clinical Nurse continuously administered CPR until he was relieved by outside Emergency Medical Technicians (EMT) when they arrived at the Health Services Area minutes later. The EMTs continued CPR, intubated Epstein, and administered medication and fluids in their efforts to revive him. At approximately 7:10 a.m., Epstein was transported by the EMTs in an ambulance to New York Presbyterian Lower Manhattan Hospital, where he was pronounced dead by an emergency room physician at 7:36 a.m. On August 11, 2019, the Office of the Chief Medical Examiner, City of New York, performed an autopsy on Epstein and determined that the cause of death was hanging and the manner of death was suicide.

The OIG conducted this investigation jointly with the Federal Bureau of Investigation (FBI), with the OIG's investigative focus being the conduct of BOP personnel. Among other things, the FBI investigated the cause of Epstein's death. The FBI determined that there was no criminality pertaining to how Epstein had died. This report concerns the OIG's findings regarding MCC New York personnel's custody, care, and supervision of Epstein during his detention at the facility from his arrest on July 6, 2019, until his death on August 10, 2019.

The OIG investigation and review identified numerous and serious failures by MCC New York staff, as well as multiple violations of MCC New York and BOP policies and procedures. Among the most significant was the failure to assign Epstein a new cellmate on August 9, 2019, after Epstein's cellmate was transferred out of MCC New York that day. Epstein was required to have a cellmate at all times pursuant to a written direction that the MCC New York Psychology Department issued on July 30 after Epstein was removed from suicide watch and psychological observation following a possible attempted suicide by him on July 23. As a result of the failure to assign him a new cellmate, Epstein was housed alone in his cell from the night of August 9 until he was found hanged in his cell by SHU staff at approximately 6:30 a.m. the following morning. In addition, we determined that SHU staff failed to conduct required inmate counts and rounds, including overnight on August 9-10, and allowed Epstein to have an excess of blankets, linens, and clothing in his cell. These failures compromised Epstein's safety, the safety of other inmates, and the security of the institution, and provided Epstein an opportunity to commit suicide while locked alone in his cell on the morning of August 10 without having been subject to overnight observation or supervision by SHU staff.

The OIG also found that an MCC New York supervisor had allowed Epstein, in violation of BOP policy, to make an unrecorded, unmonitored telephone call the evening before his death to an individual with whom he allegedly had a personal relationship. Further, 2 days before his death, during a meeting with his lawyers in a private room at the MCC New York, Epstein signed a new Last Will and Testament, which MCC New York officials did not learn about until after his death.

Additionally, the OIG determined that MCC New York staff assigned to the SHU, including the two SHU staff on duty the night of August 9–10, 2019, who were stationed at a desk that was directly outside the SHU tier in which Epstein was housed and diagonally across from Epstein's cell, had falsified BOP records to claim

---

[1] Moving an inmate requiring outside emergency medical care to the Health Services Unit provides health care staff and Emergency Medical Technicians (EMT) with immediate access to any necessary medical equipment and supplies and allows EMTs faster access to the inmate when they arrive at MCC New York because Correctional Officers (CO) can directly escort EMTs to the Health Services Unit to begin emergency treatment immediately. If EMTs had to be escorted to the housing unit, they would first need to be thoroughly screened, which would delay medical attention.

that they had conducted all of the required counts of inmates and 30-minute rounds during their shifts within the SHU. As described in greater detail in Chapter 2, inmate counts and 30-minute rounds are two means by which the BOP accounts for inmates and assesses their safety, security, and well-being. BOP and MCC New York policies require that staff members count all inmates in each housing unit within the facility at designated times each day. Additionally, BOP and MCC New York policies require that a staff member observe all SHU inmates at least once during the first 30 minutes of each hour (e.g., 12 a.m. to 12:30 a.m.) and again during the second 30 minutes of the hour (e.g., 12:30 a.m. to 1 a.m.), thus ensuring that inmates are observed at least twice per hour. BOP staff are required to document inmate counts and 30-minute rounds on official BOP forms, which are often referred to as "count slips" and "round sheets."[2]

During the OIG's investigation, the OIG obtained information that the staff assigned to the MCC New York SHU did not conduct any counts of inmates within the SHU from August 9, 2019, at approximately 4 p.m., until Epstein was found hanged in his cell on the morning of August 10, 2019. However, in documentation completed by the SHU staff on duty during that period, staff members falsely certified in the count slips that they had conducted the required counts. Additionally, the OIG investigation revealed that the staff assigned to the MCC New York SHU did not conduct any required 30-minute rounds of inmates after approximately 10:40 p.m. on August 9, 2019. Again, however, SHU staff on duty during that period had falsely certified in the round sheet that the required rounds were conducted. The combination of these and other failures led to Epstein being unmonitored and locked alone in his cell, which the OIG found contained an excessive amount of bed linens, from approximately 10:40 p.m. on August 9 until he was discovered hanged in his cell at approximately 6:30 a.m. the following day.

While the OIG determined that MCC New York staff committed significant violations of BOP and MCC New York policies and falsified records related to their conducting inmate counts and rounds, the OIG did not uncover evidence that contradicted the FBI's determination regarding the absence of criminality in connection with how Epstein died. All MCC New York staff members who were interviewed by the OIG said they did not know of any information suggesting that Epstein's cause of death was something other than suicide. Additionally, none of the 15 inmates who agreed to be interviewed in connection with this investigation, 10 of whom were housed in the SHU on August 9 and 10, had any credible information suggesting that Epstein's cause of death was something other than suicide. Further, the SHU staff and the three interviewed inmates with a direct line of sight to the door of Epstein's cell from their cells stated that no one entered or exited Epstein's cell after the SHU staff returned Epstein to his cell on the evening of August 9, which is consistent with the security measures in place within the MCC New York SHU. SHU staff told the OIG that at approximately 8 p.m. on August 9, all SHU inmates were locked in their cells for the evening and that there was no indication that any of the other inmates could have gotten out of their cells. Additionally, the OIG analyzed the available recorded video of the SHU, which was limited to the common area of the SHU, including the SHU Officers' Station, due to the MCC New York security camera system's recording issues that we detail in this report.[3] The OIG's analysis of the recorded video did not identify any Correctional Officers (CO) or other individuals approaching any of the SHU tiers, including the L Tier where

---

[2] These BOP forms are officially entitled "Official Count Slip" and "MCC New York, Special Housing Unit, 30 Minute Check Sheet."

[3] For reasons we describe below, while the camera inside the L Tier was working and transmitting live video, the video was not being recorded.

Epstein was housed, from the common area of the SHU between approximately 10:40 p.m. on August 9 and approximately 6:30 a.m. on August 10.

Finally, the Medical Examiner who performed the autopsy detailed for the OIG why Epstein's injuries were more consistent with, and indicative of, a suicide by hanging rather than a homicide by strangulation. The Medical Examiner also cited to the absence of debris under Epstein's fingernails, marks on his hands, contusions to his knuckles, or bruises on his body that evidenced Epstein had been in a struggle, which would be expected if Epstein's death had been a homicide by strangulation.

As discussed in greater detail in the Conclusions and Recommendations chapter of this report, this is not the first time that the OIG has found significant job performance and management failures on the part of BOP personnel and widespread disregard of BOP policies that are designed to ensure that inmates are safe, secure, and in good health. The OIG has investigated numerous allegations related to the falsification of official BOP documentation concerning inmate counts and rounds and has repeatedly found deficiencies with the BOP's staffing levels, the custody and care of inmates at risk for suicide, and security camera systems at BOP institutions. The combination of negligence, misconduct, and outright job performance failures documented in this report all contributed to an environment in which arguably one of the most notorious inmates in BOP's custody was provided with the opportunity to take his own life. The BOP's failures are troubling not only because the BOP did not adequately safeguard an individual in its custody, but also because they led to questions about the circumstances surrounding Epstein's death and effectively deprived Epstein's numerous victims of the opportunity to seek justice through the criminal justice process. The fact that these failures have been recurring ones at the BOP does not excuse them and gives additional urgency to the need for DOJ and BOP leadership to address the chronic problems plaguing the BOP.

Unless otherwise noted, the OIG applies the preponderance of the evidence standard in determining whether DOJ personnel have committed misconduct. The U.S. Merit Systems Protection Board applies this same standard when reviewing a federal agency's decision to take adverse action against an employee based on such misconduct. See 5 U.S.C. § 7701(c)(1)(B) and 5 C.F.R. § 1201.56(b)(1)(ii).

In Chapter 2 of this report, we provide background information, including identification and a description of significant entities and individuals; a summary of our methodology; and the applicable laws, federal regulations, and BOP policies. In Chapter 3, we outline a timeline of key events. In Chapter 4, we set forth our findings of fact relating to the BOP's custody and care of Epstein before his death. In Chapter 5, we set forth our findings of fact related to the events of August 8–10, 2019, including Epstein's death. In Chapter 6, we set forth our findings of fact related to the BOP's failure to ensure that there was a functional security camera system at MCC New York, which resulted in limited recorded video evidence relevant to Epstein's death. Finally, Chapter 7 contains our conclusions and recommendations.

Chapter 2: Background

I.   Significant Entities and Individuals

Jeffrey Epstein was born in 1953 and, prior to his arrest, worked at various jobs in the financial industry and ultimately developed considerable wealth. On July 2, 2019, a federal grand jury of the U.S. District Court for the Southern District of New York returned an indictment that charged Epstein with engaging in sex trafficking and a sex trafficking conspiracy, in violation of 18 U.S.C. §§ 371, 1591(a), (b)(2), and 2. These charges were based on allegations that between 2002 and 2005, Epstein paid girls as young as 14 years old hundreds of dollars in cash each for engaging in sex acts with him at his Florida and New York residences. The indictment further alleged that Epstein also paid each of these minor victims hundreds of dollars in cash to recruit other girls to engage in sex acts with Epstein.

On July 6, 2019, Epstein was arrested at Teterboro Airport in New Jersey upon his return to the United States from France and was transported to the Federal Bureau of Prisons' (BOP) Metropolitan Correctional Center, located at 150 Park Row in New York, New York (MCC New York). Following a detention hearing on July 15, 2019, the court ordered that Epstein be detained pending trial based on the court's finding that he was a danger to the community and a flight risk.

MCC New York is a federal administrative detention facility operated by the BOP that primarily provides pretrial detention services for the U.S. District Courts for the Southern and Eastern Districts of New York. The BOP temporarily closed MCC New York in October 2021 due to substandard conditions that are unrelated to this investigation. When it was operational, MCC New York housed approximately 750 inmates at any given time. Prior to its closure, the majority of MCC New York's inmate residents were individuals with pending criminal charges (as opposed to individuals who had been convicted of offenses and were serving a sentence of imprisonment), but whom the court had determined under applicable law should remain in custody pending trial either because they represent a danger to the community, a substantial flight risk, or both. MCC New York has several different housing units. Epstein was initially assigned to MCC New York's general inmate population, but on July 7, 2019, he was moved to the Special Housing Unit (SHU) pending reclassification due to the significant increase in media coverage and awareness of his notoriety among the other inmates. The SHU is a housing unit within MCC New York where inmates are securely separated from the general inmate population and kept locked in their cells for approximately 23 hours per day, to ensure their own safety as well as the safety of staff and other inmates.

Correctional Officer (CO) Tova Noel and Material Handler Michael Thomas began working together in MCC New York SHU at 12 a.m. on August 10, 2019.[4] During their shift, they each created and submitted falsified official BOP forms documenting inmate counts (often referred to as "count slips"), and Noel completed and signed more than 75 separate entries on an official BOP form documenting 30-minute rounds (often

---

[4] Noel worked her regular shift in the SHU from 4 p.m. to 12 a.m. on August 9, 2019, followed by an overtime shift in the SHU from 12 a.m. to 8 a.m. on August 10, 2019. Thomas did not work his regular shift as a Material Handler in a different location of MCC New York and instead worked an overtime shift in the SHU from 12 a.m. to 8 a.m. on August 10, 2019.

referred to as a "round sheet") falsely stating that she and Thomas had conducted such rounds when, in fact, they had not.[5]

On November 19, 2019, a federal grand jury of the U.S. District Court for the Southern District of New York returned an indictment that charged Noel and Thomas with one count each of conspiracy and multiple counts each of falsification of records, in violation of 18 U.S.C. §§ 371, 1001(a)(3), and 2. The indictment alleged that on August 9, 2019, Noel failed to conduct the mandatory 4 p.m. and 10 p.m. counts of inmates in the MCC New York SHU, and that on August 10, 2019, both she and Thomas failed to conduct the mandatory 12 a.m., 3 a.m., and 5 a.m. counts and mandatory 30-minute rounds within the MCC New York SHU. The indictment further alleged that Noel and Thomas created, certified, and submitted false documentation indicating that the counts and rounds had been done as required to conceal their failure to perform their assigned duties. As a result, it appeared from documentation that prisoners in the SHU, including Epstein, were being regularly monitored when, in fact, no CO had checked on Epstein from approximately 10:40 p.m. on August 9, 2019, until approximately 6:30 a.m. on August 10, 2019, when Epstein was found hanged in his cell.

On May 25, 2021, the U.S. Attorney's Office for the Southern District of New York entered into deferred prosecution agreements with Noel and Thomas. Their respective agreements, which are part of the court record in their cases, included admissions by Noel and Thomas that they falsely certified that they had conducted counts and rounds. The agreements also required each of them to truthfully and completely disclose all information related to their activities and employment with the BOP; be interviewed by the U.S. Attorney's Office of the Southern District of New York, the FBI, and the OIG; complete 100 hours of community service; refrain from violating the law; and fulfill other conditions related to pretrial supervision and their establishment of good behavior. On December 13, 2021, after Noel and Thomas successfully fulfilled the terms of their deferred prosecution agreements as determined by the prosecutors, the U.S. District Court for the Southern District of New York entered a nolle prosequi order and dismissed all charges pending against them. Prosecution was declined by the U.S. Attorney's Office for the Southern District of New York for other BOP employees assigned to the SHU who also falsely certified inmate count slips and round sheets on the day before and the day of Epstein's death.

As discussed in greater detail in Chapter 7 of this report, the OIG found that, in addition to Noel and Thomas, many other MCC New York staff members engaged in administrative misconduct, exercised poor judgment, and/or failed to adequately perform their assigned duties.

II.   Methodology

During the course of this investigation, the OIG interviewed 54 witnesses, several on more than one occasion. The witnesses interviewed included Noel, Thomas, and other MCC New York staff assigned to the SHU on August 9-10, 2019; MCC New York supervisors at the time of Epstein's death, including the Warden, Associate Wardens, Captain, and Lieutenants; medical staff; staff members responsible for the MCC New York security camera system; other BOP staff and contractors; and a relative of Epstein, who had

---

[5] These BOP forms are officially entitled "Official Count Slip" and "MCC New York, Special Housing Unit, 30 Minute Check Sheet." Each of the 6 tiers in the SHU had a separate round sheet, each of which had 13 entries reflecting 30-minute rounds were conducted, when they were not, in fact, completed.

requested to provide information.[6] The BOP employees and contractors we interviewed included employees involved in various aspects of the emergency response, who worked at MCC New York in the days leading up to the response and following the response, as well as other individuals with information pertinent to our investigation. Additionally, the OIG participated in interviews of 15 inmates who had been housed at MCC New York during time periods relevant to our investigation, including three who were housed in the L Tier of the SHU on the day Epstein died.[7] Those three L-Tier inmates were housed in cells opposite Epstein's cell and therefore had a direct line of sight to Epstein's cell on the night of August 9–10. The OIG also reached out to one of Epstein's attorneys to discuss the possibility of providing information, but ultimately the attorney declined to be interviewed, citing attorney-client privilege (the attorney-client privilege survives a client's death) and issues related to ongoing litigation involving Epstein's estate.

The OIG also collected over 127,000 documents, as well as MCC New York video and photographs. Among these were BOP documents, including staff rosters; daily logs and reports; investigative and incident reports; documentation regarding inmate counts and 30-minute rounds; inmate housing assignment documentation; inmate transfer documents; Psychology Department reports and medical records relating to Epstein; Epstein's institutional phone call records; MCC New York records of Epstein's visits with his attorneys; electronic communications, including text messages and emails of BOP employees and contractors; MCC New York security camera surveillance video; records from contractors regarding the MCC New York security camera system; service records for MCC New York's security camera system; MCC New York photographs, including photographs taken of efforts to revive Epstein on the morning of August 10, 2019; BOP policies and program statements; MCC New York Post Orders; and financial records. The OIG also conducted forensic analysis of the computers located in the SHU and BOP cellular telephones. In addition, the OIG reviewed FBI investigative records, including interview reports (FD-302), notes from witness interviews and other meetings, and electronic communications. The OIG also reviewed Epstein's autopsy report and interviewed the Medical Examiner who performed the autopsy on Epstein.

III. Applicable Law, Regulations, and BOP Policies

A. Standards of Conduct

The Standards of Ethical Conduct for Employees of the Executive Branch sets out general principles that are designed to "ensure that every citizen can have complete confidence in the integrity of the Federal Government."[8] Among other things, these standards require that every federal employee "use official time

---

[6] On a separate occasion, the relative contacted the OIG to say that the relative had "photographic proof" that the door to Epstein's cell was left open the night Epstein died. When the OIG followed up with the relative to request copies of the photographs and any information regarding this allegation, the relative stated that upon further review, the photographs did not show what the relative previously communicated to the OIG.

[7] The U.S. Attorney's Office for the Southern District of New York sought interviews from inmates housed in the L Tier of the SHU on the night that Epstein died, each of whom was represented by counsel. Three inmates agreed to be interviewed. The OIG does not have the authority to compel or subpoena testimony from individuals who are not DOJ employees.

[8] 5 C.F.R. § 2635.101(a).

in an honest effort to perform official duties."[9] The ethical regulations also mandate that federal employees not use federal property "for other than authorized activities."[10]

BOP policy (Program Statement 3420.11, Standards of Employee Conduct) imposes several additional standards of conduct on its employees. At all times, BOP employees must "[c]onduct themselves in a manner that fosters respect for the Bureau of Prisons, the Department of Justice, and the U.S. Government." Because "[i]nattention to duty in a correctional environment can result in escapes, assaults, and other incidents," BOP employees "are required to remain fully alert and attentive during duty hours." BOP policy provides that employees can use government property for authorized purposes only, and further specifies that personal use of government office equipment, such as computers, "will not take place during official working hours." BOP policy requires that employees "obey the orders of their superiors at all times."

B.   False Statements and Lack of Candor

Under federal law, "whoever, in any matter within the jurisdiction of the executive...branch of the Government of the United States, knowingly and willfully...makes or uses any false writing or document knowing the same to contain any materially false, fictitious, or fraudulent statement or entry" has violated 18 U.S.C. § 1001(a)(3). The terms "knowingly and willfully" mean that the subject acted with knowledge that the conduct was, in a general sense, prohibited by law. It is not required that the subject was aware of the existence of Section 1001.

Under BOP standards of conduct discussed above, employees are required to cooperate fully with official investigations, which includes providing "all pertinent information they may have" and "truthfully responding to questions."

C.   Relevant BOP Policies Regarding the Operation of Correctional Facilities

1.   *Special Housing Units*

SHUs within BOP facilities are governed by federal regulations, 28 C.F.R. §§ 541.21-541.33. These regulations provide that the BOP may establish SHUs "where inmates are securely separated from the general inmate population." These regulations and BOP policy (Program Statement 5270.11, Special Housing Units) explain that inmates in the SHU are either on administrative detention or disciplinary segregation status. Administrative segregation status is a non-punitive designation that removes an inmate "from the general population when necessary to ensure the safety, security, and orderly operation of correctional facilities, or protect the public." There are several reasons an inmate can be placed in administrative detention status, including when an inmate's presence in the general inmate population presents a threat to self or others, or when administrative detention status is necessary for the protection of the inmate. Assignment to the SHU for protection reasons can be based on being a victim of an assault, acting (or being perceived) as an informant, refusing to enter general population, or because of staff concerns about the inmate's safety.

---

[9] 5 C.F.R. § 2635.705(a); see also 5 C.F.R. § 2635.101(b)(5).

[10] 5 C.F.R. § 2635.101(b)(9); see also 5 C.F.R. § 2635.704(a).

Inmates in the SHU are securely separated from general population inmates and are kept locked in their cell when in their assigned tier within the SHU. As discussed in greater detail in Chapter 4, witnesses told the OIG that SHU inmates are locked in their cells for approximately 23 hours a day. BOP policy provides that, weather and resources permitting, SHU inmates will have the opportunity to exercise outside their quarters 5 hours per calendar week. Under federal regulations and BOP policy, SHU inmates ordinarily have the opportunity to shower at least 3 times a week, typically on different days in 1-hour periods. SHU inmates may also be escorted from their cells by MCC New York staff for visits, including legal visits, court appearances, medical and psychological attention. The MCC New York SHU Post Orders require that all visitors to the SHU be documented in a visitor log, and that any inmate visiting the SHU, such as inmates on work details, be searched visually and with a hand-held metal detector, without exception. The MCC New York SHU Post Orders also require that food carts be searched inside and out before being brought into a SHU cellblock and that all meals be delivered to each inmate's cell through the food slot in the inmate's locked cell door.

BOP policy provides that inmates housed in the SHU for 30 continuous calendar days are to be examined and interviewed by a mental health staff member to assess the inmate's adjustment and the threat presented to self or others.

BOP policy also requires that all staff assigned to the SHU participate in quarterly training on, among other things, orderly supervision, suicide prevention, and security procedures relating to the unit. When a staff member is assigned to the SHU at the last-minute and has not completed the quarterly training, the staff member must be advised of the general requirements of a SHU post and be permitted to ask questions about the duties.

2. Inmate Accountability[11]
a. Counts

Inmate counts serve an important security function, as they enable COs to ensure that all inmates are accounted for and present at the appropriate location within the facility. BOP policy requires that each institution "conduct, at a minimum, five official inmate counts during every 24-hour period," and that on "weekends and holidays an additional count will be conducted at 10:00 a.m." At least 1 count a day during the week and 2 counts a day on weekends and holidays must be "stand-up counts," which means that inmates are required to stand when they are counted. MCC New York SHU Post Orders designate that counts must occur at 12 a.m., 3 a.m., 5 a.m., 4 p.m., and that stand-up counts are to be conducted at 10 p.m. daily and also at 10 a.m. on weekends and federal holidays.

The BOP requires that each count be conducted by at least two officers, one of whom will count the inmates while the other observes the unit for any unauthorized movement from the end of the tier. This requirement is also set out in the MCC New York SHU Post Orders. The two officers will then switch roles and compare the count numbers. If the totals do not match, then the officers must conduct another count in the same manner. When conducting the count, officers are required to observe each inmate's body and not rely solely on movement or sound. Officers conducting the count relay the count verbally to the Control

---

[11] This section describes inmate accountability measures that are most relevant to this investigation and review. The BOP utilizes a variety of other security and inmate accountability tools in addition to those discussed in this section, which are described in BOP Program Statement 5500.14, Correctional Services Procedures Manual.

Center, which maintains the master count of all inmates, and then remain in the unit until the Control Center accepts the count. If a count reported verbally does not match the master count, then the Control Center must notify the Operations Lieutenant and the staff members must recount the inmates. If the second count does not match the master count, then the Operations Lieutenant will order a bed-book count, that is, when inmates are counted using their picture cards, which are on file in the Control Center. A Lieutenant must take at least 1 count in the morning and one in the evening.

Correctional staff prepare count slips for each count, which must be prepared in ink, signed by both officers, and retained for 30 days. Count slips may not be altered. BOP policy provides that the "official count will not be cleared until all count slips are received and verified in the Control Center."

b. 30-Minute Rounds

The BOP uses additional accountability measures for inmates who are in administrative detention or disciplinary segregation, i.e., for those detained in a SHU. In such cases, a correctional staff member must observe all inmates at least twice an hour, once during the first 30 minutes (e.g., 12 a.m. to 12:30 a.m.) and again during the second 30 minutes (e.g., 12:30 a.m. to 1 a.m.). BOP policy provides that these "rounds are to be conducted on an irregular schedule and no more than 40 minutes apart." These same requirements for rounds are also described in the Post Orders for the MCC New York's SHU.

c. Documentation Regarding Inmate Status and Confinement

BOP policy also provides that each institution must prepare a daily change/transfer sheet, which indicates changes to an inmate's status, including housing and job assignments and medical convalescence. The MCC New York SHU Post Orders require that correctional staff assigned to the SHU create a SHU file for each inmate housed in that unit and that morning watch officers audit the inmate files every night. The MCC New York SHU Post Orders further specify that all pertinent information about an inmate's confinement should be noted on a Special Housing Unit Record Form (BP-292), and that SHU officers must maintain a log of pertinent information regarding inmate activity and enter such information into the BOP computer system TRUSCOPE, which provides institution staff with detailed inmate and institution security-related information and provides unit officers an electronic event log.

d. Cell Searches

BOP policy requires that BOP staff routinely and irregularly search housing units to, among other things, maintain sanitary standards and eliminate safety hazards.[12] The MCC New York SHU Post Orders require that officers assigned to the SHU conduct searches of the SHU common areas and cells, and that the entire SHU be searched every week. BOP policy and MCC New York SHU Post Orders require written documentation of each housing unit search.

3. *Psychological Screening*
a. Initial Screening

Pursuant to BOP policy governing inmates in pretrial detention status (Program Statement 7331.04, Pretrial Inmates), all pretrial inmates must have an initial risk/needs assessment screening within 48 hours of

---

[12] BOP Program Statement 5521.06, Searches of Housing Units, Inmates, and Inmate Work Areas.

admission to the institution. The goal of this screening is to determine "the inmate's security, medical, psychological, and/or other special needs." The BOP also requires that institutions screen pretrial inmates "returning from court, as events at court may alter the inmate's separation and/or security needs." BOP policy further recognizes that there are often "high security, high profile inmates" who may present a significant threat to themselves or others, and that the "need to identify and monitor these inmates regularly is paramount."

b.   Suicide Prevention

The BOP's suicide prevention program is governed by federal regulations, 28 C.F.R. §§ 552.40-552.42, which require the BOP to establish a suicide prevention program to identify and manage potentially suicidal inmates. Pursuant to these regulations, when an inmate is identified as being at-risk for committing suicide, BOP staff must place the inmate on suicide watch until the inmate is no longer an imminent risk.

BOP policy (Program Statement 5324.08, Suicide Prevention Program) requires that medical staff screen all new inmates, ordinarily within 24 hours, for signs of suicidality. However, at MCCs, among other facilities with high rates of admissions and short lengths of stays, "comprehensive psychological intake conducted by Psychology Services ordinarily will be performed only on inmates who are suspected of being suicidal or appear psychologically unstable." Inmates in the SHU are monitored more closely, and inmates exhibiting signs of potential suicide risk are referred to the shift Lieutenant. BOP policy recognizes that inmates who are placed in the SHU due to a request for protective custody are at greater risk of committing suicide and should therefore be screened for suicidal ideation within 72 hours of arriving in the SHU. BOP policy explicitly states that "staff must never take lightly any inmate suicide threats." Any staff member who has reason to believe that an inmate may be suicidal should "ordinarily maintain the inmate under direct, continuous observation."

Every BOP institution must have one or more rooms, ordinarily in the health services area, dedicated to inmates placed on suicide watch. Suicide watch may be conducted by specially trained staff or inmates. For inmates placed on suicide watch, the specially trained staff or inmate maintains continuous observation of the inmate believed to be at risk of committing suicide. Following suicide watch and based on clinical findings following a face-to-face evaluation, the inmate will be removed from suicide watch or transferred to a medical referral or health care facility. Psychological observation is a less restrictive form of individual monitoring that is used for inmates who are stabilizing and not yet prepared for placement in general population or restrictive housing. While on suicide watch, the inmate is normally required to wear a suicide watch gown and will be allowed a suicide watch blanket.

As discussed in greater detail in Chapter 4, witnesses told the OIG that an inmate is placed on suicide watch when the inmate is believed to be imminently suicidal. During suicide watch, the inmate is under constant observation by staff; the cell lights are on 24 hours a day; and the inmate is given a special mattress, blanket, and smock to wear. Although psychological observation is a lower classification, witnesses told the OIG that at MCC New York the psychological observations was the same as suicide watch except that inmates were allowed to have their clothing and some materials, such as books, as determined by the Psychology Department. At MCC New York, psychological observation was used to see how an inmate was doing before releasing the inmate to a housing unit.

4. Suicide Response

Recognizing that failure to appropriately respond to an emergency can jeopardize the safety of staff and inmates and the security of the institution, the BOP's Standards of Employee Conduct require that "employees respond immediately, effectively, and appropriately during all emergency situations." The MCC New York General Housing Unit Post Orders outline the required response to a suspected inmate suicide. These orders require that MCC New York staff notify the Operations Lieutenant and Control Center of the situation. The orders further provide that, once there is adequate staff present, immediate action must be taken to open the inmate's airway and initiate cardiopulmonary resuscitation, even if MCC New York staff believe that the inmate "has been dead for a period of time." MCC New York staff are to continue cardiopulmonary resuscitation until they are relieved by medical staff or another rescuer. The BOP policy governing crime scenes and the collection of evidence provides that the need to immediately attend to an apparent suicide victim, undertake lifesaving measures, and ensure inmate and staff safety take precedence over efforts to preserve a crime scene.[13]

5. Inmate Discipline

Federal regulations, 28 C.F.R. §§ 541.1-541.8, and BOP policy (Program Statement 5270.09, Inmate Discipline Program) establish an inmate discipline program, which is designed to ensure the safety, security, and orderly operation of correctional facilities, as well as the protection of the public. The inmate discipline program applies to all inmates in BOP custody, including inmates with pending criminal charges. One of the guiding principles of this program is that BOP staff are to take disciplinary action when and to such a degree as necessary to regulate the behavior of inmates to promote a safe and orderly institution. "Tattooing or self-mutilation" is among the prohibited acts sanctioned through the inmate discipline program. This prohibited act falls within the second most severe category of offenses on a 4-tier scale. The BOP defines "tattooing or self-mutilation" as "[t]o put indelible patterns on the skin; to injure, disfigure or make imperfect by removing or irreparably damaging parts of the body (wrist cutting falls within this offense)."[14] The definition does not make an explicit reference to suicide attempts other than inclusion of "wrist cutting."

Among other things, BOP policy addressing the inmate discipline program identifies the prohibited acts, describes the process for adjudicating violations, and lists applicable penalties for each category of offense. As relevant to this matter, the discipline process begins when a staff member observes an inmate commit a prohibited act and issues a report documenting the incident. A BOP supervisor then investigates the alleged inmate misconduct, which includes taking a statement from the inmate regarding the incident. If an inmate appears to be mentally ill at any stage of the disciplinary process, a mental health staff member will examine the inmate and assess the inmate's competency to participate in the disciplinary process. If the inmate is found to be competent and the prohibited act falls into the first or second most severe category, the matter is referred to a discipline hearing officer, who will hold a hearing and make a determination as to whether the inmate committed the prohibited act and, if so, impose any of the sanctions that correspond to the severity of the prohibited act. At the hearing, the inmate is advised of his or her rights and permitted to

---

[13] BOP Program Statement 5510.14, Crime Scene Management and Evidence Control, is a restricted policy that is not released to the public in its entirety.

[14] BOP Elements of Prohibited Acts.

choose a staff representative, make a statement, and call witnesses. The inmate is also allowed to appeal the outcome through the BOP's administrative remedy program.

6. Conditions of Confinement
a. Telephone Calls

The federal regulations, 28 C.F.R. §§ 540.100-540.106, that govern telephone calls for inmates require that the Warden of each BOP institution establish procedures to monitor inmate telephone conversations, which is "done to preserve the security and orderly management of the institution and to protect the public." For safety and security reasons, BOP policy (Program Statement P5264.08, Inmate Telephone Regulations) requires that all inmate telephone calls be made through the Inmate Telephone System. BOP policy recognizes that "on rare occasion, during times of crisis," inmates may be permitted to make a telephone call outside of the Inmate Telephone System. In such circumstances, the telephone "must be placed in a secure area (e.g., a locked office)," and "must be set to record telephone calls." Additionally, the staff member coordinating the call must notify the BOP's Special Investigative Services via email, providing the inmate's name and register number, the date and time of the call, the number and name of the individual called, and the reason for the call. The Special Investigative Services must enter this information into the telephone recording system within 7 days.

b. Personal Effects, Medication, and Linens

Federal regulations governing BOP SHUs provide that inmates in administrative detention status ordinarily may have a reasonable amount of personal property.[15] Under BOP policy regarding SHUs, the personal property of SHU inmates "may be limited or withheld for reasons of security, fire safety, or housekeeping."[16] The BOP Chief Pharmacist issues medication each workday for inmates in the SHU. Restricted medications are administered to inmates during daily SHU rounds. Each institution determines "the medication(s) and amount (number of days) an inmate in SHU may maintain in their cell." Inmates may also purchase pre-approved over-the-counter medications at the commissary. MCC New York General Housing Units Post Orders provide that when an inmate is released or transferred out of a housing unit, the inmate will remove all limited and government-issued clothing from the cell in which the inmate was previously housed. These Post Orders further specify that all cells are to be cleaned daily by inmates occupying the cell, and that blankets, towels, and other linens will not be used as rugs or hung over inmate bunk beds at any time. Pursuant to these Post Orders, MCC New York housing unit officers on all three shifts are responsible for maintaining "a high level of sanitation" and a "safe and clean environment."

---

[15] 28 C.F.R. § 541.31(h)(1).

[16] BOP Program Statement 5270.11, Special Housing Units.

Chapter 3: Timeline of Key Events

Except as otherwise noted, the following information is derived from the Federal Bureau of Prisons (BOP) records and the Office of the Inspector General's interviews.

September 21–24, 2018	The BOP awards contracts to two companies (Company 1 and 2) to upgrade the security camera system at Metropolitan Correctional Center in New York, New York (MCC New York). At the time, images from the MCC New York's analog video cameras are recorded to a Digital Video Recorder (DVR) system, which is divided into two DVR systems. Cameras assigned to the DVR 1 system record only to the DVR 1 hard drives, and cameras assigned to DVR 2 system record only to the DVR 2 hard drives.
March 17, 2019	In connection with MCC New York's upgrade of its security camera system, the BOP's Northeast Regional Office begins arranging for technicians from other BOP institutions to perform temporary duty (TDY) assignments to MCC New York to perform necessary mechanical, electrical, plumbing, and wiring work. However, during the course of the TDY rotations, work is not consistently conducted on the camera upgrade because TDY personnel are sometimes used to cover shortages at MCC New York's custody posts.
July 2, 2019	According to court records, a federal grand jury of the U.S. District Court for the Southern District of New York returns an indictment charging Epstein with sex trafficking and conspiracy to commit sex trafficking.
July 6, 2019	Epstein is arrested at an airport in New Jersey and is transported for detention pending his initial court appearance to the MCC New York as a pretrial detainee. Epstein is placed in the general inmate population and medically screened.
July 7, 2019	An MCC New York Facilities Assistant asks the Psychology Department to evaluate Epstein because he appears "distraught, sad, and a little confused." Epstein is assigned to the MCC New York's Special Housing Unit (SHU) because of significant media attention and his notoriety among other MCC New York inmates.[17]

---

[17] The SHU is a housing unit within MCC New York where inmates are securely separated from the general inmate population and kept locked in their cells for approximately 23 hours a day, to ensure their own safety as well as the safety of staff and other inmates.

July 8, 2019	According to court records, Epstein is arraigned in federal court and enters a plea of not guilty to all charges. The court sets a detention hearing for July 15, 2019.
	MCC New York staff conducts a routine intake screening of Epstein, the records of which indicate that Epstein denies a history of any mental health problems. After the Chief Psychologist consults with the National Suicide Prevention Coordinator from BOP's Central Office, the Psychology Department conducts a further evaluation of Epstein after his return from court. Records show that Epstein denies any suicidal thoughts but was placed on psychological observation due to the presence of risk factors (high-profile case, nature of the charges, pre-trial status, and ongoing proceedings).
July 9, 2019	The Psychology Department administers a formal, in-person suicide risk assessment for Epstein. The Psychology Department continues psychological observation for another day pending a suitable housing placement.
July 10, 2019	The Psychology Department removes Epstein from psychological observation and returns him to the SHU with a recommendation that he have a cellmate. Epstein is housed with another inmate (Inmate 1).
July 11, 2019	An MCC New York psychologist meets with Epstein briefly and recommends follow-up visit to occur the next week.
July 15, 2019	According to court records, Epstein appears in court for his detention hearing.
July 16, 2019	At Epstein's request, an MCC New York psychologist meets with him during a legal visit.
July 18, 2019	According to court records, Epstein appears in court for a ruling on the issue of detention. The court orders that Epstein be detained pending trial because he presents a danger to the community and he is a flight risk.
	The Psychology Department conducts 30-day psychology reviews for the entire SHU population. Epstein is not in the SHU at the time and therefore his review is not conducted.

July 22, 2019	According to court records, Epstein files an appeal of the court's order denying Epstein pretrial release.
July 23, 2019	At approximately 1:27 a.m., SHU staff hears noises coming from Epstein's cell. Epstein's cellmate (Inmate 1) says that Epstein has attempted to hang himself. SHU staff observes Epstein lying on the floor with a piece of orange cloth around his neck. Epstein initially tells MCC New York staff that his cellmate tried to kill him. Epstein's cellmate (Inmate 1) tells MCC New York staff that while he was asleep, he felt something hit his legs and when he turned on the light, he saw Epstein with a string around his neck and called the guards.[18]
	Epstein is transferred out of the SHU and placed on suicide watch in a cell near the Psychology Department and Health Services Unit.
	Later that morning, Health Services Unit personnel conduct a medical assessment and observe that Epstein has a red mark two-thirds of the way around the front and sides of his neck. The BOP assesses Epstein for risk of suicide and determines that he should remain on suicide watch.
July 24, 2019	At approximately 8:45 a.m., Epstein is removed from suicide watch but remains under psychological observation in the same cell near the Psychology Department and Health Services Unit. Medical staff examine Epstein at 1:08 p.m. and Psychological Services staff complete a Post Suicide Watch Report. In contrast to his prior statement that his cellmate tried to kill him, Epstein says he does not remember how he sustained the injuries to his neck.
July 25–29, 2019	Epstein is seen by the Psychology Department daily and on each date adamantly denies suicidality or having any memory of what occurred on July 23, 2019.
July 29, 2019	Psychology Department staff determine that Epstein can be released from psychological observation and transferred back to the SHU.[19]

---

[18] When interviewed by the OIG, another inmate housed in the same SHU tier (Inmate 2) at the time of the July 23 incident said he heard Inmate 1 call for assistance, and that Inmate 1 later told him that Epstein had tried to kill himself by hanging himself from the bunkbed ladder.

[19] The investigation revealed that Epstein was originally scheduled to return to the SHU on July 29, 2019, but at his request he remained on psychological observation until July 30, 2019. The BOP's SENTRY database, which is a BOP

Continued

Disk failures occur in DVR 2 of MCC New York's security camera system, which results in the system being unable to record, although the cameras continue to work and broadcast live video feed. MCC New York personnel do not learn of the DVR 2 recording failure until August 8, 2 days before Epstein's death. Roughly half of MCC New York's security cameras, including those located in the SHU, are assigned to record to the DVR 2 system.

July 30, 2019   Epstein is transferred back to the SHU.[20]

An MCC New York Staff Psychologist from the Psychology Department sends an email to over 70 BOP staff members stating that Epstein "needs to be housed with an appropriate cellmate." Epstein and his new cellmate (Inmate 3) are placed in a cell within the SHU that can accommodate the electrical needs of Epstein's medical device.

MCC New York conducts disciplinary proceedings against Epstein for alleged self-mutilation and ultimately concludes that there is insufficient evidence to find that Epstein engaged in a prohibited act.[21] When Epstein is psychologically evaluated in connection with the disciplinary proceedings, he says he does not remember how he sustained the marks around his neck.

MCC New York personnel attempt to obtain an estimate from Company 1 to run the wiring and conduit for the new camera system, which would eliminate the need for BOP technicians to perform the work.

July 31, 2019   According to court records, Epstein appears in court for a status conference, at which time the court sets deadlines for motions and responses. Upon his return to MCC New York, the U.S. Marshals Service provide paperwork to BOP that indicates Epstein had "suicidal tendencies."

---

database that contains information relating to the care, classification, subsistence, protection, discipline, and programs of federal inmates, was not updated to reflect this change because it indicated that Epstein was transferred back to the SHU on July 29, 2019.

[20] The OIG's investigation revealed that at some point after he returned to the SHU from suicide watch and psychological observation, Epstein asked two different MCC New York staff members if he can be housed with the same cellmate Epstein initially said tried to kill him.

[21] The BOP's inmate discipline program and the offense with which Epstein was charged is further described in Chapter 2.

The Psychology Department conducts a clinical visit with Epstein, who denies any suicidal ideation.

August 1, 2019   MCC New York Receiving and Discharge staff notify the Psychology Department of the notation of "suicidal tendencies" on U.S. Marshals Service paperwork relating to Epstein. The Psychology Department conducts a suicide risk assessment of Epstein, who denies that he is suicidal, and determines that suicide watch is not warranted. Psychological staff recommend a follow-up in 1 week.

August 2, 2019   MCC New York Special Investigative Services complete its investigation into the incident on July 23, 2019, and finds that there is insufficient evidence to determine that Epstein harmed himself or that he was harmed by his cellmate.

August 8, 2019   Epstein is seen by the Psychology Department and denies suicidal ideation, intention, or plan.

Epstein meets with his attorneys and, unbeknownst to MCC New York personnel, changes his Last Will and Testament during the meeting.

MCC New York staff receive notice that Epstein's cellmate will be transferred out of the institution the following day, August 9.

MCC New York staff discover the disk failures that occurred in the DVR 2 system on July 29 and that resulted in approximately one half of the institution's security cameras not recording, although the cameras continued to broadcast a live video feed. MCC New York staff do not perform the work necessary to restore recording functionality of the DVR 2 system or address long-standing performance failures with the institution's camera system.

August 9, 2019   At approximately 8:30 a.m., Epstein's cellmate (Inmate 3) is transferred out of MCC New York. Two MCC New York SHU staff members said they notified supervisory staff of Epstein's cellmate's transfer and Epstein's need for a new cellmate. Other witnesses did not corroborate these statements. Epstein is not assigned a new cellmate as required by the Psychology Department.

Sometime between 8 a.m. and 9 a.m., Epstein meets with his attorneys in the SHU attorney conference room. Sometime prior to 1 p.m., Epstein's attorneys ask MCC New York staff members if Epstein could be moved to a different housing unit or housed without a cellmate.

MCC New York staff obtain the replacement hard drives to repair the institution's security camera system but do not complete the repairs necessary to restore recording functionality and address long-standing performance failures with the institution's DVR 2 system.

The U.S. Court of Appeals for the Second Circuit unseals approximately 2,000 pages of documents in civil litigation involving Ghislaine Maxwell, who is later convicted in December 2021 of conspiring with Epstein to sexually abuse minors over the course of a decade. Some of these documents contain information that may relate to the criminal charges pending against Epstein. There is extensive media coverage of information in the unsealed documents.

At approximately 6:45 p.m., Epstein leaves the attorney conference room.

At approximately 7 p.m., contrary to BOP policy but with the permission of a Unit Manager, Epstein is permitted to place an unmonitored telephone call to a number with a New York City area code, purportedly to speak with his mother. In actuality, Epstein speaks with someone with whom he allegedly has a personal relationship. After the call, Epstein is returned to his cell, where he remains without a cellmate.

MCC New York SHU staff members do not conduct the 4 p.m. or 10 p.m. inmate counts. After approximately 10:40 p.m., SHU staff members do not conduct the required 30-minute rounds.

August 10, 2019   MCC New York SHU staff members do not conduct the 12 a.m., 3 a.m., or 5 a.m. inmate counts or any of the 30-minute rounds from 12 a.m. until approximately 6:30 a.m.

At approximately 6:30 a.m., SHU staff begin to deliver breakfast to inmates in the SHU through the food slots in the locked cell doors. When SHU staff attempt to deliver breakfast to Epstein, SHU staff unlock the door to the tier in which Epstein's cell was located and then knock on the door to Epstein's cell. Epstein, who is housed alone in the cell, does not respond to SHU staff. SHU staff unlock the cell door and find Epstein hanged in his cell, with one end of a piece of orange cloth around his neck and the other end tied to the top portion of a bunkbed in Epstein's cell. Epstein is suspended from the top bunk in a near-seated position with his buttocks approximately 1 inch to 1 inch and a half off the floor and his legs extended straight out on the floor in front of him.

SHU staff immediately activate a body alarm, which notified all MCC New York staff of a medical emergency and prompted MCC New York staff in the Control Center to call for 911 emergency services. SHU staff then rip the orange cloth away from the bunkbed, which causes Epstein's buttocks to drop to the ground. SHU staff lay Epstein on the ground and immediately initiate cardiopulmonary resuscitation (CPR). At approximately 6:33 a.m., BOP medical staff respond to the SHU, continue CPR, apply the automated external defibrillator, and move Epstein to MCC New York's Health Services Unit. Minutes after arriving in the Health Services Unit, an ambulance arrives and paramedics continue CPR, intubate Epstein, and administer medications and fluids. At approximately 7:10 a.m., the ambulance takes Epstein to New York Presbyterian Lower Manhattan Hospital, where he is pronounced dead at 7:36 a.m. by the emergency room physician.

MCC New York staff unsuccessfully attempts to recover video from the DVR 2 system of the SHU and the BOP begins repairing the DVR 2 system. The FBI seizes all hard drives contained in the DVR 2 system as evidence.

August 11, 2019   The Office of the Chief Medical Examiner, City of New York, conducts an autopsy of Epstein.

August 14–15, 2019   The FBI returns to MCC New York and seizes additional components of the DVR 2 system and the entire DVR 1 system. The FBI's Digital Forensics Analysis Unit in Quantico, Virginia, begins to conduct a forensic analysis of MCC New York's DVR systems and determines that there were catastrophic disk failures in the DVR 2 system disk array and no recordings were available on the DVR 2 system after July 29, 2019.

August 16, 2019   The Office of the Chief Medical Examiner, City of New York, releases its findings publicly that the cause of Epstein's death was hanging and that the manner of death was suicide.

Chapter 4: Custody and Care of Epstein Prior to His Death

I.   Epstein's Arrest and Detention on July 6

On July 2, 2019, a grand jury of the U.S. District Court for the Southern District of New York returned a two-count indictment that charged Epstein with committing sex trafficking and a sex trafficking conspiracy, in violation of 18 U.S.C. §§ 371, 1591(a), (b)(2), and 2, based on allegations that he sexually exploited and abused dozens of minor girls, some as young as 14 years old, at his homes in New York and Florida. The indictment alleged that from at least 2002 through 2005, Epstein enticed and recruited girls, many of whom he knew were underage, to visit his homes and perform sex acts in exchange for paying each girl hundreds of dollars in cash. The indictment further alleged that Epstein, working with employees and associates, created a vast network of underage victims to sexually exploit in New York and Florida by paying some victims hundreds of dollars in cash each to recruit other minor girls to be similarly abused by Epstein. In addition to the two criminal charges, the indictment also contained forfeiture allegations, which sought to forfeit to the United States any property that was either used to commit or was a proceed of the charged sex trafficking offense, including Epstein's New York residence.

On Saturday, July 6, 2019, Epstein was arrested at Teterboro Airport in New Jersey upon his return to the United States from France. He was transported to the Metropolitan Correctional Center located in New York, New York (MCC New York), where he was initially placed in the general inmate population. MCC New York is a federal administrative detention facility operated by the Federal Bureau of Prisons (BOP). The BOP temporarily closed MCC New York in October 2021 due to substandard conditions that are unrelated to this investigation. When it was operational, MCC New York housed primarily pretrial detainees who had not yet been convicted of any offense, but whom the court had determined under applicable law should remain in custody pending trial either because they represent a danger to the community, a substantial flight risk, or both. Due to the significant media attention surrounding his arrest and his notoriety among other MCC New York inmates, the following day Epstein was moved to MCC New York's Special Housing Unit (SHU), a housing unit within MCC New York where inmates are securely separated from the general inmate population and kept locked in their cells for approximately 23 hours per day, to ensure their own safety as well as the safety of staff and other inmates. On Monday, July 8, 2019, Epstein appeared in federal court and pleaded not guilty to the charges. The court ordered that Epstein remain in custody pending a detention hearing scheduled for July 15, 2019.

At the detention hearing, Epstein sought to be placed in home detention at his New York residence with electronic monitoring and other conditions. The prosecutors sought to have Epstein detained at MCC New York pending trial. The court reviewed the parties' filings and heard argument on the matter of pre-trial release on July 15, 2019. On July 18, 2019, the court ordered that Epstein be detained pending trial. In its ruling, the court noted that because Epstein had been indicted for a violation of the federal sex trafficking statute that involved minor victims, there was a presumption in favor of detention under federal law. The court found that the United States had shown by clear and convincing evidence that Epstein threatened the safety of another person and of the community based on testimony from two victims, the allegations of repeated sexual abuse of minors, and the lewd photographs of young-looking women or girls that were found during an authorized search of Epstein's New York residence in July 2019. The court also relied on the recommendation of U.S. Pretrial Services, the seriousness of the offenses with which Epstein had been charged, evidence reflecting Epstein's harassment and intimidation of and tampering with witnesses involved in a prior Florida state criminal investigation, and Epstein's lack of compliance with his legal obligations as a registered sex offender. The court found that the United States had also shown by a preponderance of the evidence that Epstein was a flight risk based on the severity of the criminal charges and severity of the potential punishment; the strength of the evidence against Epstein; and Epstein's criminal history, sex offender registration, vast wealth and substantial liquid assets, multiple residences, a foreign residence, limited family ties in the United States, private plane(s), extensive overseas travel, and possession of a foreign passport bearing Epstein's photograph but not his name. Finally, the court found that Epstein's pretrial release proposal was inadequate because, among other things, it did not contain sworn, accurate, or comprehensive financial statements; it required excessive court involvement in routine aspects of the proposed home confinement; the proposed consent to extradition was unenforceable; and the proposed appointment of a trustee to monitor Epstein's compliance with release conditions was unacceptably vague and problematic due to the potential conflict of interest presented by monitoring the conduct of a person who paid the trustee's salary, and allegations that Epstein engaged in unlawful acts with his employees during the sex trafficking conspiracy. Epstein appealed the court's order on July 22, 2019. This appeal remained pending at the time of Epstein's death.

II.   MCC New York's Special Housing Unit

Epstein was initially assigned to MCC New York's general inmate population, but on July 7, 2019, at approximately 7:20 p.m., he was moved to the SHU pending reclassification due to the significant increase in media coverage and awareness of his notoriety among other MCC New York inmate residents. The SHU is a housing unit within MCC New York where inmates are securely separated from the general inmate population and kept locked in their cells for approximately 23 hours a day, to ensure their own safety as well as the safety of staff and other inmates. Inmates in the SHU are either on administrative detention or disciplinary segregation status. Administrative segregation status is a non-punitive designation that removes an inmate from the general population when it is necessary to do so to ensure the safety, security, and orderly operation of the correctional facility or to protect the public. The MCC New York employee who was the Acting Evening Watch Activities Lieutenant on August 9, 2019, told the Office of the Inspector General (OIG) that most inmates housed in the SHU are "locked down" in their cells for most of the day. Other witnesses told the OIG that SHU inmates are locked in their cells for approximately 23 hours a day. The Warden of MCC New York during Epstein's period of detention at that facility, along with Associate Warden 1 and the Acting Evening Watch Activities Lieutenant, explained that this was one of the reasons that conducting rounds in the SHU was so important. Unlike inmates in general population housing, SHU inmates could not physically approach a staff member; therefore, the staff member had to go to each inmate's cell.

Witnesses told the OIG that Epstein's daily routine in the SHU was to meet with his attorneys in the attorney conference room all day until approximately 8 p.m.[22] MCC New York attorney logs confirmed that Epstein had daily visits with attorneys from several different law practices throughout the period of his detention at MCC New York. This is consistent with the information available in SENTRY, a BOP database that contains information relating to the care, classification, subsistence, protection, discipline, and programs of federal inmates, which indicates that Epstein had one to two attorney visits on all but 1 day he was detained at MCC New York. BOP emails reflect that other attorneys expressed frustration to a Supervisory Staff Attorney with the BOP's Consolidated Legal Center for New York because attorneys had to wait hours or were unable to

---

[22] As discussed in Chapter 1, BOP policy provides that SHU inmates may be escorted from their cells by MCC New York staff for visits, including legal visits, court appearances, medical and psychological attention, showers, and recreation.

meet with their clients because Epstein and his attorneys were occupying the attorney conference room, even at times when Epstein had to leave the conference room for a medical visit.

At MCC New York, the SHU was located on the south side of the institution's ninth floor and was often referred to as "9 South." Primary access to the SHU was controlled by a locked door (Main Exterior Entry Door). That door was opened remotely by a staff member in MCC New York's centralized Control Center. Access into the SHU was further controlled by a second locked door (Main Interior Entry Door), to which a limited number of Correctional Officers (CO) had keys while on duty.

Secondary access to the SHU was controlled by a locked door. That door was opened remotely by a staff member in the centralized Control Center. Entry into the SHU from the secondary access point was further controlled by three additional locked doors, to which a limited number of the COs had keys while on duty. The secondary access doors were used only by staff when facilitating visits between the SHU inmates and their outside visitors.

Within the SHU, inmates were assigned to six separate tiers or groups of cells, three of which were accessible via stairs leading up from the common area on the ninth floor (Upper Tiers—G, J, and L Tiers) and three of which were accessible via stairs leading down from the common area on the ninth floor (Lower Tiers—H, K, and M Tiers). The entrance to each tier could be accessed only via a single locked door at the top or bottom of the staircase leading to the individual tier. A limited number of keys to open the locked tier doors were available only to a limited number of COs while on duty. Each tier had eight cells, each of which could house either one or two inmates. Each individual cell, which was made of cement and metal, could be accessed only through a single locked door, to which only a limited number of COs had keys while on duty. The SHU cell doors were made of solid metal with a small glass window and small locked slots that correctional staff used to handcuff inmates and provide food or toiletries to inmates. As a further security measure, during each shift the keys to the SHU tier doors and SHU cell doors were carried by different COs.

As noted above, inmates in the SHU are securely separated from the general inmate population and are kept locked in their cell when in their assigned tier within the SHU. Witnesses told the OIG that SHU inmates are locked in their cells for approximately 23 hours a day. BOP policy provides that, weather and resources permitting, SHU inmates will have the opportunity to exercise outside of their quarters 5 hours per calendar week. Under federal regulations and BOP policy, SHU inmates ordinarily have the opportunity to shower at least 3 times a week, typically on different days in 1-hour periods. SHU inmates may also be escorted from their cells by MCC New York staff for visits, including legal visits, court appearances, medical and psychological attention. The MCC New York SHU Post Orders require that all visitors to the SHU be documented in the SHU visitor log, and that any inmate visiting the SHU, such as inmates on work details, be searched visually and with a hand-held metal detector, without exception. The MCC New York SHU Post Orders also require that food carts be searched inside and out before being brought into a SHU cellblock and that all meals be delivered through the cell door food slot of the locked cell door.

Figure 4.1

Primary SHU Entrance (Ninth Floor)

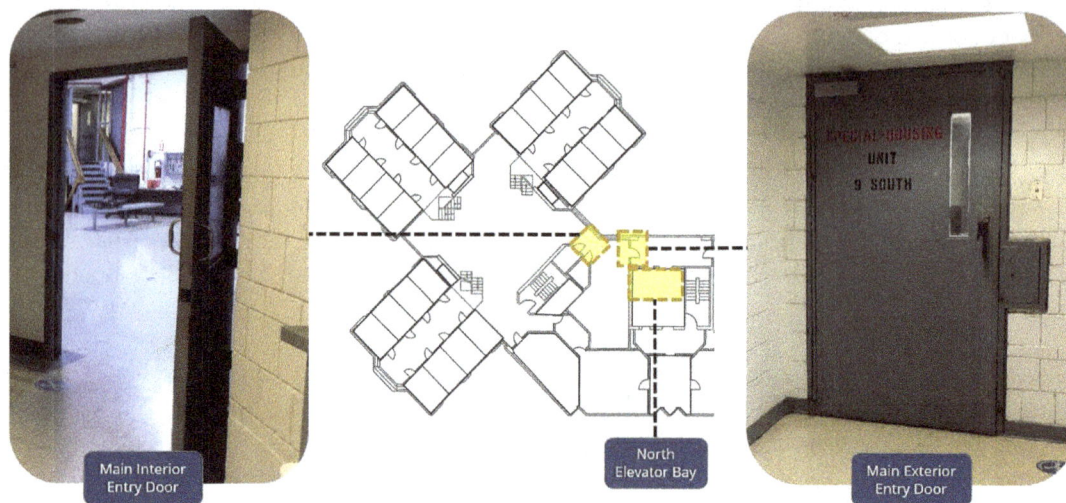

Main Interior Entry Door

North Elevator Bay

Main Exterior Entry Door

Note: The photograph on the right has been modified for security reasons.

Source: DOJ OIG photographs and DOJ OIG schematic drawing depicting the MCC New York SHU

Figure 4.2

Secondary SHU Entrance (Ninth Floor)

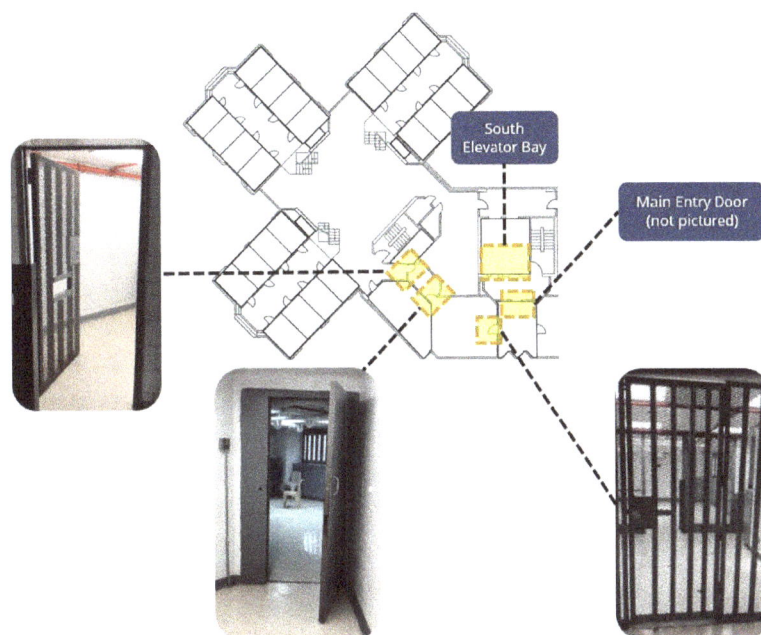

Note: The photograph on the right has been modified for security reasons.

Source: DOJ OIG photographs and DOJ OIG schematic drawing depicting the MCC New York SHU

Figure 4.3

Tiered Structure of SHU (2-Dimensional)

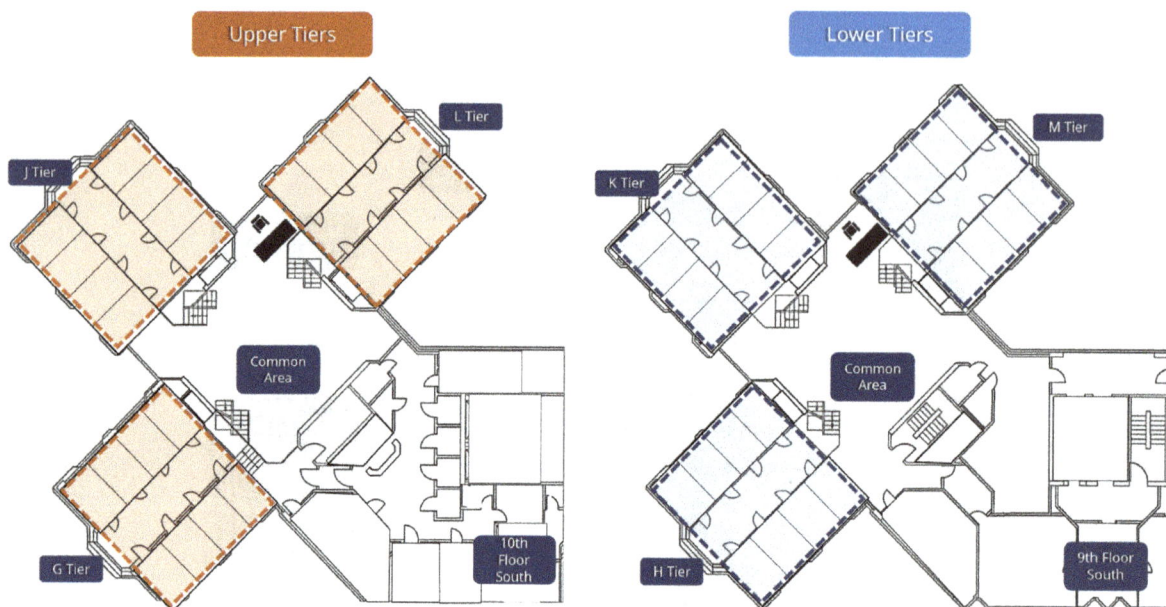

Source: DOJ OIG schematic drawings depicting the MCC New York SHU

Figure 4.4

Tiered Structure of SHU (3-Dimensional)

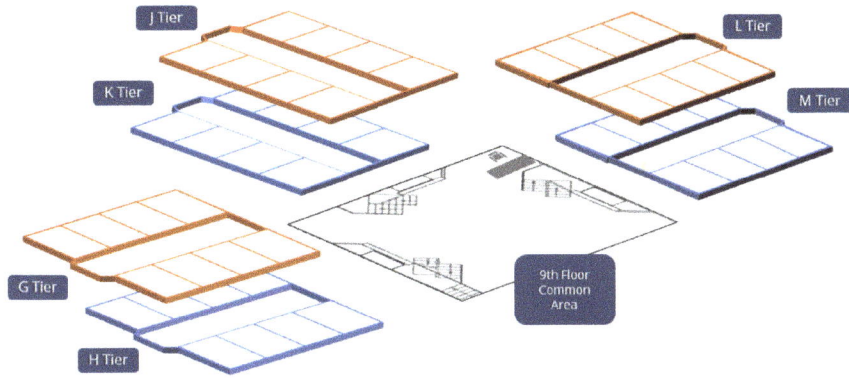

Source: DOJ OIG schematic drawing depicting the MCC New York SHU

Figure 4.5

Stairways Leading to SHU Upper and Lower Tiers

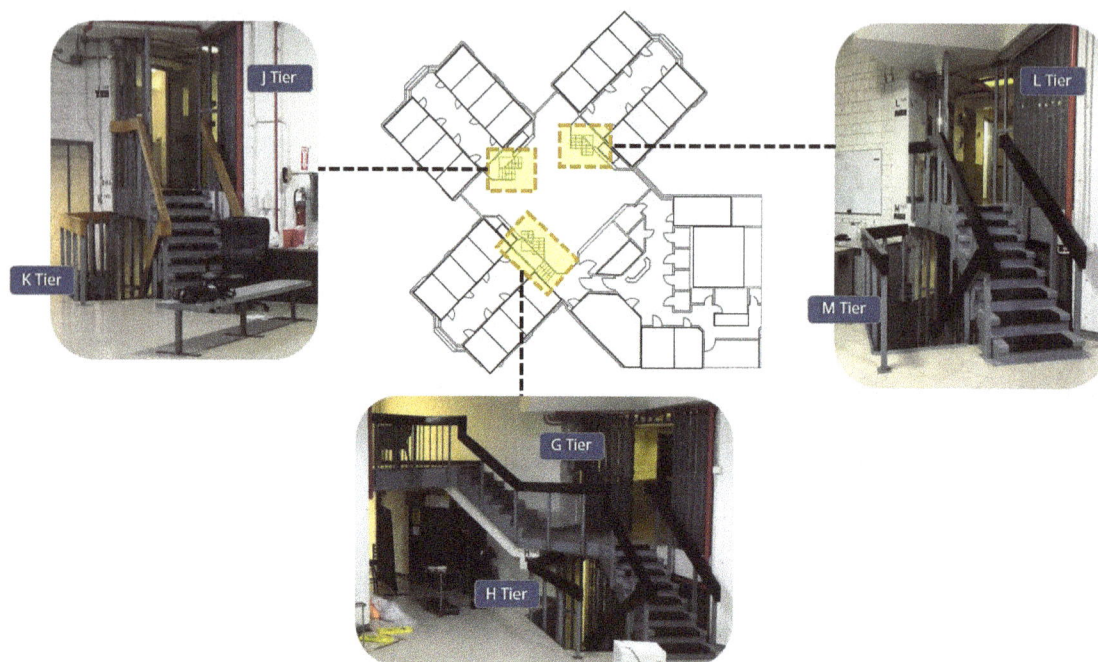

Note: The photograph on the right has been modified for privacy reasons.

Source: DOJ OIG photographs and DOJ OIG schematic drawing depicting the MCC New York SHU

III.   Epstein's Initial Cell and Cellmate Assignment from July 7 to July 23

According to the Warden, MCC New York typically housed inmates in the SHU with a cellmate. Upon Epstein's initial transfer to the SHU on July 7, 2019, he was assigned a cell in the M Tier of the SHU with Inmate 1. The Warden explained that Epstein was a high-profile inmate and that he initially selected Inmate 1 to be Epstein's cellmate because Inmate 1 was another high-profile inmate, and the Warden believed Inmate 1 to be the least likely SHU inmate to harm Epstein.[23] Epstein and Inmate 1 were housed together in cell Z05-124.

---

[23] In 2008, Epstein pleaded guilty in a Florida state court to a felony charge of procurement of minors to engage in prostitution in violation of Florida Statute § 796.03. As a result of this conviction, Epstein was required to register as a sex offender.

IV. Events of July 23 and the Placement of Epstein on Suicide Watch and Psychological Observation from July 23 to July 30

According to BOP documents, at approximately 1:27 a.m. on July 23, 2019, Senior Officer Specialists 1 and 2 heard noise coming from the M Tier in the SHU, the tier where Epstein was housed. Senior Officer Specialist 2 documented in a BOP report that upon checking cell Z05-124, he saw Epstein laying down near his bunk with "a piece of handmade orange cloth" around his neck, and Senior Officer Specialist 1 wrote in a BOP report that Epstein's cellmate (Inmate 1) said Epstein had attempted to hang himself. In his interview with the OIG, Senior Officer Specialist 1 said that Inmate 1, who appeared shaken up, told him that he had been asleep on the floor of the cell and was awoken when he felt Epstein land on him. Senior Officer Specialist 2 reported that after he had been alerted by the noise, he grabbed the door keys, called the Control Center for assistance, and then he and Senior Officer Specialist 1 entered the cell, where they secured and removed Epstein's cellmate. Senior Officer Specialist 1 reported that he then reentered the cell, placed Epstein on his side, and removed "an orange homemade rope" from his neck. In his interview with the OIG, Senior Officer Specialist 1 said Epstein had a sheet around his neck, which was attached to the bunkbed ladder in the cell. Senior Officer Specialist 1 said that Epstein was sitting on the floor of the cell with his back against the bunkbed ladder. Senior Officer Specialist 1's report said that Epstein was breathing, but unresponsive, so he began chest compressions, at which time the Morning Watch Operations Lieutenant and other staff arrived. Senior Officer Specialist 1 confirmed in his OIG interview that they started cardiopulmonary resuscitation but stopped when they realized that Epstein was already breathing. The Morning Watch Operations Lieutenant documented in a BOP report that when she arrived at the SHU, she saw Epstein lying in the fetal position in his cell, breathing heavily and snoring, wearing only a t-shirt and boxers. The Morning Watch Operations Lieutenant observed that Epstein's neck was red, but she saw no further injuries. She called out to Epstein, who flickered his eyes and continued snoring. The COs unsuccessfully tried to get Epstein to stand on his own, and then placed him on a stretcher and took him to the Health Services Unit.

According to BOP records, at approximately 1:40 a.m., Epstein was transferred out of the SHU and placed on suicide watch. As previously noted in Chapter 2, inmates on suicide watch are housed in a dedicated room, typically in the health services area, where they are continuously monitored by specially trained staff or inmates.

Senior Officer Specialist 3 documented in a BOP report that when he and others responded to the call for assistance and gained access to the SHU, he saw Epstein lying on the floor of his cell snoring. He and the other officers verbally instructed Epstein to stand up, but Epstein did not. He and other officers then lifted Epstein onto a stretcher to remove him from the cell.

Senior Officer Specialist 4 wrote in a BOP report that he responded to a body alarm in the SHU and helped remove Epstein from his cell, placed him on a stretcher, and took him to the second floor for a medical assessment. Senior Officer Specialist 4 further reported that, while he was observing Epstein in the Health Services Unit, Epstein told Senior Officer Specialist 4 that he thought his cellmate had tried to kill him. Epstein further stated that his cellmate had tried to extort him and that for the last week his cellmate had threatened to beat him if he did not pay him. Epstein told Senior Officer Specialist 4 he had not reported this to MCC New York staff, but that he had told his lawyers.

The Morning Watch Operations Lieutenant documented in a BOP report that when she returned to the Health Services Unit, Senior Officer Specialist 4 informed her that Epstein had said that his cellmate had tried to kill Epstein and had been harassing him. The Morning Watch Operations Lieutenant then spoke with the cellmate (Inmate 1), who said he was wearing headphones and was asleep when he felt something hit his legs. Inmate 1 said he called out to Epstein and when Epstein did not answer, he got up, turned on the light, and saw Epstein sitting on the floor, leaning to the side with a string around his neck. Inmate 1 told the Morning Watch Operations Lieutenant that he then called the guards. Inmate 1 provided a similar statement to BOP officials at approximately 2:50 p.m. on July 23, 2019.

The Morning Watch Operations Lieutenant's report notes that she also spoke with Epstein, who told her that he had returned to his cell after an attorney visit at approximately 8 p.m. the previous day, at which time his cellmate was reading the *Daily News* newspaper. Epstein's said his cellmate turned to a page of the newspaper that had Epstein's picture and reported that Epstein was worth $77 million. Epstein told the Morning Watch Operations Lieutenant that he looked at his picture, balled it up, and threw it in the garbage. Epstein further stated that he woke up at approximately 1 a.m. to get a drink of water, returned to his bunk, and the next thing he remembered was that he was snoring and MCC New York staff were inside his cell. When asked about the allegations against his cellmate, Epstein said he had been told that if his cellmate hurt him, MCC New York staff would not care.

Inmate 2, who was housed in the same SHU tier as Epstein on July 23, told the FBI about an incident that occurred in the SHU around 1:20 a.m. to 1:30 a.m. on an unspecified date. Inmate 2 said he was reading a book when he heard an inmate scream and bang on the cell door to get the SHU officers' attention. Inmate 2 said he could only see the cell door and not inside. According to Inmate 2, Senior Officer Specialist 2 responded to the cell and then left and returned with additional officers. The FBI was further told by Inmate 2 that the officers opened the cell door, removed an inmate, placed the inmate in handcuffs, and put the inmate in the shower area. Inmate 2 stated that the officers reentered the cell and Inmate 2 heard a thump as if something had hit the floor. The officers then pulled the other inmate out of the cell, placed him on a stretcher, and took him away. Inmate 2 also told the FBI that, later in the evening, around 2:10 a.m. to 2:15 a.m., the COs returned to the cell where the incident had occurred earlier. He said he further observed the officers clean out the cell and use a video camera to record the inside of the cell. Inmate 2 said he saw the officers remove from the cell orange clothing items that had been tied together. Inmate 2 also said that the first inmate to be removed from the cell later told Inmate 2 that he was sleeping when his cellmate had tried to kill himself by hanging himself from the ladder of the bed.

According to BOP records, medical staff evaluated Epstein at approximately 6:20 a.m. on July 23, 2019, and observed friction marks and superficial reddening of his neck and one knee. The red mark spanned two-thirds of Epstein's neck (front and sides) and was 2 inches wide. Epstein told the medical staff that he did not know what had caused his injuries, and that he went to drink a little water and woke up snoring.

Later that morning, the MCC New York Staff Psychologist conducted a suicide risk assessment and determined that Epstein should remain on suicide watch. During the assessment, Epstein denied any knowledge of how he sustained the marks on his neck. The Staff Psychologist noted in the assessment report that it was unclear whether Epstein had placed the string around his neck or if someone else did. Medical staff examined Epstein at approximately 1:08 p.m. the following day, July 24, 2019, and observed that the central part of the red mark on Epstein's neck had some abrasion. According to BOP records, Epstein told the medical staff that he still did not want to talk about how he sustained his injuries, but he believed that his cellmate had something to do with it. BOP's Special Investigative Services (SIS) opened an investigation into this incident but was unable to determine whether Epstein harmed himself or had been assaulted.

On July 24, 2019, at approximately 8:45 a.m., Epstein was removed from suicide watch. However, Epstein remained in the same cell that he was placed in the previous day and was under psychological observation until July 30, 2019.[24]

The MCC New York Chief Psychologist told the OIG that an inmate is placed on suicide watch when the inmate is believed to be imminently suicidal. During suicide watch, the inmate is under constant observation by staff; the cell lights are on 24 hours a day; and the inmate is given a special mattress, blanket, and smock to wear. The Chief Psychologist explained that although psychological observation is a lower classification, at MCC New York the psychological observations were the same as suicide watch except that inmates were allowed to have their clothing and some materials, such as books, as determined by Psychology Department. At MCC New York, psychological observation was used to see how an inmate was doing before releasing the inmate to a housing unit.

The Chief Psychologist told the OIG that the Psychology Department independently makes the decision who goes on and off suicide watch. The Chief Psychologist also stated that the Psychology Department makes recommendations to the institution's management about where inmates are housed when they come off of suicide watch. According to her, the Psychology Department always recommends that inmates coming off of suicide watch be housed with other inmates; however, she said the recommendations cannot always be carried out due to other security factors. When that occurs, the Psychology Department recommends conducting increased rounds and keeping an eye on those inmates.

The Chief Psychologist further told the OIG that, based on a conversation with the BOP's National Suicide Prevention Coordinator from the BOP's Central Office, she passed along to the MCC New York executive staff the recommendation that Epstein be housed with an alleged sex offender in the SHU.[25] The Chief Psychologist stated that the MCC New York Warden and Associate Wardens decided who Epstein would be housed with and the Psychology Department was not involved in that decision.

According to BOP records, as a result of the July 23 incident, MCC New York subsequently conducted disciplinary proceedings against Epstein for alleged self-mutilation, but ultimately found that there was insufficient evidence to find that Epstein engaged in a prohibited act. When Epstein was psychologically evaluated on July 30, 2019, in connection with disciplinary proceedings, Epstein said he did not remember how he obtained the marks around his neck. On August 2, 2019, the SIS investigation into the July 23, 2019, incident was completed and found insufficient evidence to support either that Epstein had harmed himself or that he had been harmed by his cellmate.

---

[24] Epstein's BOP medical records reflect that he was removed from psychological observation and returned to the SHU on July 30, 2019.

[25] Neither of Epstein's cellmates at MCC New York were alleged to be sex offenders.

Senior Officer Specialist 1 told the OIG that after Epstein came off of suicide watch, Epstein asked if he could be paired up with Inmate 1 again. Senior Officer Specialist 1 told Epstein that his request was something he would need to raise with the Operations Lieutenant. Senior Officer Specialist 1 told the OIG that Epstein replied, "Yeah, but I don't understand, you know, we were bunkies, everything was cool." The Chief Psychologist also told the OIG that Epstein mentioned to her that he wanted Inmate 1 to continue to be his cellmate.

V. The Psychology Department's Post-July 23 Determination that Epstein Needed to Have an Appropriate Cellmate

Following the events of July 23, the MCC New York Psychology Department determined that Epstein needed to be housed with an appropriate cellmate. To ensure Epstein's cellmate requirement was disseminated to MCC New York staff, on July 30, 2019, at 12:30 p.m., the Staff Psychologist sent an email to over 70 MCC New York staff members which read, "Inmate Epstein #76318-054 is being taken off Psych Observation and needs to be housed with an appropriate cellmate." A review of the email recipients showed that the email was sent to, among others, the Warden, Associate Warden 2, the Captain, the SHU Lieutenant, the SIS Lieutenant, the Day Watch Operations Lieutenant, the Evening Watch Operations Lieutenant, the Morning Watch Operations Lieutenant, the Day Watch Activities Lieutenant, and CO 1. The Staff Psychologist also completed a "Post-Watch Report," which stated that the "SHU L[ieutenant] informed inmate Epstein needs to be housed with an appropriate cellmate."

The Warden told the OIG that the Chief Psychologist had advised him that Epstein was not suicidal and was ready to return to the SHU. According to the Warden, when he spoke with the Chief Psychologist regarding Epstein, she told him to assign Epstein a cellmate. He added that MCC New York would typically house an inmate who was previously on suicide watch with a cellmate. The Warden stated there was no BOP policy mandating that an inmate coming off of suicide watch have a cellmate, but they usually housed such an inmate with a cellmate.

During their interviews with the OIG, Associate Warden 1, the Captain, and the SHU Lieutenant each said they had verbally informed the SHU staff of Epstein's cellmate requirement and were confident that all SHU staff members knew of Epstein's cellmate requirement. Additionally, the Captain said he visited the SHU on multiple occasions and directed his staff to be alert and attentive about Epstein's special needs.

According to Associate Warden 1, the Captain was in charge of correctional services, including the SHU. Associate Warden 1 said the Captain should have told the SHU Lieutenant, and that the SHU Lieutenant should have told the SHU staff about the cellmate requirement. Associate Warden 1 further told the OIG that the SHU Lieutenant was responsible for ensuring that everything within the SHU was in compliance. Associate Warden 1 told the OIG that the SHU staff knew that Epstein was required to have a cellmate, and said she personally heard it being discussed on more than one occasion when she would visit the SHU while performing her rounds.

The Captain, who supervised all of the Lieutenants and COs working in MCC New York, said that after the cellmate requirement was issued for Epstein, he spoke with the SHU Lieutenant and directed him to ensure that Epstein had a cellmate. Similar to the Warden, the SHU Lieutenant told the OIG that while there is no BOP policy addressing the necessity of assigning cellmates to individuals coming off of suicide watch, it was common practice in the BOP for prisoners coming off of suicide watch to be assigned a cellmate. The SHU Lieutenant confirmed that a BOP psychologist told him that Epstein had to be housed with a cellmate when Epstein returned to the SHU and said that he passed the directive down to the SHU staff.

Additionally, the Day Watch SHU Officer in Charge on August 9, 2019, said he and all other SHU staff were aware of Epstein's cellmate requirement. MCC New York Psychology Department personnel told the OIG that MCC New York staff members knew of Epstein's cellmate requirement because it was discussed during staff meetings, department head meetings, SHU meetings, morning meetings, and during required staff training.

Forensic Psychologist 1 told the OIG that on August 9, 2019, she was present during a meeting in which one of Epstein's attorneys opposed Epstein having a cellmate. Forensic Psychologist 1 said she explained to the attorney that Epstein needed to have a cellmate because he was housed in the SHU and he was a sex offender.

VI. Selection of Epstein's Cellmate After Psychological Observation

The Captain told the OIG that he compiled a list of possible cellmates for Epstein, vetted those inmates, and provided the list of names to the MCC New York Warden. The Warden told the OIG that he identified two potential cellmates and tentatively decided on Inmate 3. The Warden said he passed this information on to the BOP Director's Chief of Staff and later received word that he should assign Inmate 3 to be Epstein's cellmate.

The Warden told the OIG that no inmates were pre-vetted to replace Inmate 3 if he left MCC New York. The Warden and the Captain told the OIG that if Inmate 3 had been removed as Epstein's cellmate, they would have had to review a new list of potential cellmate candidates to ensure that Epstein was housed with an appropriate inmate. According to the Warden and the Captain, if Inmate 3 was no longer detained at MCC New York, SHU staff should have informed a Lieutenant on duty, who should have informed the Captain, who would have ensured that the process of selecting a new cellmate for Epstein would begin.

VII. Epstein's Cell Assignment from July 30 to August 10

As a result of Epstein's cellmate requirement, on July 30, 2019, following his release from psychological observation, Epstein was initially assigned to cell Z04-206 with Inmate 3 in the J Tier of the SHU.[26] A BOP

---

[26] SENTRY, which is BOP's database of information relating to the care, classification, subsistence, protection, discipline, and programs of inmates, inaccurately reflected that this move from his psychological observation cell to the SHU occurred the previous day (July 29, 2019). The investigation revealed that Epstein was originally scheduled to return to the SHU on July 29, 2019, but, at his request, he remained on psychological observation until July 30, 2019.

SENTRY was not updated to reflect either the actual date of Epstein's transfer back into the SHU or the cell to which he and Inmate 3 were assigned after the initial cell change necessitated by the electrical needs of Epstein's medical device. The administrative error in BOP's SENTRY records regarding Epstein's cell assignment had no effect on the events the OIG investigated and reviewed.

According to OIG interviews with MCC New York staff members, it does not appear that there were any checks to ensure
Continued

medical record note reflected that, on this same date, Epstein was provided with his personally-owned medical device. BOP witnesses told the OIG that on that same date, Epstein and Inmate 3 were moved to cell Z06-220 in the L Tier of the SHU to accommodate the electrical needs of Epstein's medical device. Of all the cells in the SHU, cell Z06-220 was the closest cell with a direct line of sight to the SHU Officers' Station in the common area of the SHU, which was approximately 15 feet away.

Inmate 3 told the OIG that when he and Epstein were first assigned as cellmates in cell Z06-220 in the L Tier, the Day Watch Operations Lieutenant told Inmate 3 that he had a "cool bunkie" for him, an "old guy" who would not bother Inmate 3. Inmate 3 said he told the Day Watch Operations Lieutenant that he slept on the bottom bunk, and the Day Watch Operations Lieutenant said that would not be a problem because his new cellmate slept on the floor. Inmate 3 said he was surprised by this response because he understood that sleeping on the floor was not allowed and he had previously been disciplined for doing so.

When Epstein arrived in the cell, Inmate 3 recognized him and said he (Inmate 3) told the Day Watch Operations Lieutenant that the Day Watch Operations Lieutenant had "jammed up" Inmate 3. Inmate 3 said he knew Epstein had tried to hang himself and had just come from suicide watch. According to Inmate 3, the Day Watch Operations Lieutenant told Inmate 3 not to worry, that Epstein was okay, and that Inmate 3 should keep an eye on him. Inmate 3 asked the Day Watch Operations Lieutenant if he was supposed to serve as a suicide prevention advocate, that is, an inmate who is assigned to the suicide watch area. Inmate 3 said the Day Watch Operations Lieutenant laughed and brushed off Inmate 3's comment.

According to Inmate 3, COs brought two mattresses to the cell for Epstein and placed them on the floor. Epstein put the mattresses on the right side of the cell, which is only partially visible through the cell door window when the cell door is closed. Inmate 3 noted that Epstein also had two extra blankets, which Inmate 3 said was also unusual because none of the inmates had extra blankets.

Inmate 3 said he asked Epstein to please not kill himself or hang himself while Inmate 3 was his cellmate because Inmate 3 had a chance to go home soon. Epstein told Inmate 3 not to worry and that he was not going to cause Inmate 3 any trouble.

---

that inmates were physically located in the cells to which they were assigned in SENTRY. Associate Warden 1 told the OIG that the error would have been identified if SHU staff members had conducted a bed-book count, but there was no requirement to do a bed-book count every certain number of days. Associate Warden 1 explained that during a bed-book count, the staff members have a roster with them while conducting the count of inmates assigned to their housing unit to ensure all inmates are accounted for and in their assigned cells. The OIG's investigation revealed that these and other cell assignment and recordkeeping errors would have been uncovered had MCC New York SHU staff been undertaking inmate accountability measures, such as rounds, counts, census checks, and bed-book checks.

Figure 4.6

SHU L Tier

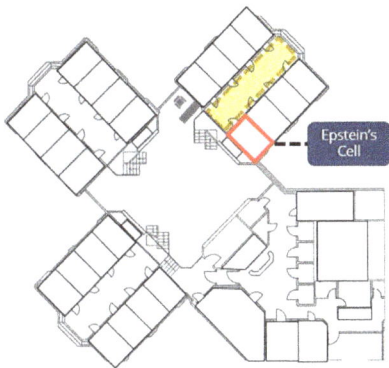

Sources: DOJ OIG schematic drawing depicting the MCC New York SHU; and photograph taken by the Office of the Chief Medical Examiner, City of New York (OCME)

Figure 4.7

Exterior Views of Epstein's Cell

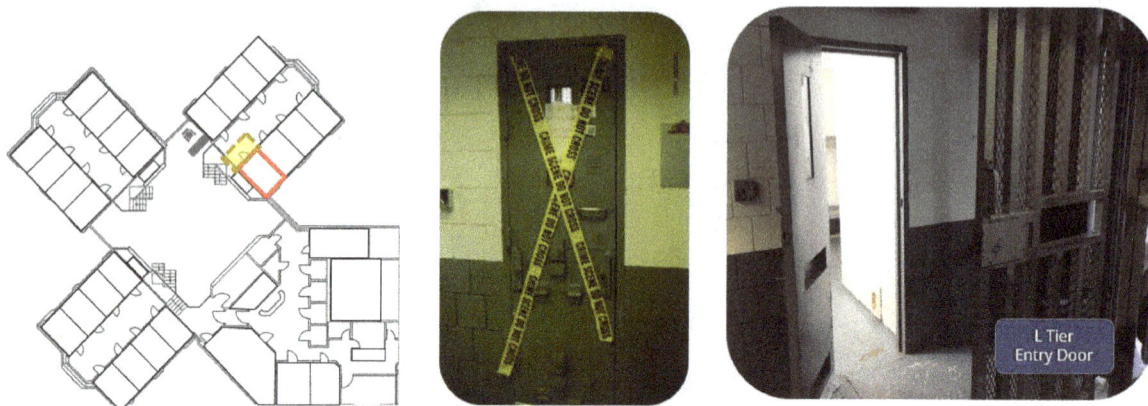

Note: Both photographs have been modified for security reasons and the left photograph has been modified for privacy reasons.

Sources: DOJ OIG schematic drawing depicting the MCC New York SHU; OCME photographs

Figure 4.8

The Door to the Cell Occupied by Epstein and Inmate 3 from July 30 to August 9

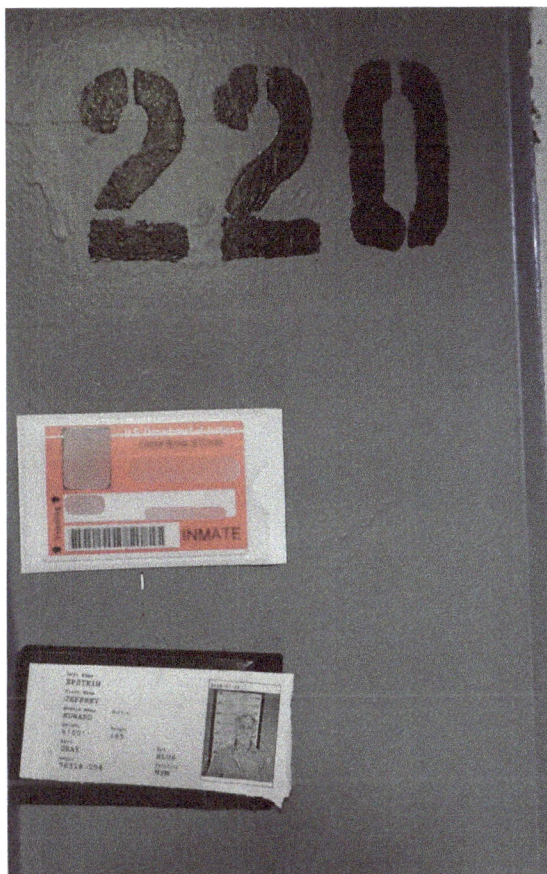

Note: The photograph has been modified for privacy reasons.

Source: OCME

Figure 4.9

View of Epstein's Empty Cell from Cell Door Window

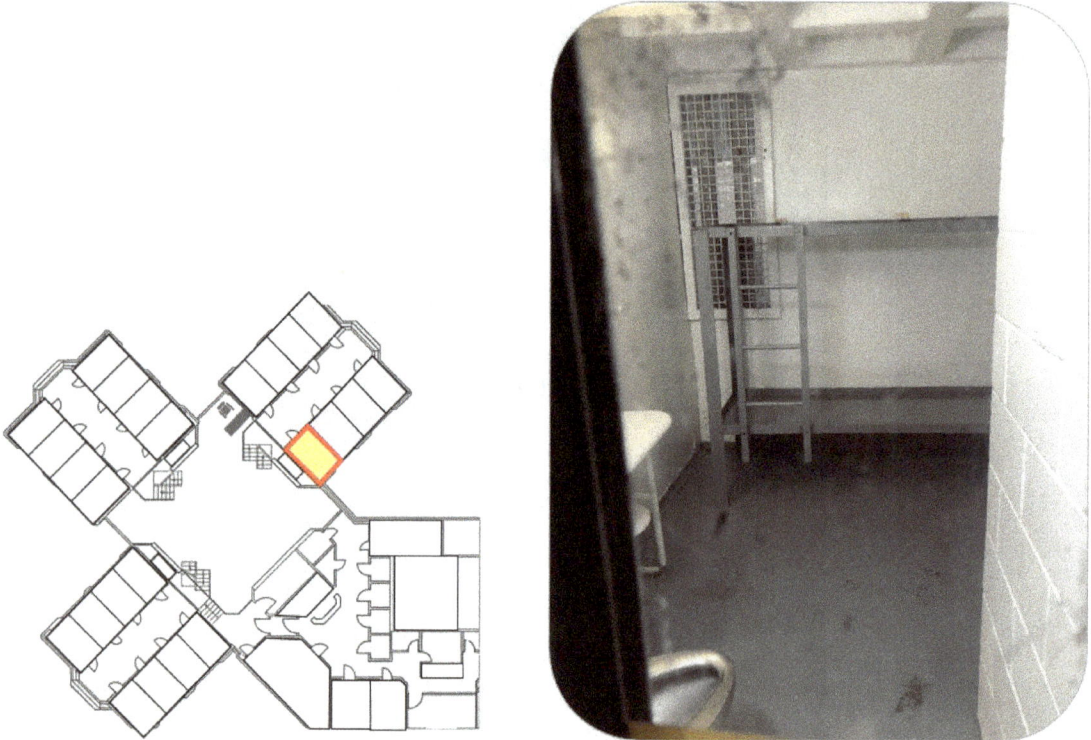

Source: DOJ OIG photograph and DOJ OIG schematic drawing depicting the MCC New York SHU

Figure 4.10

Interior View of Epstein's Empty Cell from Just Inside the Cell Door

Source: DOJ OIG photograph and DOJ OIG schematic drawing depicting the MCC New York SHU

Figure 4.11

View of Epstein's Cell Door from the SHU Officers' Station

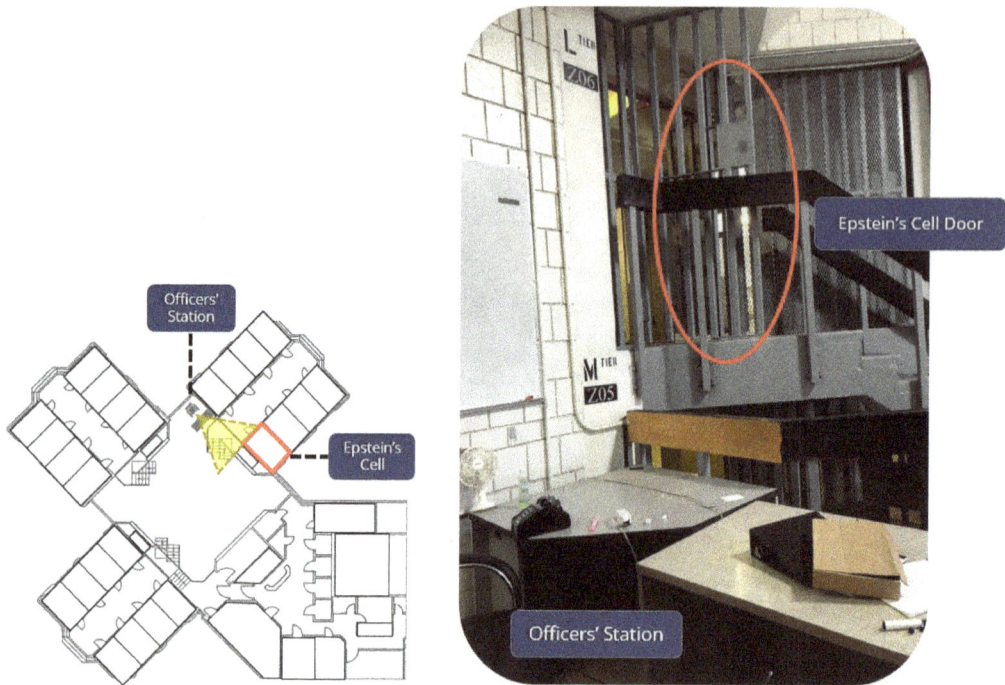

Note: The photograph has been modified for security and privacy reasons.

Source: DOJ OIG photograph and DOJ OIG schematic drawing depicting the MCC New York SHU

Figure 4.12

View of the SHU Officers' Station from Epstein's cell

Note: The photograph has been modified for security reasons.

Source: DOJ OIG photograph and DOJ OIG schematic drawing depicting the MCC New York SHU

VIII. Psychological Evaluations of Epstein from July 6 to August 9

During Epstein's detention at MCC New York, a variety of medical professionals, including a Medical Doctor, a Clinical Nurse, and Physician Assistant 1, who is a Mid-Level Practitioner, conducted multiple medical appointments with Epstein, and Epstein was prescribed a variety of medications for various ailments and health needs. Epstein was also given an eye and dental exam, as well as a blood panel screening. This section details Epstein's psychological evaluations while he was in MCC New York custody prior to his death.

On Saturday, July 6, 2019, at 9:38 p.m., upon Epstein's intake into MCC New York, he was medically screened by Physician Assistant 2. The screening included taking vital signs and asking various medical history questions, including questions related to Epstein's mental health. Among other things, Physician Assistant 2 annotated that Epstein did not have current suicidal ideation and had denied having a history of suicide attempts. Physician Assistant 2 instructed Epstein how he could obtain medical, dental, and mental health care.

At 2:58 a.m. on Sunday, July 7, 2019, a Facilities Assistant emailed the Psychology Department asking that someone evaluate Epstein because he appeared "distraught, sad, and a little confused."

On July 8, 2019, Forensic Psychologist 1 of the Psychology Department conducted an Intake Screening of Epstein that included a self-report, staff observation, and a review of information in SENTRY. Forensic

Psychologist 1 noted that during Physician Assistant 1's initial intake evaluation, on the intake questionnaire, Epstein denied having a history of mental health treatment and any history of mental health symptoms. Additionally, Forensic Psychologist 1 noted no suicidal ideations, attempts, or self-harm; no history of substance abuse or treatment; and no sexual offense convictions.

During the evaluation, Epstein stated he had been previously incarcerated for 3 months for "prostitution," and that he was currently charged with sex trafficking. Epstein denied recent or present morbid thoughts and denied passive or active suicidal ideation. It was noted in BOP records that Epstein's verbalizations were future-oriented and did not have indications of helpless or hopeless thinking.

According to Forensic Psychologist 1, Epstein did not meet the criteria for any psychological diagnosis and was designated as Mental Health Care Code 1. This is indicative of an inmate who does not show any significant level of functional impairment associated with a mental illness and does not demonstrate a need for regular mental health intervention. Epstein was educated on emergency procedures for contacting the Psychology Department staff, and Epstein agreed to contact staff if he needed Psychology Department services in the future.

The MCC New York Chief Psychologist told the OIG that based on the Psychological Services Intake Questionnaire, inmates have four different Care Code ratings.[27] Code 1 means there are no concerns about the inmate's mental health status; they have no needs and will not be followed up with unless requested by staff or the inmates. Code 2 means there is some history of mental health issues, but the inmate has them under control and the Psychology Department will follow up monthly. Code 3 is more severe, requiring weekly visits by the Psychology Department to ensure the inmate is stable and if unstable would be moved to observation. Code 4 inmates are seen daily by the Psychology Department and are under constant psychological observation. The Chief Psychologist stated that a Code 1 inmate can be on suicide watch. Suicide watch is for inmates who are showing immediate and exigent signs of being suicidal.

Subsequent to the intake screening, on July 8, 2019, the Chief Psychologist consulted with the National Suicide Prevention Coordinator from the BOP's Central Office, regarding the various risk factors associated with Epstein for suicidality. These risk factors were that Epstein was involved in a high-profile case with media attention, had been charged with sex offenses, was on pretrial status, and there was the potential for bad news from a court proceeding that day. A determination was made that upon Epstein's return from court, staff were to notify the psychologist and place Epstein on a "watch status" until a thorough suicide risk assessment could be conducted.

When Epstein returned from court on July 8, 2019, it was after duty hours and MCC New York staff contacted the Psychology Department and informed them that Epstein denied suicidality. However, for precautionary reasons, Epstein was placed on psychological observation status until Psychology Department staff could conduct a suicide risk assessment the following day. During Epstein's period of psychological observation, inmate companions continuously observed him and kept a log that detailed Epstein's activities in 15-minute increments. Under BOP policy, on a case-by-case basis, the Warden may authorize such an inmate

---

[27] Upon reviewing a draft of this report, the Chief Psychologist noted that mental health care is classified into "levels," not "codes."

companion program at an institution to utilize inmate observers, who are selected, trained, and supervised by the institution's Suicide Prevention Program Coordinator.

On July 9, 2019, the Chief Psychologist conducted a suicide assessment of Epstein. She reviewed Epstein's medical record and interviewed him, which revealed that he possessed some risk factors for suicidality. Epstein denied having any past or present suicidal ideation, intention, or plan, and also denied having any history of mental health treatment or any current mental health symptoms. The Chief Psychologist's assessment was that Epstein had "protective" factors present that could decrease his risk of suicide. The Chief Psychologist assessed factors that included his willingness to engage in treatment, view of death as negative, future orientation, and the fact that he adamantly denied any suicidal ideation, intention, or plan. The Chief Psychologist's assessment was that Epstein had numerous protective factors that outweighed his risk factors for suicidality and that he had a positive outlook regarding his legal case. Epstein remained on psychological observation pending a suitable cell assignment, and the Chief Psychologist noted that a suicide watch was not warranted at the time of her report.

On July 10, 2019, the Chief Psychologist met with Epstein for a psychological observation and noted that, according to the psychological observation logbook, Epstein had been eating his meals, sleeping, and interacting with other inmates. During this meeting with the Chief Psychologist, Epstein voiced concerns over being housed in the SHU. Epstein asked the Chief Psychologist to be "single-celled" if he were to be housed in the SHU and had also requested a shower, his property, pen, and paper. The Chief Psychologist stated Epstein had been provided a shower on this date. She provided Epstein with coping skills strategies, to which he was receptive. Epstein continued to deny any suicidal ideation, intention, or plan; and Epstein stated he was looking forward to his upcoming court hearing regarding pretrial release. The Chief Psychologist's assessment was that Epstein was psychologically stable at the time and that he could be released from the psychological observation area. She noted that Epstein would be housed in the SHU with a cellmate and would be seen the following morning to evaluate his mental status and stability. Following this July 10 assessment, Epstein was taken off of psychological observation and returned to the SHU with documented recommendations for a cellmate and next-day contact by the Psychology Department.

The following day, July 11, 2019, the Staff Psychologist attempted to see Epstein in the morning and afternoon, but he was meeting with his attorneys. Since the Staff Psychologist was unable to meet with Epstein, the Chief Psychologist met with Epstein in the attorney conference area for a psychological observation follow-up. During this meeting, Epstein expressed concerns about a number of issues, including not yet receiving his property, not having enough water during his attorney conference, and a desire to attend recreation. Epstein was upset about having to wear an orange uniform and the Chief Psychologist explained the orange uniform was because he was being housed in the SHU. During this clinical contact, the Chief Psychologist provided Epstein with additional coping strategies, to which he was receptive. Additionally, Epstein was educated about routine and emergency procedures for contacting the Psychology Department staff and reminded of self-help books and audiotapes available through the Psychology Department. Epstein continued to deny any suicidal ideation, intention, or plan and was scheduled to be seen again the following week. The Chief Psychologist told the OIG that Epstein and his attorney mocked her for thinking Epstein was suicidal.[28]

On July 16, 2019, at Epstein's request, the Chief Psychologist met with Epstein during his attorney conference. The Chief Psychologist noted that Epstein did not have any psychological concerns and denied suicidality. The Chief Psychologist noted that she provided Epstein with psychoeducation regarding additional coping strategies. Epstein was educated about routine and emergency procedures to contact Psychology Department staff and reminded of self-help books and audiotapes that are available to him. The Chief Psychologist noted in her clinical contact report that there was no need for follow-up and that Epstein would be seen in the SHU for rounds and monthly SHU reviews.

According to the BOP After Action Review submitted by the Southeast Regional Director, the Chief Psychologist's meeting with Epstein on July 16, 2019, at Epstein's request during his attorney conference was inappropriate. The Southeast Regional Director wrote in the report that Epstein attempted to "bring his attorneys into the fray regarding the mental health treatment being provided by the institution." In the After Action Review, the Southeast Regional Director wrote that it was not typical for the BOP to provide psychological intervention in the presence of others, nor was it appropriate for a BOP psychologist to meet with an inmate's attorney. When asked by the OIG about these findings, the Chief Psychologist stated that the intention was to check on Epstein, not to breach any security.

On July 18, 2019, the Chief Psychologist conducted a monthly SHU review and noted that Epstein was unavailable due to a meeting with his legal team and that she would attempt to interview Epstein in the near future to complete his monthly review.

As noted previously, at approximately 1:27 a.m. on July 23, 2019, Epstein was found lying on the floor of his cell with a piece of homemade orange cloth around his neck. The Chief Psychologist made a general administrative note in Epstein's file that she was contacted by the Operations Lieutenant at approximately 2 a.m., and informed that Epstein was being placed on suicide watch after he was found with a string loosely hanging around his neck. That morning, Physician Assistant 1 assessed Epstein for injuries and noted in BOP records that Epstein was cooperative, alert, and oriented. According to BOP's medical records, Epstein did not appear distressed and was smiling during the clinical assessment. Epstein said he did not know what had happened and could not explain the mark on his neck. Physician Assistant 1 noted that Epstein had a circular line of erythema, i.e., superficial redness on the skin, that was 2 inches wide and spanned two-thirds of the way around the front and sides of the base of his neck. According to the BOP report, one section of the erythema (or redness) in the front of his neck had marks of friction, and there was no inflammation, deformities, hematomas, lacerations, or tenderness. The BOP report stated that Epstein was able to move his neck without any restriction and denied having any pain, discomfort, or respiratory problems. Physician Assistant 1 further noted there was another small erythema (or redness) on Epstein's left knee about 2 centimeters in diameter, which was noted as mild. Physician Assistant 1's assessment was that the injury was unspecified and was self-inflicted.

---

[28] Upon reviewing a draft of this report, the Chief Psychologist noted that Epstein's attorneys were not "mocking" her; the attorneys and Epstein were simply laughing at the fact that she was inquiring as to whether Epstein was suicidal and dismissing the possibility that Epstein could be suicidal.

Also on July 23, 2019, the Staff Psychologist conducted a suicide risk assessment that included a clinical interview of Epstein and a review of Epstein's medical record, the psychology data system, and a review of the SENTRY database. According to the Staff Psychologist's report, Epstein denied knowing why he was placed on suicide watch. BOP records state that Epstein recalled getting a drink of water the night prior and then went back to bed. Epstein's next recollection was hearing himself snoring. The BOP assessment records reflect that Epstein wanted to know why he was on suicide watch and he was informed that he had been found with a string on his neck. The Staff Psychologist noted that it was unclear whether Epstein had placed the string around his neck or if someone else did. Epstein denied current suicidal or self-harm thoughts or ever having these thoughts; denied a history of self-harm and suicide attempts; and denied feeling hopeless and fearing for his safety. Epstein told the Staff Psychologist that he lived to enjoy life and that his future plans included fighting his criminal case and getting back to his normal life. The Staff Psychologist noted that Epstein was to remain on suicide watch for further observation. The Staff Psychologist told the OIG she had advised BOP staff that Epstein would need a cellmate.

The Chief Psychologist said she considered three possibilities to explain the July 23 incident: (1) Epstein and/or Inmate 1 were gaming the system to get something they wanted that they were not getting; (2) Epstein, who really was suicidal, had conducted a rehearsal; or (3) Inmate 1 had assaulted Epstein. The Chief Psychologist told the OIG that after Epstein told her he wanted to be housed with the same cellmate he originally said had assaulted him, she began to think that the third possibility (assault by Inmate 1) was less plausible than the other two possibilities, although she did not know for certain.

The following day, July 24, medical staff examined Epstein at approximately 1:08 p.m., and observed that the central part of the red mark on Epstein's neck had some abrasion. Epstein told the medical staff that he still did not want to talk about how he sustained his injuries, but he believed that his cellmate had something to do with it. BOP's SIS opened an investigation into this incident but was unable to determine whether Epstein had harmed himself or had been assaulted.

On July 24, 2019, after 31 hours and 5 minutes, Epstein was removed from suicide watch. Epstein remained in the same cell that he was in under suicide watch and was under psychological observation until July 30, 2019.[29] Also on July 24, 2019, Forensic Psychologist 2 completed a Post Suicide Watch Report. According to Forensic Psychologist 2's report, Epstein continued to claim a lack of memory regarding how he sustained the scar around his neck. The BOP report further stated that Epstein adamantly denied suicidal ideation, intentions, and plans, that Epstein identified reasons to live and was future-oriented, and that Epstein was assessed for a willingness to engage in treatment. The BOP report reflected that Forensic Psychologist 2 inquired further if Epstein could recall the previous day's incident and Epstein stated that he had been trying to remember. Forensic Psychologist 2 asked Epstein why he told another inmate that Epstein's cellmate had tried to kill him but was now claiming he has no memory of the incident. Epstein told Forensic Psychologist 2 that he did not recall himself or his cellmate tying a string or rope around his neck.

Following Forensic Psychologist 2's examination of Epstein, she determined that he should be removed from suicide watch. Forensic Psychologist 2 told the FBI that she discussed the decision to step Epstein down to psychological observation from suicide watch with the Chief Psychologist and Associate Warden 2, who both

---

[29] Epstein's BOP medical records reflect that he was removed from psychological observation and returned to the SHU on July 30, 2019; however, SENTRY inaccurately reflects that Epstein was transferred back to the SHU on July 29, 2019.

concurred with her determination. Epstein was therefore taken off suicide watch and placed on psychological observation, during which time BOP records reflect that he was continuously observed by inmate companions and seen daily by Psychology Department staff. Forensic Psychologist 2 annotated in the Post Suicide Watch Report that the reason for removing Epstein from suicide watch was due to Epstein stating he had no interest in killing himself; he had described having a wonderful life; and Epstein had said it would be crazy to take his own life and he would not do that to himself. Forensic Psychologist 2 told the FBI that following her clinical visit with Epstein on July 24, 2019, she was cautious with Epstein's case and his self-reporting of what had occurred the previous day. Forensic Psychologist 2 stated that she observed signs of positivity and that Epstein "adamantly denied suicide." Nevertheless, she was not comfortable taking Epstein off suicide watch and instead opted to place Epstein on psychological observation, which was a step down from suicide watch. Forensic Psychologist 2 told the FBI that "I made the decision with the consent" of the Chief Psychologist and Associate Warden 2, with whom she had consulted. Forensic Psychologist 2 told the FBI that placing Epstein on psychological observation allowed him to possess hygiene products, two novels, attend legal visits, and take showers. It also allowed him to have standard inmate clothing, a flex pen, a toothbrush and toothpaste, soap, and deodorant. However, Forensic Psychologist 2 explained that it was not healthy for inmates to stay on suicide watch for extended periods of time and they are re-evaluated on a day-to-day basis.

According to Forensic Psychologist 2's Post Suicide Watch Report, Epstein expressed a feeling of safety being housed in the psychological observation area rather than the SHU and asked if there was a safer unit for him to be housed. Forensic Psychologist 2 informed Epstein that he would remain on psychological observation for the near future, but his long-term housing would need to be revisited because it is not ideal to remain in psychological observation for extended periods of time. The BOP report states that Epstein was again educated on routine and emergency procedures for contacting Psychology Department staff.

According to BOP records, between July 25-29, 2019, Epstein was seen daily by the Chief Psychologist or the Staff Psychologist while he was on psychological observation. On each of these dates, according to BOP reports, Epstein adamantly denied any suicidality and denied having any memory of what occurred on July 23, 2019, which resulted in him being placed on suicide watch. Additionally, on each date, Epstein was provided with supportive and coping skill interventions to which he was receptive. BOP records state that Epstein expressed concerns about being housed again in the SHU because he felt it was dangerous; he could not sleep well due to noise from other inmates; and it was difficult for him to work on his legal case. The Chief Psychologist told the FBI and the OIG that she met with Epstein on July 25, 2019, and he was in good spirits. She said that during this clinical visit, Epstein said he was baffled over the July 23, 2019 incident and asked the Chief Psychologist to give him some cues to help him remember. The Chief Psychologist told the OIG that she kept Epstein on psychological observation because he had not answered her questions regarding the possible suicide attempt. The Chief Psychologist told the OIG that she coordinated with the BOP's National Suicide Prevention Coordinator, who recommended that Epstein be housed with a sex offender in the SHU. The Chief Psychologist notified Associate Warden 2 of this recommendation via email. BOP records further reflect that, during his clinical visit on July 28, 2019, Epstein told the Staff Psychologist that he was agitated for hours the previous night because of a non-stop toilet flushing and that the noise was similar to when he was housed in the SHU. The Staff Psychologist informed Epstein that he would be moving to a different cell.

On July 29, 2019, according to BOP records, Epstein reported to the Chief Psychologist that his memory of the July 23, 2019 incident may be impaired because of his sleep apnea. On this date, Epstein was to receive his personally owned medical device. BOP records state that Epstein was aware he would be returning to the SHU but reported that he did not feel well due to lack of sleep and other medical concerns. Epstein asked to stay on psychological observation, where he felt safe, for one more night to get some sleep and then return to the SHU with a cellmate the following day. According to BOP records, the Chief Psychologist informed Epstein that he could stay 1 more night and explained that there were no mental health issues precluding him from returning to the SHU the following day. The Chief Psychologist explained to Epstein that he would be placed in a safe situation in the SHU. Epstein again was provided supportive interventions and psychoeducation regarding additional coping strategies. BOP records state that Epstein was somewhat receptive but more concerned with getting phone calls, recreation, and housing placement concerns.

On July 30, 2019, according to BOP records, Epstein reported to the Staff Psychologist that he had not slept well, and Epstein discussed how he did not think he would be able to sleep well in the SHU because of the noise. The Staff Psychologist annotated in the clinical contact summary that documentation revealed Epstein had eaten and taken a shower the day prior (July 29) and also had eaten breakfast on July 30. The Staff Psychologist annotated, Epstein did not display indications of disturbed thought process or content and denied current suicidal or self-harm ideation. BOP records further stated that Epstein agreed to immediately report to staff if he began to have suicidal or self-harm thoughts and that Epstein was future-oriented and did not appear to be a danger to himself. The Staff Psychologist noted in her clinical contact report that she had consulted with the Chief Psychologist and that psychological observation of Epstein would be discontinued. According to her clinical contact report, the Staff Psychologist educated Epstein about routine and emergency procedures for contacting Psychology Department staff and noted that Epstein would be seen the following day to monitor his mental status and provide further intervention if needed. The Staff Psychologist also noted in her report that the SHU Lieutenant was informed that Epstein needed to be housed with an appropriate cellmate.

Also on July 30, 2019, the Staff Psychologist completed an evaluation of competency related to Epstein being able to proceed with the disciplinary process. Epstein had been charged by BOP with a prohibited act, specifically tattooing or self-mutilation, for the incident that occurred on July 23, 2019. In conducting the evaluation of competency, the Staff Psychologist reviewed the suicide risk assessment completed by the Chief Psychologist on July 9, 2019, in which Epstein had denied a history of mental health treatment and having any past or present suicidal ideation, intention, or plan. The Staff Psychologist also reviewed the suicide risk assessment that she herself completed, dated July 23, 2019, which stated that it was unclear at the time if Epstein had placed the string around his neck or if it was done by someone else. According to the Staff Psychologist's notes from her competency evaluation on July 30, the determination of an inmate's competency to proceed with the disciplinary process was based on a clinical assessment of the inmate's ability to understand the nature of the proceedings and his or her ability to assist in his or her own defense. After a review of available psychological and psychiatric records and information related to the offense, the Staff Psychologist found that Epstein was competent to proceed with the disciplinary process.

That same day, July 30, Epstein was removed from psychological observation and transferred back to the SHU, consistent with what he had been told by the Chief Psychologist the prior day.

On July 31, 2019, according to BOP records, Forensic Psychologist 3 conducted a clinical visit with Epstein and noted that he was in a pleasant mood, generally slept well, and was getting readjusted to being in the SHU. Epstein told Forensic Psychologist 3 that he was getting along with his cellmate. According to her report, Epstein explicitly denied recent and current suicidal ideation or intent and denied having thoughts of harming others. Epstein also agreed to contact staff immediately if he experienced any suicidal thoughts or psychological distress. Forensic Psychologist 3's report further stated that Epstein was receptive to her utilization of cognitive behavioral therapeutic techniques. She wrote that there did not appear to be a need for follow-up at the time and Epstein expressed a willingness to self-refer to Psychology Department staff if needed. According to the report, Epstein would continue to be seen during routine SHU rounds and SHU reviews.

On August 1, 2019, according to BOP records, BOP Receiving and Discharge staff, who are responsible for processing inmates who enter or leave the facility, notified the Staff Psychologist that the previous day when the U.S. Marshals Service (USMS) had brought Epstein back to MCC New York from court, they had provided a form on which it was noted that Epstein had "suicidal tendencies." The OIG reviewed the USMS Prisoner Schedule Report for July 31, 2019, as well as the USMS Prisoner Custody Alert Notice that had annotated in the remarks that Epstein had "Mental Concerns: Suicidal Tendencies." The Chief Psychologist told the OIG that the USMS annotates suicidal tendencies for many inmates if the USMS was aware the inmate was previously on suicide watch. Therefore, the Chief Psychologist said the annotation was not abnormal since Epstein had just come off suicide watch and Epstein may have told the USMS that he had been on suicide watch.

Following receipt of this information from the Receiving and Discharge staff, the Staff Psychologist conducted a suicide risk assessment on August 1 that included a review of Epstein's previous clinical encounters, medical records, and data in the Psychology Department and SENTRY systems. According to the Staff Psychologist's assessment, Epstein denied stating he was suicidal and was surprised that the form noted that he had suicidal tendencies. The Staff Psychologist said that Epstein told her that the incident report he received for the marks on his neck arising from the July 23 event had been expunged. The OIG confirmed that the incident report was expunged. Epstein also said his cellmate talked at night and kept Epstein awake but that Epstein wanted to give it 3 to 4 more days before determining if he wanted another cellmate. The Staff Psychologist concluded in her report that Epstein did not appear to be a danger to himself and denied current suicidal or self-harm ideation and agreed to immediately inform staff if he had any of these thoughts. Epstein told her that he had social supports in the community and that he had reasons to live and positive future plans. The Staff Psychologist noted that Epstein was currently psychologically stable and that suicide watch was not indicated at the time. The Staff Psychologist concluded that Epstein's overall acute suicide risk was low, and the overall chronic suicide risk was absent. Epstein was again provided supportive and educative interventions and educated about routine and emergency procedures for contacting Psychology Department staff. The Staff Psychologist's report noted that Epstein would continue to be seen during routine SHU rounds and SHU reviews and that he would be seen by Psychology Department staff the following week to monitor his mental status and provide further intervention, if needed.

On August 8, 2019, the Chief Psychologist conducted a clinical follow-up session with Epstein. According to her report, Epstein described his sleep as fair and requested that he be placed in general population. The report further stated that Epstein denied feelings of depression, anxiety, and any suicidal ideation, intention, or plan. Epstein told the Chief Psychologist that he received the necessary documentation to make phone calls and asked if his previous phone calls over the speaker phone counted as his monthly phone contact. The Chief Psychologist stated in her report that Epstein had no mental health concerns and did not appear to be in any distress. The Chief Psychologist wrote that SHU staff had not reported any unusual behaviors related to Epstein. She provided Epstein with supportive interventions and psychoeducation regarding additional coping strategies, to which Epstein was receptive. Epstein was educated on routine and emergency procedures for contacting Psychology Department staff and also reminded of self-help books and audiotapes that are available to him. The Chief Psychologist wrote that Epstein would be seen in weekly SHU rounds and monthly for SHU reviews. The Chief Psychologist told the OIG that the fact that Epstein underwent three suicide risk assessments was unusual.[30]

---

[30] Upon reviewing a draft of this report, the Chief Psychologist noted that it was not unusual for someone with static risk factors like Epstein to have received multiple suicide risk assessments. According to the Chief Psychologist upon reviewing a draft of this report, what was unusual was the fact that Epstein was in attorney conference "day and night on a daily basis due to his financial resources." She noted that it was difficult for Psychology Department staff to interview Epstein because he had a right to his attorney visits, which would last throughout the working day.

Chapter 5: The Events of August 8–10, 2019, and Epstein's Death

I.   Epstein Signs a New Last Will and Testament on August 8

In the weeks following Epstein's death, multiple media outlets reported that Epstein signed a new Last Will and Testament on August 8, 2019. At least one media organization published a copy of the notarized document showing that it was signed by Epstein and two of his attorneys and notarized on August 8, 2019. Attorney visitor logs from the Metropolitan Correctional Center in New York, New York (MCC New York) confirmed that those attorneys and the notary public visited Epstein on that date. The Office of the Inspector General (OIG) confirmed via court records that the August 8, 2019 will and other probate-related documents were filed in the Superior Court of the Virgin Islands on August 15, 2019. Among the court filings was an affidavit from another attorney who stated that she received the August 8, 2019 will from Epstein. The OIG confirmed via attorney visitor logs that this attorney also visited Epstein at MCC New York on August 8, 2019. The OIG's investigation and review revealed that MCC New York personnel were unaware that Epstein had changed his will 2 days before he died.

The Chief Psychologist said she had heard that Epstein had changed his will from media reporting following his death. The Chief Psychologist did not know if the media reporting was accurate, but she thought that if it were true, it would have been useful information to know because it would have been a red flag. The Staff Psychologist and the Chief Psychologist told the OIG that if Epstein's attorneys had notified them or the Psychology Department that Epstein had changed his will, such information would have been a factor warranting a review of Epstein's mental state and Epstein probably would have been placed back on suicide watch or some type of observation.

II.   Court Order on August 9 Releasing Epstein-Related Documents in Pending Civil Litigation

On August 9, 2019, the U.S. Court of Appeals for the Second Circuit ordered the unsealing of the summary judgment filings from a defamation lawsuit filed by Virginia Roberts Giuffre, a woman who alleged that Epstein had victimized her when she was a teenager, against Ghislaine Maxwell.[31] As a result of the court's order, that same day approximately 2,000 pages of documents were released into the public domain, which contained considerable derogatory information about Epstein and some may have related to the criminal charges pending against him. Additional high-profile public figures were also named in the released documents. There was significant media coverage of information contained within the unsealed court filings.

---

[31] Maxwell was subsequently indicted and, in December 2021, convicted of conspiring with Epstein to sexually abuse minors.

III. Transfer of Epstein's Cellmate on August 9 to Another Institution and Failure to Replace Him with Another Inmate

A. Notice on August 8 of the Impending Transfer of Epstein's Cellmate on August 9

As noted above, since July 30, consistent with the Psychology Department's determination that Epstein needed to have a cellmate, Epstein had been housed with Inmate 3, whom the Warden and the Federal Bureau of Prisons (BOP) executive leadership had selected as an appropriate cellmate. At 10:33 a.m. on August 8, 2019, the U.S. Marshals Service (USMS) sent an email to MCC New York personnel assigned to Receiving and Discharge, the area within the Correctional Services Department that is responsible for processing inmates who enter or leave the facility, with the subject "Transfer of Prisoners from NYM [MCC New York] to GEO."[32] The body of the email identified Inmate 3 as one of the prisoners to be transferred and further stated, "Please schedule the transfer for Friday 8/9/19."

At 3:36 p.m. on the same day, the USMS sent a second email to a number of MCC New York personnel, including Associate Warden 2, the Captain, the SHU Lieutenant, the Day Watch Operations Lieutenant, the Day Watch Activities Lieutenant, the Evening Watch Operations Lieutenant, another Lieutenant, and the Special Investigative Services Lieutenant, with the subject "Prisoner Production 08-09-2019." This email contained two attachments, one of which was the Prisoner Schedule Report for MCC New York for August 9, 2019. The first page of this attachment reflects that Inmate 3 was scheduled to be transferred from MCC New York to GEO (Queens Detention Facility) on August 9, 2019. This attachment also includes the acronym "WAB" within the Destination/Description portion of the document, which MCC New York personnel told the OIG means "with all belongings." During their OIG interviews, MCC New York staff members further explained that the "WAB" notation meant that Inmate 3 was being permanently removed from MCC New York on August 9, 2019. Notwithstanding this email, as detailed below, several of the email recipients identified above, including the Captain, the Day Watch Operations Lieutenant, and the Day Watch Activities Lieutenant told the OIG that they believed Inmate 3 had gone to court on August 9, and they did not know he had been transferred to another facility.

B. MCC New York Staff Reject Epstein Attorney's Request that Epstein be Housed Without a Cellmate

Forensic Psychologist 1 told the OIG that on August 9, 2019, she was present during a meeting in which one of Epstein's attorneys opposed Epstein having a cellmate. Forensic Psychologist 1 explained to the attorney that because Epstein was housed in the SHU and he was a sex offender, he needed to have a cellmate.

Additionally, the OIG investigation revealed that on the day of Epstein's death, a Supervisory Staff Attorney with the BOP's Consolidated Legal Center for New York, sent an email to the Warden to inform him that on the previous day (August 9, 2019), two of Epstein's attorneys separately contacted him. One of the attorneys asked for Epstein to be moved to a different, specific housing unit within MCC New York; the other attorney asked for Epstein to be housed without a cellmate in the SHU. The Supervisory Staff Attorney said he informed the first attorney that the suggested housing unit was not available for pretrial detainees such as

---

[32] GEO refers to the Queens Detention Facility, a contract detention facility located in Queens, New York, that is managed by The GEO Group, Inc.

Epstein, and he said he told the second attorney that Epstein could not be housed without a cellmate because of his prior suicide attempt.

C. Removal on August 9 of Epstein's Cellmate from MCC New York

According to MCC New York reports, including the Daily Log and the Lieutenant's Log, on August 9, 2019, at approximately 8:38 a.m., Epstein's cellmate, Inmate 3, was "pre-removed" and transferred out of MCC New York in a routine, pre-arranged transfer. The Daily Log tracks inmate movements throughout MCC New York each day, while MCC New York Lieutenants utilize the Lieutenant's Log to document the daily activities that took place within the institution during their respective shifts.

The Supervisory Correctional Systems Specialist was the supervisor of Receiving and Discharge on August 9, 2019, and was responsible for overseeing all inmate movements in and out of the institution that day. The Supervisory Correctional Systems Specialist verified that Receiving and Discharge would have used the USMS emails sent on August 8, 2019, to coordinate Inmate 3's transfer out MCC New York, and since Inmate 3 was listed as "WAB" on the USMS emails, that meant he was being transferred from the facility and not coming back. She explained to the OIG that if Inmate 3 had been going to court, as many pretrial inmates held at MCC New York often did, the Daily Log would have reflected "court," rather than "pre-remove." Since the Daily Log listed Inmate 3 as "pre-remove," the Receiving and Discharge personnel who entered the information into the report were made aware that Inmate 3 was being transferred from MCC New York on or before the morning of August 9, 2019. The Supervisory Correctional Systems Specialist told the OIG that the language in the USMS emails ("WAB," i.e., "with all belongings") and MCC New York reports ("pre-removed") made it clear that Inmate 3 would not be returning to the SHU or MCC New York.

The OIG also interviewed the Correctional Systems Officer, who was the Receiving and Discharge officer who handled inmate movement in and out of MCC New York on August 9, 2019. The Correctional Systems Officer confirmed that the Daily Log reflected that Inmate 3 was "pre-removed" on August 9, 2019, at 8:38 a.m., because he was being officially moved from the institution to another prison. She explained to the OIG that the ordinary process was that Receiving and Discharge personnel would enter the information regarding Inmate 3 into SENTRY, along with information pertaining to other inmates who would be leaving their MCC New York housing units. Receiving and Discharge used this information to create the daily call out list, which had all of the inmates' names and times that they were to be moved. The Correctional Systems Officer told the OIG that the call out list from August 9, 2019, was no longer available because the call out lists were printed and hand-delivered to the housing units each day, and then discarded by the units at the end of the day. She also said each day's call out list was only maintained electronically for a 24-hour period, and then it was updated (overwritten) with the next day's list. In her OIG interview, the Correctional Systems Officer explained what would have occurred on this date based on her experience. Receiving and Discharge personnel would have printed copies of the call out list for August 9, 2019, which the MCC New York internal officer would distribute to the various housing units within the facility. Based on the other records reflecting Inmate 3's transfer, the Correctional Systems Officer said the call out list created for August 9, 2019, would have listed "WAB" next to Inmate 3's name, which meant that he was departing from the institution and not returning.

Correctional Officer (CO) 1 told the OIG that on the morning of August 9, 2019, he and Day Watch SHU Officer in Charge escorted Inmate 3 to Receiving and Discharge and Epstein to his legal visit.

D. Failure to Assign Epstein a New Cellmate on August 9

1. *Day Watch Staff Actions on August 9*

The SHU Lieutenant told the OIG that he worked at MCC New York on August 8, 2019, from approximately 6 a.m. until approximately 2 p.m., and that he was off on August 9, 2019. The SHU Lieutenant, whose shift ended over an hour before the USMS sent the second email regarding Inmate 3's impending transfer, told the OIG he was not aware that Inmate 3 was scheduled to be transferred out of MCC New York, and therefore he did not notify the Captain that Epstein would require a new cellmate. According to the SHU Lieutenant, as soon as the SHU staff learned that Inmate 3 would be transferred, they should have notified a Lieutenant on duty. The Day Watch Operations Lieutenant and the Day Watch Activities Lieutenant told the OIG that on August 9, 2019, they had oversight of the SHU from approximately 6 a.m. until 2 p.m. due to their position descriptions and because of the SHU Lieutenant's absence.

According to the MCC New York Staff Roster, on August 9, 2019, SHU Officer #1 was listed as Senior Officer Specialist 5. Although SHU Officer #1 is typically the Officer in Charge, another Senior Officer Specialist told the OIG that, in actuality, he was the Day Watch SHU Officer in Charge on August 9 from approximately 6 a.m. until 2 p.m. The Day Watch SHU Officer in Charge said that since he had the most experience and seniority, he was considered by everyone to be the SHU Officer in Charge, which the SHU Lieutenant confirmed. The Day Watch SHU Officer in Charge told the OIG that he knew that Epstein had to have a cellmate. He said that, as a general practice, every inmate who is transferred from suicide watch and/or psychological observation to the SHU is placed with a cellmate. He also confirmed that the SHU Lieutenant had instructed him that Epstein was to be housed with a cellmate at all times. According to the Day Watch SHU Officer in Charge, between July 30 and August 9, 2019, he told all other MCC New York staff members who worked in the SHU of Epstein's cellmate requirement and further stated that everyone who worked in the SHU should have known that Epstein was required to have a cellmate due to their knowledge, training, and experience.

The Day Watch SHU Officer in Charge confirmed that on the morning of August 9, 2019, the SHU staff received an inmate call out list that listed Inmate 3 as "WAB," which he explained meant that Inmate 3 was being removed from MCC New York. He told the OIG that sometime between 8 a.m. and 9 a.m., he escorted Epstein from the SHU to the attorney conference room for Epstein's daily legal visit, during which time Epstein joked around with him. The Day Watch SHU Officer in Charge said that he and Epstein were accompanied by CO 1, who was escorting Inmate 3 to Receiving and Discharge. The Day Watch SHU Officer in Charge and CO 1 both told the OIG that Inmate 3 was escorted to Receiving and Discharge with all of his belongings, and both said that during the escort the Day Watch SHU Officer in Charge informed Epstein that he would be assigned a new cellmate due to Inmate 3's departure and the requirement that Epstein have a cellmate. In his interview with the OIG, CO 1 confirmed this conversation between the Day Watch SHU Officer in Charge and Epstein, but he did not provide any additional information regarding notifications made either by him or the Day Watch SHU Officer in Charge. The Day Watch SHU Officer in Charge told the OIG that when he and CO 1 left the SHU with Epstein and Inmate 3, both the Day Watch Operations Lieutenant and the Day Watch Activities Lieutenant should have been physically present in the Lieutenants' Office and should have seen that Inmate 3 was departing the institution when they passed the office.

The Day Watch SHU Officer in Charge said that while he did not expect Inmate 3 to return to MCC New York, there had been times when inmates had been escorted to Receiving and Discharge as an expected removal, only to be returned to the SHU later that same day due to unforeseen circumstances. According to the Day

Watch SHU Officer in Charge, he did not select a new cellmate for Epstein because he was not certain that Inmate 3 had been discharged from the institution, although he assumed that Inmate 3 would not return to the SHU. The Day Watch SHU Officer in Charge told the OIG that when his shift ended at approximately 2 p.m., he informed the Evening Watch SHU Officer in Charge and Senior Officer Specialist 5 that, if Inmate 3 did not return to the SHU, Epstein would need a new cellmate upon Epstein's return from his attorney visit. The Day Watch SHU Officer in Charge said he specifically recalled telling the Evening Watch SHU Officer in Charge, in the presence of Senior Officer Specialist 5, "Make sure this guy gets a bunkie," to which the Evening Watch SHU Officer in Charge replied, "All right." The Day Watch SHU Officer in Charge said that, at some point that day, it was likely that he also informed the Day Watch Operations Lieutenant, but he could not specifically recall if he had done so.

The Day Watch SHU Officer in Charge told the OIG that a replacement cellmate should have been identified as soon as it was confirmed that Inmate 3 had left the institution. He said a new cellmate could have been reassigned before the 4 p.m. SHU count if it was known that Inmate 3 was not coming back, but the SHU staff members had until Epstein returned from his attorney visit to assign Epstein a new cellmate. According to the Day Watch SHU Officer in Charge, SHU staff definitely should have realized that Inmate 3 was not returning both during the 4 p.m. count and when Epstein returned from his attorney visit later that evening. The Day Watch SHU Officer in Charge told the OIG that Epstein's daily routine was that he would be with his attorneys in the attorney conference room until approximately 8 p.m., so SHU personnel had time to make a new cellmate assignment. He said all SHU staff members shared the responsibility to find a replacement cellmate and that anyone assigned to the SHU could have found another inmate to replace Inmate 3. However, he also said that due to Epstein's high profile, the SHU personnel should have asked a Lieutenant to contact the Psychology Department to see which inmate should be placed with Epstein.

On August 12, 2019, following Epstein's death, the Day Watch SHU Officer in Charge wrote a memorandum to the Warden stating, "On Friday August 9, 2019 at approximately 1:50 p.m., I S/O/S [the Day Watch SHU Officer in Charge] passed on to oncoming staff member [the Evening Watch SHU Officer in Charge] and present shift staff [Senior Officer Specialist 5] and [CO 2] that Inmate [3] was going WAB [i.e., with all of his belongings] and possibly may not return. Also that Inmate Epstein #76318-054 will be needing a cell mate upon arrival from his attorney visit." The Day Watch SHU Officer in Charge departed the SHU at approximately 2 p.m. and worked an overtime shift as a driver for MCC New York. He stated that he did not follow up with the SHU staff to verify that Epstein had been assigned another cellmate.

MCC New York staff with responsibility for oversight and staffing of the SHU during the Day Watch, including the Warden, Associate Warden 1, the Captain, the SHU Lieutenant, the Day Watch Operations Lieutenant, the Day Watch Activities Lieutenant, and the Day Watch SHU Officer in Charge, told the OIG that they all knew Epstein was required to have a cellmate pursuant to the Psychology Department's determination. They also confirmed that everyone who regularly worked in the SHU knew of this requirement, and that it was the responsibility of all SHU staff to notify a supervisor upon learning that Epstein needed to be assigned a new cellmate due to Inmate 3's transfer to another prison. The Day Watch SHU Officer in Charge and CO 1, however, were the only two MCC New York staff members working the Day Watch on August 9, 2019, who told the OIG that they were aware of Inmate 3's transfer and the need to assign Epstein a new cellmate. CO 1's immediate superior (the Day Watch SHU Officer in Charge) was already aware of the need to assign Epstein a new cellmate. While the Day Watch SHU Officer in Charge told the OIG that he made a number of notifications, other witnesses could not confirm that he had passed on information regarding Epstein's need for a new cellmate.

The Day Watch Operations Lieutenant and the Day Watch Activities Lieutenant both told the OIG that they did not know Inmate 3 had been transferred out of the facility, despite the fact that both were recipients of the second email the USMS sent on August 8 that included the information about Inmate 3's impending transfer out of MCC New York on August 9. Rather, the Day Watch Operations Lieutenant and the Day Watch Activities Lieutenant told the OIG that they believed Inmate 3 had been removed from MCC New York for a court appearance.

The Day Watch Activities Lieutenant did not recall Inmate 3 departing the institution with all of his belongings or having any conversations with the Day Watch SHU Officer in Charge or anyone else regarding Inmate 3's departure from MCC New York. According to the Day Watch Activities Lieutenant, he did not know that Epstein was without a cellmate. Other senior officials, including the Warden, Associate Warden 1, and the Captain, were also unaware of Inmate 3's transfer and the need to assign Epstein a new cellmate. These officials concurred that while all SHU staff and supervisors were responsible for notifying a supervisor in the chain-of-command of the need to assign Epstein a new cellmate, the Day Watch SHU Officer in Charge bore primary responsibility for the notification because he was the SHU Officer in Charge and one of two people who saw Inmate 3 leave the facility with all of his belongings. The Captain told the OIG that since Epstein was in the attorney conference room all day, no one may have even thought about it, and may have only become aware when they put Epstein back in his cell after his attorney visit that evening. The Captain said as soon as the SHU staff became aware that Epstein was without a cellmate, they should have notified the Evening Watch Operations Lieutenant. The Captain said that if he had been informed, he would have taken immediate action to ensure that Epstein was either assigned a new cellmate or monitored until that assignment occurred. The Captain, however, was one of the recipients of the USMS August 8 email that notified members of MCC New York supervisory staff of Inmate 3's transfer to another facility. The Warden and Associate Warden 1 did not receive this email.

The Warden told the OIG that he was off duty on August 9, 2019. The Warden said that in the event Epstein was without a cellmate, the plan was to review the situation and decide who should replace Inmate 3, but that no inmate in the SHU was preselected to replace Inmate 3 if this event occurred.

2. Evening Watch Staff Actions on August 9

The Evening Watch SHU Officer in Charge told the OIG that he was the SHU Officer in Charge on August 9 from approximately 2 p.m. until 10 p.m. The Evening Watch SHU Officer in Charge said he relieved the Day Watch SHU Officer in Charge from his duties and worked in the SHU with Senior Officer Specialist 5, a Material Handler, CO 2, and CO Tova Noel. The Evening Watch SHU Officer in Charge stated that when he began his shift, Epstein was visiting with his attorneys in the attorney conference room. The Evening Watch SHU Officer in Charge told the OIG that he did not recall having a conversation with the Day Watch SHU Officer in Charge about Epstein needing a cellmate. When advised that the Day Watch SHU Officer in Charge was confident about their conversation, the Evening Watch SHU Officer in Charge stated, "I don't necessarily want to call anyone a liar[] per se, but I don't remember him speaking to me about this. So, maybe he spoke to [Senior Officer Specialist 5], and maybe I was standing there, and he thought I heard him." The Evening Watch SHU Officer in Charge said if Inmate 3 had left MCC New York with all of his belongings, then someone should have found another inmate to replace him because Epstein was required to have a cellmate.

The Evening Watch SHU Officer in Charge told the OIG that he eventually learned later that evening that Epstein did not have a cellmate. According to the Evening Watch SHU Officer in Charge, after Epstein returned from his attorney visit and placed a telephone call, he escorted Epstein to his cell and saw that Inmate 3 was not there. According to the Evening Watch SHU Officer in Charge, after he realized that Epstein did not have a cellmate, he, Noel, and the Material Handler, all of whom were working in the SHU that evening, talked about Epstein needing a new cellmate. The Evening Watch SHU Officer in Charge said SHU staff could not just put anyone in the cell with Epstein. In his interview with the OIG, the Evening Watch SHU Officer in Charge stated that he called someone (he could not recall who) and notified that person that Epstein did not have a cellmate. OIG interviews did not identify an individual who received such a call or who witnessed the Evening Watch SHU Officer in Charge making it.

Senior Officer Specialist 5 told the OIG that on August 9, he worked in the SHU from approximately 8:45 a.m. until 4 p.m. Senior Officer Specialist 5 said when he reported for duty, Epstein was already with his attorneys, Inmate 3 had already left the SHU, and neither inmate returned to the SHU prior to his departure. Senior Officer Specialist 5 told the OIG that he did not know Inmate 3 had been released from MCC New York and that no one told him Epstein would need a new cellmate, including the Day Watch SHU Officer in Charge, the Captain, the SHU Lieutenant, or anyone from the Psychology Department.

CO 2 told the OIG that on August 9, he worked in the SHU from 8 a.m. until 4 p.m. CO 2 said he did not recall Inmate 3 departing the SHU that day, and that he was unaware that Epstein needed a new cellmate.

The Evening Watch Operations Lieutenant told the OIG that he was the Operations Lieutenant at the MCC on August 9 from approximately 2 p.m. until 10 p.m. The Evening Watch Operations Lieutenant said he was aware that Epstein was required to have a cellmate due to a mass email that was sent to all of the MCC New York Lieutenants. According to the Evening Watch Operations Lieutenant, everyone who regularly worked in the SHU should have known that Epstein was required to have a cellmate. The Evening Watch Operations Lieutenant told the OIG that he did not know Inmate 3 had left MCC New York earlier that day and was unaware that Epstein did not have a cellmate. He said that if Inmate 3 had been transported to Receiving and Discharge as "WAB" and the SHU Lieutenant was off, then another supervisor should have been notified. The Evening Watch Operations Lieutenant told the OIG that SHU personnel assigned to his shift should have notified him that Epstein was without a cellmate, but he had not been informed. The OIG's investigation revealed, however, that the Evening Watch Operations Lieutenant was one of the recipients of the USMS email notifying MCC New York supervisory staff of Inmate 3's scheduled transfer out of MCC New York on August 9. According to the Evening Watch Operations Lieutenant, the Acting Evening Watch Activities Lieutenant conducted the Lieutenant round in the SHU on August 9, and she only would have known that Epstein was without a cellmate if someone from the SHU told her or if she walked through the SHU tiers during the round. The Evening Watch Operations Lieutenant said he believed that if the Evening Watch Acting Activities Lieutenant knew that Epstein did not have a cellmate, she would have notified him.

Both the Acting Evening Watch Activities Lieutenant and the Morning Watch Operations Lieutenant told the OIG that they were unaware that Epstein needed to have a cellmate. The Acting Evening Watch Activities Lieutenant, who was serving in this position on August 9 from approximately 4 p.m. until 10 p.m., told the OIG that because her ordinary position was a Senior Officer Specialist, she was not aware that Epstein was required to have a cellmate. The Acting Evening Watch Activities Lieutenant recalled hearing that Epstein had been placed on suicide watch, but said she never received specific instructions regarding Epstein. She said the SHU staff did not tell her about the requirement that Epstein have a cellmate or that his cellmate had left MCC New York. The Acting Evening Watch Activities Lieutenant did not receive the August 8 USMS email regarding Inmate 3's transfer. The Morning Watch Operations Lieutenant, who was the Operations Lieutenant from approximately 10 p.m. on August 9 until 6 a.m. on August 10, told the OIG that she did not know that Epstein was required to have a cellmate, and that the Captain never spoke with her about this issue. The Captain confirmed that he did not specifically tell the Morning Watch Operations Lieutenant that Epstein needed a cellmate; however, the Captain said he believed that the Morning Watch Operations Lieutenant should have known of the requirement, and she was one of the recipients of the email from the Psychology Department on July 30, 2019, that informed MCC New York staff that Epstein needed to have an appropriate cellmate. The Morning Watch Operations Lieutenant also received the August 8 USMS email notifying MCC New York supervisory staff of Inmate 3's scheduled transfer out of MCC New York. The Morning Watch Operations Lieutenant told the OIG that if SHU staff knew that Epstein required a cellmate and did not have one, they should have informed her when she visited the SHU at approximately 4 a.m. on August 10, as part of her Lieutenant rounds.

The Material Handler said the SHU was not his regular post and he had not attended SHU training, but he had worked in the SHU approximately 10 to 20 times. According to the Material Handler, on August 9 he reported for a voluntary overtime shift from 12 a.m. to 8 a.m. and then worked his regular 8 a.m. to 4 p.m. shift in the warehouse. At some point during the day shift, the Day Watch Operations Lieutenant called and asked the Material Handler if he could work overtime in the SHU, and he agreed. The Material Handler said he worked the 4 p.m. to 12 a.m. shift in the SHU with the Evening Watch SHU Officer in Charge and Noel. The Material Handler told the OIG that he felt pressured to work the third shift, which resulted in him working 24 hours straight, from 12 a.m. on August 9 through 12 a.m. on August 10. After the Evening Watch SHU Officer in Charge left at 10 p.m., the Material Handler and Noel were the only employees working in the SHU from 10 p.m. to 12 a.m. The Material Handler recalled that Epstein came back to the SHU from meeting with his attorneys at approximately 8 p.m., which was later than the rest of the inmates, and was returned to his cell on L Tier. After the Material Handler and Noel gave Epstein his food, the Material Handler said they left the L Tier area. The Material Handler said Epstein was alone in his cell, but he was unaware that Epstein needed a cellmate.

Noel told the OIG that she worked in the SHU from approximately 4 p.m. on August 9 until 8 a.m. on August 10, which was a double shift of 16 hours. Noel said the SHU was her regular post during the time that Epstein was housed within the SHU. According to Noel, inmates housed within the MCC New York SHU were typically assigned cellmates, but she did not know if they were required to have cellmates. Noel said Epstein was assigned a cellmate while he was housed within the SHU but said that no one spoke with her about a requirement that Epstein have a cellmate. Noel said she did not know that Inmate 3 had been removed from MCC New York on August 9, and stated she was not aware that Epstein should have been assigned a new cellmate if Inmate 3 had been removed from MCC New York.

Material Handler Michael Thomas told the OIG that he worked a shift in the SHU on August 10 from 12 a.m. until 8 a.m. Thomas said the SHU was not his normal post, but he had worked in the SHU on numerous previous occasions and was familiar with the SHU protocols and procedures. Thomas said he knew that if an inmate came off suicide watch or psychological observation, they should be assigned a cellmate, and he said he was aware that Epstein had previously been on suicide watch and psychological observation. Therefore, Thomas assumed that Epstein was required to have a cellmate but said no one had spoken with him about that requirement. Thomas said the SHU staff should have notified the Operations Lieutenant as soon as they knew that Epstein's cellmate had departed MCC New York on August 9. However, Thomas said

57

he did not know that Inmate 3 was removed from MCC New York on August 9, and that Epstein was without a cellmate during his shift on August 10.

IV.   Epstein is Allowed to Make an Unmonitored Telephone Call on August 9

For safety and security reasons, BOP policy requires that all inmate telephone calls be made through the Inmate Telephone System. BOP records reflect that Epstein placed an unrecorded, unmonitored telephone call to a telephone number in the local 646 area code using a non-Inmate Telephone System line on August 9, 2019, from 6:58 p.m. to 7:19 p.m. No other BOP records exist regarding the unmonitored call, including identity of the person called or a summary of the conversation. The OIG found no evidence that Epstein signed an Acknowledgement of Inmate form, as required by BOP policy and necessary for him to use a non-Inmate Telephone System line. The Acknowledgement of Inmate form provides, among other things, that the BOP reserves the authority to monitor and record non-attorney conversations on any telephone located within the institution to preserve the security and orderly management of the institution and to protect the public. The OIG did not find that any notification was made to the MCC New York's Special Investigative Services staff advising the telephone call had been made, the date and time of the telephone call, the name of the person being called, Epstein's name and register number, or a brief statement explaining the purpose of Epstein's telephone call, as BOP policy requires.

The Evening Watch Operations Lieutenant told the OIG that when he was preparing to escort Epstein back to the SHU from the attorney conference room on August 9, 2019, a Unit Manager said to the Evening Watch Operations Lieutenant that he was going to escort Epstein, so he could provide Epstein with the opportunity to place a telephone call using an unrecorded legal telephone line that is utilized by inmates to call their attorneys. The Unit Manager was the Institutional Duty Officer the week of Epstein's death. The Northeast Regional Director told the OIG that an Institutional Duty Officer is a supervisor who monitors the facility on non-duty hours on behalf of the Warden when the Warden is not present.

The Captain told the OIG that he had authorized the Unit Manager to provide Epstein with a telephone call from the SHU on August 9, 2019, because he wanted to accommodate Epstein's request for a telephone call since Epstein was assigned to the SHU and had limited ability to place telephone calls. The Captain explained that when the Unit Manager was escorting Epstein from his attorney visit back to the SHU, he told the Unit Manager in the elevator that Epstein could place a telephone call from the SHU, but it had to be monitored and logged.

The Unit Manager told the OIG that he worked on August 9 from approximately 11 a.m. to 7 p.m. The Unit Manager explained that on August 9, Epstein asked to call his mother and that it was his understanding that Epstein had not been able to obtain the necessary documentation to use the Inmate Telephone System for various reasons, including the fact that Epstein was with his attorneys during normal working hours. As described below, Epstein had, in fact, completed the requisite BOP paperwork that allowed him to place calls through the Inmate Telephone System. The Unit Manager said the decision to allow Epstein to place the call was his alone as the Unit Manager and because, as the Institutional Duty Officer, he was representing the Warden, who was not physically within MCC New York at that time. The Unit Manager said he did not recall having a conversation with the Captain about permitting Epstein to make the call, and he would have allowed the call even if the Captain did not want him to, given it was his decision to make as the Unit Manager. The Unit Manager explained that he viewed ensuring that inmates had family socialization as a part of his job, and he would allow inmates to place telephone calls if they were unable to make calls under ordinary circumstances.

The Unit Manager told the OIG that at approximately 6:45 p.m., he and Senior Officer Specialist 1 escorted Epstein from the attorney conference room to the SHU so that Epstein could place a telephone call. The Unit Manager said he put Epstein in the shower area to make the telephone call because COs were present in that area. The Unit Manager explained that he also chose the shower area because that location ensured Epstein would not be able to pull the phone cord into his cell and use it to harm himself. The Unit Manager said he plugged the telephone line into the legal line, which was not recorded, and dialed the telephone number that Epstein provided. As noted above, the number that was dialed was in the local 646 area code. The Unit Manager said he allowed Epstein to place the telephone call on the unrecorded legal line because he believed that Epstein had not set up his Inmate Telephone System account that would have allowed him to call on the institutions recorded lines. According to the Unit Manager, a male answered, and the Unit Manager handed the receiver to Epstein. The Unit Manager heard Epstein say, "Hey, how are you doing? How's everything?" The Unit Manager admitted that he should have verified who was on the line, as Epstein had requested to make a telephone call to speak with his mother, and it was a male who answered the phone. The Unit Manager said he could not verify the phone number because he believed that Epstein did not have his Inmate Telephone System account set up, and he did not have any phone numbers associated with his account. The Unit Manager told the OIG that after he handed the telephone to Epstein, his shift ended so he left the SHU and left MCC New York for the day.

The Unit Manager said that when he left the SHU, Epstein was still on the call and the Evening Watch SHU Officer in Charge and Noel were at the officers' desk, and that Senior Officer Specialist 1 was also present. According to the Unit Manager, when he was leaving, he told the officers, "Hey, make sure he gets his 15-minutes, and after that, he's done." The Unit Manager said he did not provide the SHU staff with instructions to monitor the call. He said that after he left, he contacted Noel on the SHU telephone and asked her to make sure that Epstein's call had ended because his time was up.

The Unit Manager acknowledged that he did not stay and monitor the call as he should have done. The Unit Manager said the proper way to have an inmate place a telephone call on an unmonitored line would be to bring the inmate out and place him in a belly chain because then he would be handcuffed in the front. The Unit Manager said he should have provided Epstein with the phone, with a counselor or unit team member present, and placed the call on speaker so the call was monitored.

The OIG investigation determined that Epstein did not, in fact, speak with his mother, who, according to public records, died in 2004. The OIG found that Epstein actually spoke with Individual 1, who declined to be interviewed by the OIG.[33] Individual 1's lawyer told the U.S. Attorney's Office for the Southern District of New York during an attorney proffer that Individual 1 spoke with Epstein on August 9, 2019, at about 7 p.m., for approximately 20 minutes. Individual 1's attorney proffer was that Individual 1 was in the country of Belarus at the time of the call.[34] Individual 1's attorney told the U.S. Attorney's Office that during the

---

[33] The OIG does not have the authority to compel or subpoena testimony from individuals who are not Department of Justice employees.

[34] The OIG did not investigate the factual accuracy of this proffer. We note that there are methods by which a call to the 646 area code could connect to a telephone in Belarus.

telephone call, Epstein told Individual 1 that the press had gotten crazy, and they discussed personal things such as books, music, and hygiene while incarcerated. According to the representations by Individual 1's counsel, Epstein told Individual 1, "They are trying to keep me safe," and that his case would take a little longer than he originally thought. He told Individual 1 he loved her, to be strong, and that he would not be able to call her again for another month.

Senior Officer Specialist 1 told the OIG that he was not a witness to Epstein's August 9 call, but he had previously discussed telephone calls with Epstein and knew that Epstein had the requisite paperwork that allowed him to place calls through the Inmate Telephone System. Senior Officer Specialist 1 told the OIG that Epstein was issued the necessary documentation to make telephone calls when Inmate 1 was his cellmate. Senior Officer Specialist 1 also advised the OIG about an interaction that he had with one of Epstein's attorneys prior to August 9 when he was on an elevator with Epstein and the attorney. According to Senior Officer Specialist 1, Epstein's attorney asked him about getting Epstein the necessary documentation to make calls. Senior Officer Specialist 1 said he then verified that Epstein was able to make calls through the Inmate Telephone System. When Senior Officer Specialist 1 asked Epstein why he had said he was unable to make calls, Epstein responded, "[T]hey said they monitor those phone calls." Senior Officer Specialist 1 said that in a subsequent conversation with Epstein's attorney, the attorney asked how Epstein could get an unmonitored call. Senior Officer Specialist 1 told Epstein's attorney that decision had to be made by a Lieutenant or Unit Manager.

Noel told the OIG that after Epstein's attorney conference on August 9, the Unit Manager plugged a telephone line in the legal line, and placed Epstein in a shower area within the SHU where he was afforded a telephone call. The OIG investigation determined that the legal line is an unrecorded telephone line outside of the Inmate Telephone System, which is designed for inmates to use when speaking with their counsel and therefore is not recorded. Noel said that after the Unit Manager set Epstein up with the call, he left the SHU and did not instruct Noel, or anyone else to Noel's knowledge, to monitor Epstein's call. According to Noel, the call was not monitored or logged. Noel said that approximately 15 to 20 minutes later, while Epstein was still using the telephone, the Unit Manager called the SHU staff via telephone, told Noel that Epstein's time was up, and asked that Noel retrieve the telephone from Epstein. Noel estimated that Epstein's call lasted for 20 minutes and said the Evening Watch SHU Officer in Charge and the Material Handler were also present in the SHU during Epstein's phone call. Noel reported that she took the phone back from Epstein, left Epstein alone in the shower, and went to use the bathroom on 10 South. Noel said that upon her return, Epstein was already placed back in his cell.

The Evening Watch SHU Officer in Charge told the OIG that he was present in the SHU on August 9 during the time of Epstein's telephone call but did not overhear Epstein's conversation. The Evening Watch SHU Officer in Charge also said that while Epstein was having his telephone call, the officers were distracted by the actions of another inmate. The Material Handler said he did not recall seeing the Unit Manager or Epstein in the shower area on the night of August 9, and did not have any knowledge or information regarding a phone call made by Epstein that night.

The Northeast Regional Director told the OIG that if Epstein's call was authorized by an MCC New York official, then it should have been done on a speaker phone while being monitored by a staff member, and the call should have been logged and a record of the call should have been created. The Northeast Regional Director said Epstein's unmonitored telephone call was extremely concerning because "[w]e don't know what happened on that phone call. It could have potentially led to the incident [Epstein's death], but we don't, we will never know."

V. Failure to Conduct SHU Inmate Counts and Staff Rounds on August 9–-10

A. SHU Inmate Counts

As detailed in the BOP policies section of Chapter 2, the BOP requires COs assigned to guard inmates to conduct institution-wide counts of inmates at regularly scheduled intervals each day to ensure that all inmates are present and accounted for at the appropriate location within the facility. Performing an institutional count is one of the basic and essential aspects of a CO's job, and the count was one of the basic and essential components of the daily operation of MCC New York. The Captain told the OIG that counts are a core responsibility of COs and ensure accountability of the inmates. The Evening Watch Operations Lieutenant said that it is very important that the institutional count is accurate because that is how staff members know if all inmates are present and if anyone has escaped.

On weekdays, MCC New York conducted institutional counts at 12 a.m., 3 a.m., 5 a.m., 4 p.m., and 10 p.m. The 10 p.m. count was a stand-up count, which meant that inmates were required to stand when they were counted. Pursuant to BOP policy and MCC New York SHU Post Orders, two COs were required to perform the institutional count for each housing unit, including the SHU. To perform the institutional count in the SHU, BOP policy and MCC New York SHU Post Orders required two officers to walk from tier to tier to observe and count each individual inmate. During each count, one CO would count the inmates while the other officer observed the inmates. The two officers would then switch roles and compare the count numbers. If the totals did not match, then the officers had to conduct another count in the same manner. COs had to document their performance of inmate counts on an official MCC New York form often referred to as a count slip.[35]

On the count slip, COs were required to fill in the date and time the count had been performed, write the total number of inmates physically present in the unit counted, and then both COs printed their name and signed the count slip. Once the COs had completed and signed the count slip, the count slips were then collected and delivered to the Control Center. Officers assigned to the Control Center were responsible for comparing the count slips from each housing unit to the institution's inmate roster to ensure that each inmate was accounted for. Only after all the count slips had been collected from each housing unit, and the numbers on the slips had been matched to the institution's inmate roster, could the institutional count be deemed "cleared" or completed. If a housing unit's count slip was incomplete or did not match the number of inmates that were supposed to be in the unit, then the count had to be redone in that housing unit via a more intensive version of the institutional count, called a bed-book count, which is when inmates are counted using their picture cards. Records of each institutional count, including the count slips, were provided to a supervising official and retained by MCC New York.

The OIG's investigation found that none of the required SHU inmate counts were conducted from 4 p.m. on August 9, 2019, until Epstein was discovered hanged in his cell at approximately 6:30 a.m. on August 10, 2019. Further, the OIG determined that SHU staff did not conduct any 30-minute rounds after approximately 10:40 p.m. on August 9, and that the count slips and round sheets had been falsified. As a

---

[35] This BOP form is officially entitled "Metropolitan Correctional Center; New York, New York; Official Count Slip."

result, many SHU staff and supervisors were unaware that Epstein did not have a cellmate as the Psychology Department had determined was necessary, and Epstein was alone and unobserved in his cell for an extended period of time.

1. The 4 p.m. SHU Count on August 9

The OIG's investigation determined that the 4 p.m. SHU inmate count on August 9, 2019, was inaccurate because SHU staff did not physically count the inmates as required by BOP policy and instead relied upon a predetermined number of inmates believed to be in the SHU at that time. However, Epstein, who was in the SHU attorney visitation room, was correctly accounted for during the 4 p.m. and subsequent SHU counts. The OIG determined that the error in the 4 p.m. SHU count was carried over into the next inmate count at 10 p.m. that counted an inmate who had been transferred out of the SHU. The SHU inmate count was not corrected until 12 a.m. when the Morning Watch Operations Lieutenant reviewed the master institutional count and housing unit count slips and informed SHU staff of the correct number of inmates in the SHU at that time.

Senior Officer Specialist 5 told the OIG that prior to his departure from the SHU at approximately 4 p.m., he told the Evening Watch SHU Officer in Charge what the SHU count should be. In addition, the Day Watch SHU Officer in Charge told the OIG that SHU staff maintain a "cheat sheet," which lists the number of inmates believed to be in the SHU at any given time.

When interviewed by the OIG, the Day Watch SHU Officer in Charge reviewed the 4 p.m. SHU count slip from August 9, 2019, which was signed by the Evening Watch SHU Officer in Charge and CO Noel. Based on his review, the Day Watch SHU Officer in Charge told the OIG that the Evening Watch SHU Officer in Charge and Noel probably did not count the inmates in the SHU. He said they likely wrote down the numbers they thought should have been entered for the count because the count slip inaccurately included an inmate (Inmate 4) among the number of inmates in the SHU after that inmate had been transferred to another housing unit. According to what he told the OIG and wrote in an email on August 9, earlier that afternoon the Day Watch SHU Officer in Charge observed Inmate 4 attempt to retrieve an unknown item from his visitor in the MCC New York SHU visiting room. The Lieutenant's Log from August 9, 2019, reflected that following this incident, Inmate 4 was removed from the SHU at 3:15 p.m. and transferred to the Receiving and Discharge dry cell, which is a secure location where inmates are taken for observation when they are believed to have ingested or secreted contraband on their person. According to the Day Watch SHU Officer in Charge, the inaccurate 4 p.m. count slip told him "that the count was not done and they just assumed and went by the cheat sheet because the body wasn't even there," referring to Inmate 4, who was transferred from the SHU to Receiving and Discharge. The Day Watch SHU Officer in Charge told the OIG that if the 4 p.m. SHU count had been accurately conducted, then the Evening Watch SHU Officer in Charge and the SHU staff should have realized that Inmate 4 was no longer in the SHU.

In his interview with the OIG, the Evening Watch SHU Officer in Charge acknowledged that neither he nor any other SHU staff member conducted the 4 p.m. SHU count on August 9. The Evening Watch SHU Officer in Charge verified that it was his handwriting and signature on the 4 p.m. SHU count slip and said he had prepared the count slip ahead of time because "[t]here was so much going on" in the SHU that day. The Evening Watch SHU Officer in Charge confirmed that Noel's name and signature also appeared on the 4 p.m.

count slip.[36] During his OIG interview, the Evening Watch SHU Officer in Charge reviewed BOP documents regarding the inmate's transfer from the SHU and acknowledged further that based on that transfer, the number of inmates listed on the SHU count slip he and Noel submitted for the 4 p.m. count, the count slip was incorrect.

Noel admitted in the deferred prosecution agreement she entered into with the U.S. Attorney's Office for the Southern District of New York that she completed false count slips on August 9 and 10. Noel initially told the OIG that she did not conduct the 4 p.m. count on August 9, but after acknowledging that she signed the 4 p.m. SHU count slip, Noel said she did not recall if she conducted the count. According to Noel, she and other SHU staff filled out the count slip before conducting the counts because they knew the number of inmates they were supposed to report.

2. The 10 p.m. SHU Count on August 9

At the time of the 10 p.m. count, all inmates in the MCC New York SHU, including Epstein, were locked in their cells for the night. At or around that time, the two officers assigned to the SHU were responsible for conducting the 10 p.m. stand up count. At 10 p.m. on August 9, the two assigned SHU officers were Noel and the Material Handler. Through review and analysis of the SHU security camera video, witness statements, and BOP records, the OIG determined that MCC New York staff did not perform the 10 p.m. count in the SHU.[37] Nonetheless, Noel and the Material Handler completed and signed the 10 p.m. SHU count slip. The 10 p.m. SHU count slip listed the total number of inmates as "73 + 1." According to the MCC New York master count sheet for the 10 p.m. count on August 9, 2019, all units had verbally reported their inmate counts to the Control Center by 10:30 p.m.[38] At approximately 10:36 p.m., the Control Center completed all paperwork and officially cleared the 10 p.m. institutional count.

The Material Handler said he was present at the time of the 10 p.m. count, but that the count was not conducted because everyone was tired. The Material Handler noted that on August 9, he had worked an overtime shift from 12 a.m. until 8 a.m., his regular shift from 8 a.m. to 4 p.m., followed by his SHU overtime shift from 4 p.m. to midnight. Thus, at the time of the 10 p.m. count, he had worked 22 consecutive hours at MCC New York. The Material Handler verified that he and Noel signed the 10 p.m. count slip and believed that Noel called the Control Center with their count numbers. He did not know why the count slip listed "73 + 1".

Noel told the OIG that she had conducted the SHU count alone at 10 p.m. and that the Material Handler signed the count slip even though he did not conduct the count with her. However, the OIG's review and analysis of the SHU security camera video conflicts with Noel's statement that she conducted the 10 p.m. count. Specifically, the video reflects that it was not until between 10:29 p.m. and 10:36 p.m. when Noel walked to different tiers inside the SHU. Yet, as described above, MCC New York records reflect that counts from all MCC New York housing units were reported to the Control Center by 10:30 p.m., as the count

---

[36] Prosecution was declined for BOP employees (other than Noel and Thomas) who falsely certified inmate counts and rounds on the day before and the day of Epstein's death.

[37] The quality of the SHU video footage was poor. Therefore, in conjunction with reviewing the video, the OIG analyzed witness statements and BOP records to better determine what the video depicted.

[38] The official name for the document used to record an institutional count is "Bureau of Prisons Count Sheet."

documentation shows the count was verbally cleared by the Control Center at 10:30 p.m. It therefore appears that the video depicts Noel conducting a later round in the SHU, as she was required to do every 30 minutes during her shift, and not the 10 p.m. SHU count.

Noel said she wrote the 73 on the count slip but she did not remember if she or someone else had written "+ 1" on the count slip and she did not know why "+1" was on the count slip. Noel claimed that, unlike the 4 p.m. count slip, which the Evening Watch Officer in Charge pre-filled, she did not prepare the 10 p.m. count slip in advance of the count. Noel said she did not know that the 10 p.m. SHU count slip, which listed 73 inmates, was inaccurate, and she could not explain why the 12 a.m. count also inaccurately listed that 73 inmates were physically present in the SHU, whereas the 3 a.m. and 5 a.m. count slips accurately listed 72 inmates in the SHU.

Senior Officer Specialist 6 told the OIG that on August 9, 2019, he worked in the Control Center from approximately 4 p.m. until 12 a.m., and then he worked as an Internal Officer from 12 a.m. until 8 a.m. on August 10. According to Senior Officer Specialist 6, he took the August 9 10 p.m. institutional count by himself in the Control Center, and assisted with the 12 a.m., 3 a.m., and 5 a.m. counts on August 10 as an Internal Officer. Senior Officer Specialist 6 confirmed to the OIG, as MCC New York records reflect, that he had received verbal counts from all units by 10:30 p.m., and further stated that he had cleared the institutional count at 10:36 p.m., which was when paperwork was complete and the count was officially complete.

Senior Officer Specialist 6 reviewed the MCC New York 10 p.m. institutional count, which showed that the SHU had 73 inmates assigned, whereas the Receiving and Discharge Department had zero inmates assigned to the unit. When questioned by the OIG about the 10 p.m. SHU count slip that listed "73 + 1" inmates and was signed by the Material Handler and Noel, Senior Officer Specialist 6 told the OIG that he believed that the "+ 1" on the count slip was in his handwriting. Senior Officer Specialist 6 also reviewed the 10 p.m. Receiving and Discharge count slip, which listed "9S + 1" on the count slip and told the OIG that it was his handwriting.[39] Senior Officer Specialist 6 explained that the "9S + 1" on the SHU count slip meant that he was "ghost counting" the inmate (Inmate 4) who had been moved from the SHU, located in the 9 South area, to the Receiving and Discharge area earlier that day. Senior Officer Specialist 6 said that because there were, in actuality, only 72 inmates in the SHU during the 10 p.m. count, he should have written "73 - 1" on the SHU count slip rather than "73 + 1".

---

[39] According to BOP records and witness interviews, "9S" refers to the SHU, which was located in 9th Floor South section of MCC New York.

Figure 5.1

10 p.m. Count Slips from the SHU and Receiving and Delivery on August 9

Metropolitan Correctional Center
New York, New York
Official Count Slip

95 + 1

Unit: R&D Date: 8/9/2019

Count: 1 Time: 10.00pm

1. Print Name:

1. Signature:

2. Print Name:

2. Signature:

Metropolitan Correctional Center
Official Count Slip

Unit: ZA Date: 8.9.19

Count: 73 + 1 Time: 10 00 pm

Print Name:

Signature:

Print Name:

Signature:

Note: The images have been modified for privacy reasons.

Source: BOP

Senior Officer Specialist 6 did not recall if he wrote on the count slips at the time of the 10 p.m. count or during the 12 a.m. count when Inmate 4 was transferred in SENTRY from the SHU to Receiving and Discharge. Senior Officer Specialist 6 told the OIG that if he had made the notations at the time of the 10 p.m. count, he should not have cleared the count. Instead, he should have created a new master count sheet and requested that the SHU staff conduct a new count, provide a new count slip, and discard the inaccurate SHU count slip. Senior Officer Specialist 6 told the OIG that an Operations Lieutenant would have needed to authorize him to do the "ghost count" and write on the count slips, although he could not recall precisely who gave him the authorization or when he had done so. The OIG investigation and review determined that the only Operations Lieutenant on duty at the time was the Morning Watch Operations Lieutenant, who started her shift at 10 p.m. on August 9. When questioned by the OIG, the Morning Watch Operations Lieutenant adamantly denied having authorized a "ghost count" and the OIG identified no record or witness (other than Senior Officer Specialist 6) to indicate that she had done so. The OIG interviewed other MCC New York personnel, who said "ghost counting" was not permitted, and stressed the importance of an accurate physical count of inmates.

3. *The 12 a.m., 3 a.m., and 5 a.m. SHU Counts on August 10*

The Morning Watch Operations Lieutenant told the OIG that she supervised the August 10 12 a.m. institutional count from the Control Center. During the count, the Morning Watch Operations Lieutenant said she identified the issue with the inaccuracy of the SHU count slip because it counted Inmate 4 as present in the SHU, when in actuality he had been removed from the SHU and placed in the Receiving and Discharge dry cell the previous day (August 9, 2019). The Morning Watch Operations Lieutenant said that after learning of the discrepancy, she made the appropriate update reflecting the inmate transfer in SENTRY. This update is reflected in Inmate 4's Inmate History Quarters, which states that Inmate 4 was transferred out of the SHU into a different housing unit on August 10, 2019, at 12:35 a.m. The Morning

Watch Operations Lieutenant told the OIG that she believed she told the SHU staff to conduct a new count and create a new count slip, but she did not know if they had actually done so.

During his interview with the OIG, Senior Officer Specialist 6 reviewed BOP records relating to the inmate transfer, the 12 a.m. institutional count, and the housing unit count slips. Based on his review of this material, Senior Officer Specialist 6 said the 12 a.m. SHU count slip was inaccurate because it continued to list 73 inmates instead of the 72 inmates who were physically present in the SHU at that time. Senior Officer Specialist 6 reviewed the institutional counts and SHU count slips for the 3 a.m. and 5 a.m. counts and told the OIG that they were accurate because they listed the SHU as having 72 inmates.

At approximately 12 a.m. on August 10, 2019, Material Handler Thomas replaced the other Material Handler, and he and Noel were the only two staff members on duty in the SHU. Noel and Thomas were responsible for conducting the 12 a.m., 3 a.m., and 5 a.m. counts in the SHU. Through review and analysis of the SHU security camera video, witness statements, and BOP records, the OIG determined that Noel and Thomas did not perform any of these counts. Nonetheless, Noel and Thomas completed and signed SHU count slips for each of the three counts, and in reliance on the count slips, the Control Center cleared the 12 a.m., 3 a.m., and 5 a.m. institutional counts at approximately 12:49 a.m., 3:24 a.m., and 5:30 a.m., respectively. Noel and Thomas both admitted to the OIG that they did not conduct the 12 a.m., 3 a.m., and 5 a.m. counts on August 10, and that they had falsified the respective count slips.

Noel told the OIG that she signed the August 10 12 a.m., 3 a.m., and 5 a.m. count slips that Thomas had prefilled. Noel said she did not know why the 12 a.m. count slip documented that there were 73 inmates in the SHU, whereas the 3 a.m. and 5 a.m. slips documented there were only 72 inmates. Noel recalled that Thomas had spoken with someone and then they changed the count slips.

Noel told the OIG that she and CO 3 conducted the 3 a.m. and 5 a.m. counts in MCC New York's 10 South Unit, which is the single-celled secure unit adjacent to the SHU. Noel said that when she left the SHU to assist CO 3, she took the SHU keys with her and that no one could have accessed the SHU while she was gone because she had to physically open the door for anyone who came into the SHU. Noel also told the OIG that when the Morning Watch Operations Lieutenant arrived to conduct a round at approximately 4 a.m., Noel let her into the SHU. The OIG's review and analysis of the SHU video shows that the Morning Watch Operations Lieutenant arrived in the SHU at approximately 4 a.m., visited the 10 South Unit at 4:04 a.m., returned to SHU at 4:11 a.m., and left the SHU at 4:14 a.m. According to Noel, no one other than the Morning Watch Operations Lieutenant and CO 3, as detailed later below, entered the SHU during her shift.

Thomas told the OIG that since he had begun working with the BOP in 2007, he had worked in the SHU fairly regularly and he was familiar with how to work in the SHU and how the SHU operated. Thomas described his responsibilities while working in the SHU as to maintain the count of inmates, make sure the inmates are fed, and, depending on the shift, make sure they get their showers. Thomas's Overtime Schedule showed that he worked 21 shifts in the SHU during morning watch from May through August 2019. The overtime schedule also showed that Thomas worked 12 overtime shifts in the SHU when Epstein was assigned to the SHU in July and August 2019.

Thomas acknowledged that neither he nor Noel conducted any rounds or counts in the SHU during their shift between approximately 12 a.m. and approximately 6:30 a.m. Thomas said the August 10, 2019 round sheets were signed, but the rounds were not conducted because he was tired that day. Thomas recalled "dozing off from here and there" during his shift, but he did not know if Noel slept.

Thomas did not recall having a conversation with anyone concerning the discrepancy between the 12 a.m. SHU count slip, which listed 73 inmates, and the institutional count, which listed 72 inmates in the SHU. Thomas said he had filled out and signed the 3 a.m. SHU count slip, which listed 72 inmates in the SHU. Thomas did not know why the number of inmates was different on the 12 a.m. and 3 a.m. count slips and did not recall speaking with the Morning Watch Operations Lieutenant about the 12 a.m. count. Thomas told the OIG that he knew he was falsely certifying the count slips when he signed them on August 10, 2019.

B. Staff Rounds in the SHU

1. CO Rounds

As detailed in the BOP Policies section of Chapter 2, in addition to inmate counts, BOP policy and MCC New York SHU Post Orders required that COs assigned to the SHU conduct rounds to observe all inmates at least twice an hour. As part of their assigned duties, MCC New York SHU officers had to walk each of the tiers of the SHU twice an hour on an irregular schedule, once during the first 30 minutes and again during the second 30 minutes, with both rounds occurring no more than 40 minutes apart. COs working in the SHU were required to complete and initial an official MCC New York form, often referred to as a "round sheet," which was reviewed and signed by a supervisor, documenting the date and time of each 30-minute round in each tier of the SHU.[40]

The Day Watch SHU Officer in Charge told the OIG that SHU staff spoke about conducting rounds on Epstein every day. He said that the Warden, Lieutenants, and other MCC New York staff members frequently told the SHU staff to conduct rounds and to keep an eye on Epstein. To reinforce this message, the Day Watch SHU Officer in Charge created a sign on orange paper that he hung on a computer in the SHU officer's area that said, "MANADATORY [sic] ROUNDS MUST BE CONDUCTED EVERY 30 MINUTES ON EPSTEIN # 76318-054 AS PER GOD!!!!" The Day Watch SHU Officer in Charge said the sign was hanging on the computer on August 9 and 10, 2019, and it was clearly visible to everyone who worked in the SHU. The Acting Evening Watch Activities Lieutenant confirmed that written instructions to conduct rounds on Epstein were posted on the SHU computer.

---

[40] This BOP form is officially entitled "MCC New York, Special Housing Unit, 30 Minute Check Sheet."

Figure 5.2

Sign Created by the Day Watch SHU Officer in Charge

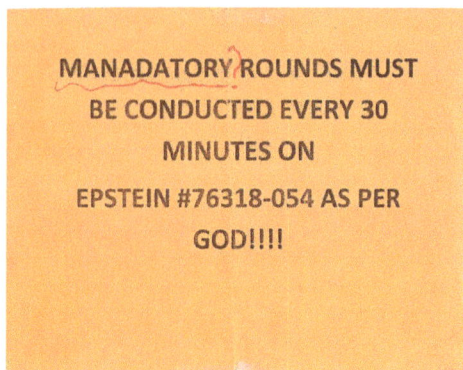

MANADATORY ROUNDS MUST BE CONDUCTED EVERY 30 MINUTES ON EPSTEIN #76318-054 AS PER GOD!!!!

Note: The image has been modified for privacy reasons.

Source: BOP

The Evening Watch SHU Officer in Charge told the OIG that Noel filled out the round sheet on behalf of everyone who was working in the SHU during his shift. The Evening Watch SHU Officer in Charge was not certain if all of the rounds were actually conducted. The Material Handler said he believed the rounds listed on the round sheet as having occurred between 4:01 p.m. to 7:36 p.m. probably had been done, but he was uncertain about the remaining rounds. The Material Handler said he had seen officers "blow off" 30-minute rounds in the past. Noel told the OIG that, as a general practice, when the COs went to the various SHU tiers to distribute food or supplies, they counted that as a round. Noel said she was aware that she was supposed to conduct two rounds every hour during their shift, but that she had never actually completed rounds every 30 minutes while working in the SHU. When asked which rounds she conducted on August 9, 2019, Noel responded, "That's hard for me to tell because I didn't conduct it every 30 minutes. It was give out food, pick up the trays, give out toilet paper, go down. So those were the rounds I conducted." Noel verified that her initials were on the round sheets for August 9 and 10, 2019, and said, consistent with her usual practice, she filled out the round sheets and initialed the round sheets at the start of the 4 p.m. and the 12 a.m. shifts.

Noel and Thomas both admitted to the OIG that they did not conduct any of the rounds reflected on the SHU Round Sheet on August 10, 2019, from 12 a.m. until Epstein was found hanged in his cell at approximately 6:30 a.m. Nonetheless, Noel completed and signed more than 75 separate 30-minute entries stating that she and Thomas had, in fact, conducted such rounds.[41] Through review and analysis of the SHU video footage, witness statements, and BOP records, the OIG determined that Noel and Thomas did not enter the tiers in the SHU to conduct any of the rounds and counts between 12 a.m. and approximately 6:30 a.m. on August 10. Noel and Thomas can be seen at the SHU Officers' Station, moving in the SHU common area, and in the SHU laundry and entrance/exit area throughout the morning of August 10. Additionally, from approximately 1 a.m. to 3 a.m., Noel and Thomas were seated at the SHU Officers' Station without moving and appeared to be sleeping. OIG analysis of the activity on the SHU computers revealed that Noel used the computer periodically throughout the night, including to search the Internet for furniture sales and benefit websites and to read a news article about Epstein. Thomas used the computer briefly around 1 a.m. and 6 a.m. to search for motorcycle sales and sports news.

Noel told the OIG that she went through each tier in the SHU at approximately 10 p.m., and at the time she went to Epstein's cell and saw him laying on a mattress on the floor, which she said was typical for him. Epstein asked Noel for his medical device, so she plugged it in for him. Noel saw that Epstein was in the cell by himself and without a cellmate, but she maintained that she did not know that Epstein was required to have a cellmate. Noel told the OIG that Epstein's cell was approximately 15 feet away from the SHU Officers'

---

[41] Each of the 6 tiers in the SHU had a separate round sheet, each of which had 13 entries reflecting 30-minute rounds were conducted, when they were not, in fact, completed.

Station. Noel said that during her shift on August 10, 2019, no one went to Epstein's cell and no one other than the Morning Watch Operations Lieutenant and CO 3 came into the SHU.

Through review and analysis of the SHU video footage, witness statements, and BOP records, the OIG determined that at approximately 10:40 p.m. a CO, believed to be Noel, carried linen or inmate clothing up to the L Tier, which was the last time any CO approached the only entrance to the SHU tier in which Epstein was housed.

2. Lieutenant Rounds

BOP policy requires that a Lieutenant visit the SHU during each shift to ensure that all procedures are being followed. BOP training for new Lieutenants instructs that the Operations Lieutenant must visit the SHU at least once per shift and "[t]his visit will be substantially more than just entering the unit, signing the log book, and talking with staff." Additionally, when the SHU Lieutenant is unavailable, the Operations Lieutenant should make rounds in the SHU on each shift. The training instructs that while in the SHU the Operations Lieutenant must walk each range (tier), inspect logs and records, observe activities, and periodically observe SHU inmate counts. The training further outlines that the SHU Lieutenant is responsible for the direct supervision of the unit, including enforcement of rules, review of paperwork, coordination of activities, movement of inmates, and cell searches. The SHU Lieutenant should make rounds on the ranges (tiers) each day.

The statements of multiple witnesses were consistent with BOP training materials. The Northeast Regional Director, the Warden, Associate Warden 1, the Captain, and the Day Watch SHU Officer in Charge all told the OIG that Lieutenants should have walked down all of the SHU tiers when conducting a Lieutenant round in the SHU. Noel said the SHU Lieutenant walked the tiers all the time, however, other Lieutenants did not always walk down the tiers. Multiple witnesses also told the OIG that it was standard practice for the BOP to store the SHU round sheets at the end of each tier in the SHU. This practice was designed to ensure that the assigned COs and Lieutenants walked down each tier when conducting rounds to observe every cell and inmate during the round before initialing the round sheet. On August 9 and 10, 2019, however, the MCC New York SHU round sheets were kept at the SHU Officers' Station in the common area of the SHU rather than at the end of each tier.

None of the Lieutenant rounds conducted on August 9 and 10 alerted the supervisory staff to the fact that Epstein lacked a cellmate. According to MCC New York records, the Day Watch Activities Lieutenant conducted a round in the SHU at 11:27 a.m. on August 9. The Day Watch Activities Lieutenant said he did not specifically recall if he conducted a round in the SHU, but he believed that he did conduct the round. As discussed in greater detail above, the Day Watch Activities Lieutenant told the OIG that he did not know that Epstein's cellmate had been removed from MCC New York or that Epstein was without a cellmate during his shift on August 9. The Acting Evening Watch Activities Lieutenant told the OIG that she conducted a Lieutenant round in the SHU on August 9 sometime between 5 p.m. and 8 p.m. The Acting Evening Watch Activities Lieutenant told the OIG that she did not know that Epstein's cellmate had departed from MCC New York or that Epstein required a cellmate because she was only the Acting Activities Lieutenant and had not attended SHU or department head meetings. The Evening Watch Operations Lieutenant reviewed the August 9 round sheets and said that although his signature is on one of the forms as if he conducted a round in the SHU, it was actually the Acting Evening Watch Activities Lieutenant who had conducted the round. The Evening Watch Operations Lieutenant said he did not know why his signature was on the form because he did not conduct any rounds within the SHU on August 9 and he did not recall signing the form. The Morning Watch Operations Lieutenant confirmed that she conducted her round in the SHU at approximately 4 a.m. on August 10. The Morning Watch Operations Lieutenant said she went up to the 10 South Unit and then back down to the SHU because she needed to sign the round sheets. Contrary to BOP training for new Lieutenants, which she attended in 2011, the Morning Watch Operations Lieutenant told the OIG, "We are not required to go to each individual cell and look at the inmates. When we make rounds, we get with the officers." The Morning Watch Operations Lieutenant said she did not conduct a round to observe the inmates when she visited the SHU. Noel confirmed that the Morning Watch Operations Lieutenant visited the SHU but did not walk down the tiers.

Through review and analysis of the SHU security camera video, witness statements, and BOP records, the OIG determined that at approximately 4 a.m. on August 10, 2019, the Morning Watch Operations Lieutenant briefly visited the SHU as part of her supervisory duties and conferred with Noel and Thomas, who were seated at and around the SHU Officers' Station in the common area of the SHU. Noel told the OIG that at approximately 5:30 a.m., Thomas went to the 10 South Unit, which was adjacent to the SHU, to relieve CO 3, and that CO 3 briefly walked through the SHU common area as he left and returned from his break. The OIG's review and analysis of the video footage revealed that, aside from those two officers, no one entered the SHU and no one conducted any counts or rounds.

VI.   Epstein's Death on August 10

A.   Discovery of Epstein Hanged in Cell and Emergency Response

On August 10, 2019, shortly after 6 a.m., the doorbell to the SHU rang, indicating that a delivery of breakfast carts had arrived at the SHU. Noel and Thomas retrieved the breakfast carts from the double-locked entrance to the SHU and brought them inside the SHU. At the time, Thomas and Noel were the only officers in the SHU. At approximately 6:30 a.m., MCC New York security camera video recordings show Noel and Thomas walking toward the L Tier. Noel and Thomas told the OIG that at this time they were entering the L Tier, in which Epstein was housed, to deliver breakfast to the inmates. As discussed previously, between approximately 10:40 p.m. on August 9 and approximately 6:30 a.m. on August 10, the OIG did not observe on the available recorded video any COs or other individuals approach the L Tier where Epstein was housed from the common area of the SHU.

Noel told the OIG that she unlocked the door to the L Tier so Thomas could deliver the breakfast trays. Thomas told the OIG that he knocked on Epstein's cell door, saw a portion of Epstein through the window but could not make out what he saw, so he said to Epstein, "Come to the door, come to the door." Thomas said he did not observe any movement or hear a response, so he unlocked the cell door, entered the cell, and saw Epstein hanged as described further below. Thomas said he immediately yelled for Noel to get help, and that Noel activated a body alarm, signaling a medical emergency, and began taking the steps described below.

Figure 5.3

Photograph of a Piece of Orange Cloth Hanging from the Bunkbed in Epstein's Cell Following His Death

Source: Office of the Chief Medical Examiner, City of New York

Thomas explained that when he first entered Epstein's cell, Epstein had an orange string, presumably from a sheet or a shirt, around his neck. The end of the string was tied to the top portion of the bunkbed. Epstein was suspended from the top bunk in a near-seated position, with his buttocks approximately 1 inch to 1 inch and a half off the floor and his legs extended out straight on the floor. Thomas said Epstein did not look discolored or very different from when he last saw Epstein alive. Thomas said he immediately ripped the orange sheet or shirt away from the bunkbed, and Epstein's buttocks dropped approximately 1 inch to 1 inch and a half to the ground. Thomas then lowered Epstein's entire body to the floor and, because he did not believe Epstein was breathing, Thomas immediately began providing chest compressions until responding MCC New York staff members arrived approximately 1 minute later. Thomas said he did not provide rescue breaths and was unaware if Epstein was dead or alive because he never checked for a pulse before initiating chest compressions. Thomas said medical personnel took over the emergency response, including chest compressions and use of an automated external defibrillator (AED), when they arrived. Thomas said he assisted with bringing Epstein down to the Health Services Unit on the second floor, and that he left MCC New York at approximately 8 a.m. Thomas said he had received cardiopulmonary resuscitation (CPR) training during MCC New York annual refresher training and had responded to medical emergencies in the past, but this was the first time he was the first responder.

Thomas said he was present in the SHU for his entire shift on August 10, 2019, from 12 a.m. until the time he attempted to deliver breakfast to Epstein at approximately 6:30 a.m. and did not see anyone go inside Epstein's cell during his shift. Thomas said that he would have known if someone went in or out of Epstein's cell and said no one did. Thomas told the OIG that he could see Epstein's cell door from the SHU Officers' Station, but he could not see inside the cell from that vantage point. Thomas said that it was not possible for anyone to have entered the SHU without his knowledge because he or Noel would have had to open the SHU door for anyone to gain entry. The only other key to the SHU was located elsewhere in the institution; no other MCC New York staff members had the keys required to gain access to the SHU. Moreover, Thomas said that anyone attempting to access the L Tier where Epstein was located would have had to walk directly in front of the SHU Officers' Station where Thomas was seated, and no one did. Thomas denied that he or Noel had any role in Epstein's death.

Noel told the OIG that on the morning on August 10, when it was time to deliver food to the inmates, she unlocked the door to the L Tier and stood by it while Thomas took the food to the inmates. Noel said that when Thomas knocked on Epstein's door, there was no response. Noel said Epstein's cell door was locked, so Thomas used a key to open it and went inside. Noel heard Thomas call out for her to retrieve the cutter

71

and then she heard Thomas rip something. Noel said she observed Thomas lifting Epstein from under his arms and dragging him back out of the corner of the cell and laid him down on the ground to perform CPR. According to Noel, within seconds of Thomas calling out for the cutter she hit the body alarm, which is a button on an MCC staff member's radio that is used to signal distress or an emergency. Noel recalled hearing Thomas say, "Breathe, Epstein, breathe," and "We're going to be in so much trouble." Noel said she stood at the door about a foot away from Epstein's cell and never went in. Noel said Thomas only performed chest compressions and said she did not see Thomas checking for breath or pulse. Noel said that when she saw Epstein, he looked blue and did not have a shirt on or anything around his neck. Noel said she did not get the cutter because Thomas did not need it based upon the ripping sound she heard.

Noel said an MCC New York Lieutenant who responded to the alarm asked her what happened, and before she got the chance to answer, Thomas stated, "Oh, it's not her fault, we fucked up." Noel did not recall making any comments or statements to the Lieutenant. Other than the Lieutenant, Noel did not recall which COs responded to the alarm and she did not know what happened in the cell after MCC New York staff arrived because she was waiting at the bottom of the steps outside the L Tier. Noel said she was alone in the SHU for 20 minutes after they left with Epstein and she kept calling the Control Center to get status updates.

Noel told the OIG that Epstein's cell was approximately 15 feet from the SHU Officers' Station. Noel said she would have known if someone went in or out of Epstein's cell overnight and no one did. She also said that there was no indication that any of the inmates could have gotten out of their cells. Noel said she never slept during her shift on August 9-10, 2019. Noel said that when she is seen on the camera at the desk not moving, she was on the computer. Noel then clarified by saying that she worked 5 days of overtime leading up to her shift, so she would begin to doze off; however, she caught herself and never slept.

The Lieutenant told the OIG that he was the Operations Lieutenant who relieved the Morning Watch Operations Lieutenant on August 10, 2019, at approximately 5:30 a.m. The Lieutenant said that at approximately 6:33 a.m., he heard a call for a medical emergency in the SHU and immediately responded to the alarm. When he arrived, Noel told him, "Epstein hung himself." Once inside, the Lieutenant observed that Thomas was performing CPR on Epstein. The Lieutenant stated that he asked, "Where's his bunkie at?" and that Noel responded, in substance, that Epstein did not have a cellmate. Noel also told the Lieutenant, "We didn't do rounds at 3 a.m. and 5 a.m." Thomas stated, "We didn't do the rounds. We messed up." The Lieutenant took over administering CPR and asked SHU staff to retrieve an AED and call for the duty nurse.

The MCC New York Electronics Technician told the OIG that he responded to the emergency call at 6:33 a.m. When the Electronics Technician first arrived in the SHU, Thomas and other MCC New York staff members were picking Epstein up and placing him on a stretcher. The Electronics Technician said he and Senior Officer Specialist 6 performed chest compressions on Epstein while he was on the stretcher and being transported to the Health Services Unit on the second floor.[42] The Electronics Technician stated that he

---

[42] Moving an inmate requiring outside emergency medical care to the Health Services Unit provides health care staff and Emergency Medical Technicians (EMT) with immediate access to any necessary medical equipment and supplies, and allows EMTs faster access to the inmate when they arrive at MCC New York because COs can directly escort EMTs to the Health Services Unit to begin emergency treatment immediately. If EMTs had to be escorted to the housing unit, they would first need to be thoroughly screened, which would delay medical attention.

then returned to the SHU and worked there for approximately 1 hour, along with the Morning Watch Operations Lieutenant and Noel. The Electronics Technician believed he was in the SHU prior to 7 a.m. and until approximately 8 a.m., but he was not positive with regard to the times. The Electronics Technician said he delivered food to the inmates on one tier while the Morning Watch Operations Lieutenant did the same on another tier while Noel unlocked the doors outside of the tiers for the Electronics Technician and the Morning Watch Operations Lieutenant. The Electronics Technician said that when they were delivering food to the inmates, he heard the inmates saying, "You killed him. You weren't making rounds. You killed him." The Electronics Technician told the OIG that the inmates also said Thomas and Noel just sat at the SHU Officers' Station and never checked on the inmates. The Electronics Technician told the OIG he understood the inmates to be saying that Thomas and Noel were responsible for Epstein's death because they had not conducted rounds during their shift. The Electronics Technician said he believed that Epstein took his own life and said he had no reason to believe otherwise.

Senior Officer Specialist 6 said he responded to the emergency call at 6:33 a.m. and when he arrived, staff members were already performing CPR on Epstein. Senior Officer Specialist 6 said he assisted with transporting Epstein to the Health Services Unit, taking Epstein to the ambulance, and then followed the ambulance to the hospital in another vehicle, and stayed at the hospital until he was relieved from duty.

The OIG also reviewed photographs that were taken in the MCC New York Health Services Unit of EMTs attempting to resuscitate Epstein. The photographs show, among other things, Epstein on his back with an intravenous line in his arm, his orange BOP-issued shirt ripped open and laying around his arms, and him wearing orange BOP-issued boxer shorts. None of the photographs taken at MCC New York show Epstein in a hospital gown, although the OIG did review photographs taken at New York Presbyterian Lower Manhattan Hospital which show Epstein in a hospital gown.

Additionally, the OIG participated in interviews of three inmates assigned to the same SHU tier as Epstein at the time of his death and who were housed in cells opposite Epstein's cell and therefore had a direct line of sight to Epstein's cell.[43] One such inmate was Inmate 5, who was assigned to a cell directly across from Epstein's cell on the left side of the tier and who told the OIG that he could see all the cells on the right side of L Tier, where Epstein was housed. Inmate 5 believed a count was last conducted within the SHU on August 9, 2019, a little before 12 a.m., and said that no additional count was conducted after that time. Inmate 5 did not see anyone, or hear anyone, go into Epstein's cell on the night of August 9 or the morning of August 10 prior to a male CO discovering Epstein on the morning of August 10. Inmate 5 said the male CO knocked on Epstein's assigned cell, looked in, and then opened the door. Inmate 5 could only see Epstein's legs from the knee down but could tell that Epstein was laying down on his back because his feet were pointed upward. The male CO bent down to shake Epstein and was saying, "Epstein, Epstein." The male CO then tried to pick up Epstein from behind, with his arms wrapped around Epstein. Inmate 5 said both the officer and Epstein fell back to the floor, with Epstein falling to the side of the officer. Inmate 5 said that once the two fell, he could then see that it was Epstein. The CO then started giving Epstein chest compressions and mouth-to-mouth resuscitation. At this point, the officer said, "Fuck!" and asked the female CO, who was standing near the L Tier gate, if she has pressed the button. The female officer said, "Yeah, a long time ago." A Lieutenant then arrived at Epstein's cell along with a male nurse who tried to

---

[43] As noted previously, the U.S. Attorney's Office for the Southern District of New York sought interviews from all of the inmates housed in the L Tier of the SHU on the night that Epstein died.

revive Epstein. Epstein was not responsive. Inmate 5 said Epstein looked dead when the male CO tried to pick him up and they both fell. Inmate 5 said officers had trouble getting Epstein onto the stretcher because Epstein was basically dead weight. When the officers did get Epstein on the stretcher, Epstein still had on headphones.[44] Inmate 5 did not see any marks around Epstein's neck, and he did not see a rope around Epstein's neck. However, Inmate 5 saw a male CO come out of Epstein's cell with a sheet that had a loop and knot.

Figure 5.4

Location of the Cells Assigned to Inmates 5-7 in Relation to Epstein's Cell in the L Tier

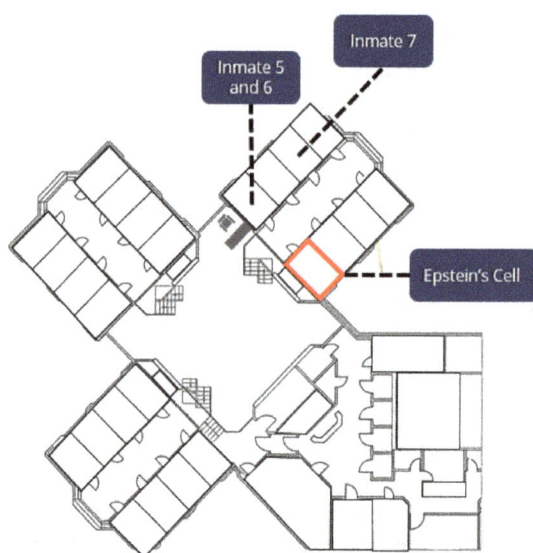

Source: DOJ OIG schematic drawing depicting
the MCC New York SHU

Inmate 6 told the OIG that on August 9 and 10, 2019, he was housed within the SHU on L Tier in a cell directly across from Epstein's cell. Inmate 6 last saw Epstein's cellmate, Inmate 3, on August 9 when Inmate 3 said, "See you later. I'm going to court." Inmate 6 said Inmate 3 did not return that night and said the SHU officers never conducted their required 30-minute rounds. Inmate 6 believed the COs last checked on the inmates in the SHU on August 10 between 12:30 a.m. and 1 a.m. Inmate 6 did not observe anyone entering Epstein's cell after Epstein returned from his legal visit on August 9, 2019; did not hear noise that night; and said Epstein's door was not opened during the night. Inmate 6 said a male officer discovered Epstein dead during breakfast delivery on August 10. Inmate 6 said he observed the male CO entered Epstein's cell and began performing CPR, while the female CO, who appeared panicked, stayed outside of the cell. Inmate 6 said he observed Epstein on the floor but did not see a rope over Epstein's head. However, when Epstein was removed from his cell, Inmate 6 observed the COs holding a rope and a

---

[44] An MP3 player with headphones was obtained as evidence by the Federal Bureau of Investigation (FBI).

defibrillator. Inmate 6 did not see marks on Epstein's neck but did see bruising on his face and observed earphones that were still in place on Epstein's ears.

Inmate 7, who was two cells down from Epstein's cell and on the other side of the tier, told the OIG that he could not see into Epstein's cell but he could see the cell door. Inmate 7 said that after dinner was brought to Epstein's cell on the evening of August 9, 2019, Inmate 7 did not recall seeing anyone going in or out of Epstein's cell until the following morning at around 6 a.m. He further stated that he did not hear any door "pop open" that evening. Inmate 7 said he remembered waking up around 6 a.m. on August 10, 2019, and hearing a voice, possibly male, saying "Breathe." Inmate 7 said he saw Epstein removed from his cell on a stretcher.

In addition, the OIG and the Federal Bureau of Investigation (FBI) interviewed seven inmates assigned to other tiers in the SHU, none of whom had any direct knowledge of how Epstein died. These inmates consistently reported that the SHU officers did not systematically conduct the counts and rounds as required on the evening Epstein died and that the last round was either between 9:30–10 p.m. or 12:30–1 a.m. Several inmates told the OIG that before Epstein died the SHU staff never conducted rounds at night.

According to the BOP Form 583 Report of Incident, on August 10, 2019, at approximately 6:33 a.m., while delivering the breakfast meal, Epstein was found unresponsive in his cell. Consistent with the required response to a suspected suicide outlined in the MCC New York General Housing Unit Post Orders that are described in Chapter 2, staff called for assistance and began life-saving measures.[45] At 6:39 a.m., Epstein was taken to the MCC New York Health Services Unit, and Emergency Medical Services (EMS) arrived to MCC New York at 6:43 a.m. Epstein was transported to the local hospital, New York Presbyterian Lower Manhattan Hospital, at 7:10 a.m., and was pronounced deceased at 7:36 a.m.

According to a memorandum attached to the Form 583 from the Clinical Nurse dated August 10, 2019, when the medical emergency involving Epstein was called over the radio, the Clinical Nurse immediately responded to the call and upon arrival, saw Epstein on the floor within his cell unresponsive with CPR in progress by COs. The Clinical Nurse's memorandum reads that Epstein was cold, with circumferential bruising around his neck and posterior mottling, pupils fixes and dilatated, and no palpable pulses were felt. According to the memorandum, at 6:35 a.m., a call was placed for EMS, CPR continued, and an AED was utilized and indicated "No Shock Advised," so CPR continued. Epstein was then transported to the MCC New York Health Services Unit treatment room with CPR in progress. Upon arrival, Epstein's pulse was checked, and the AED indicated "No Shock Advised." EMS and paramedics arrived on the scene, intubated Epstein, and gave him medications and fluids.[46] Epstein was transported to the local emergency room with CPR in progress at approximately 7:10 a.m.

---

[45] As noted in Chapter 2, BOP policy provides that the need to immediately attend to an apparent suicide victim, undertake lifesaving measures, and ensure inmate and staff safety take precedence over efforts to preserve a crime scene.

[46] The EMS arrival time on the Clinical Nurse's memorandum is listed as 6:56 a.m. Based on the OIG's review of other documentation and interviews, we believe the arrival time reflected on those other documents (6:43 a.m.) is more likely the time of EMS's arrival. We noted that the Clinical Nurse, at the time of EMS's arrival, was actively engaged in administering CPR to Epstein and responding to the health emergency.

According to a memorandum attached to the Form 583 from the Correctional Systems Officer dated August 10, 2019, after Noel called the medical emergency, the Correctional Systems Officer received a call from staff in the SHU instructing her to call 911 for an ambulance. The Correctional Systems Officer notified the New York Police Department (NYPD) via the MCC New York institutional NYPD telephone. The Correctional Systems Officer then informed NYPD that MCC New York needed an ambulance and medical assistance for one of the inmates. The New York City Fire Department and EMS arrived at MCC New York at 6:43 a.m. and were escorted to the second-floor medical area. EMS departed MCC New York with Epstein and a BOP escort via ambulance and chase car to the local hospital at 7:10 a.m.

The Morning Watch Operations Lieutenant told the OIG that she was relieved as the Operations Lieutenant prior to 6 a.m. on August 10, 2019, but was still working on things like the Daily Activity Reports and Lieutenant Logs that she did not get to finish during her shift. At some point, the Morning Watch Operations Lieutenant heard that there was a medical emergency in SHU, so she went to assist because she knew that inmates would need to be given food and other things would need to be done. The Morning Watch Operations Lieutenant estimated that she went to the SHU around 7 a.m. to help with the inmate meals, and believed the Electronics Technician was also helping out. Noel was there, but she was not helping with delivering food to the inmates. The Morning Watch Operations Lieutenant said that after the meals were delivered, she finished up and went home.

All MCC New York staff members who were interviewed by the OIG said they did not know of any information suggesting that Epstein's cause of death was something other than suicide. Additionally, no inmate provided the OIG with information suggesting that anyone assisted Epstein with taking his own life or had any credible information suggesting that Epstein's cause of death was something other than suicide. Some MCC New York staff told the OIG that Epstein's death could have been prevented if, among other things, Epstein had been assigned a new cellmate after Inmate 3's departure and rounds and counts had been conducted in the SHU as required. Some witnesses also faulted MCC New York staffing shortages, which resulted in excessive overtime and meant that MCC New York staff members were often overtired during their shifts. Other MCC New York staff members told the OIG that even if inmate safety and accountability measures had been property executed, an inmate who wanted to take his life would have found a way to do so.

B.   Items Found in Epstein's Cell on August 10 Following His Death

Following Epstein's death, the BOP and FBI collected many of the items found inside Epstein's cell. The FBI inspected the cell and retrieved what it believed to be relevant to its investigation into the cause of Epstein's death, which included one torn sheet, miscellaneous papers, and an MP3 player. The FBI did not recover any weapons inside of the cell. After the FBI's inspection, the BOP recycled the linens from Epstein's cell and collected the remaining items, which included various over-the-counter medications, books (including religious books), BOP pamphlets, toiletries, batteries, headphones, glasses, mail and envelopes, a brown paper bag, an orange homemade rope, AED pads, and a medical device.

Figure 5.5

Photograph of a Piece of Orange Cloth Tied into a Noose Recovered from Epstein's Cell After His Death[47]

Source: Office of the Chief Medical Examiner, City of New York

The photographs of Epstein's cell on August 10, 2019, show an excess of blankets, linens, and clothing. Some of the linens had been ripped into thin strips, which were tied to the desk and bunkbed inside the cell. Some of the strips were tied like a noose. When shown a picture of Epstein's cell, Noel verified that it contained a lot of linen and extra clothing. Noel said the mattress on the floor was Epstein's, as he always slept on the mattress on the floor. As detailed in the BOP policies section of Chapter 2, MCC New York SHU Post Orders required that COs assigned to the SHU during the daytime tours of duty conduct at least five cell searches each day, and that the entire SHU, including all common areas and cells, be searched every week. The OIG investigation revealed, however, that on August 9, 2019, the SHU staff logged only one cell search in TRUSCOPE, and the search was not of Epstein's cell.[48] BOP records did not indicate when Epstein's cell was last searched.

The Day Watch SHU Officer in Charge told the OIG that at least five cell searches should be conducted on the day and night watch shifts within the SHU, and that cell searches are conducted in cells every time the inmate departs the cell. He said the SHU Officer in Charge was responsible for making sure the searches were conducted and logged into the BOP TRUSCOPE database. The Day Watch SHU Officer in Charge said that only one cell search was entered into TRUSCOPE on August 9, 2019, because cell searches were tedious to enter, and he was busy. He did not believe that it was a problem that only one cell search was logged on August 9 because he said the SHU staff would have gone into every cell when the inmates took their showers. He said that during the period of Epstein's custody, SHU inmates showered on Mondays, Wednesdays, and Fridays. The Day Watch SHU Officer in Charge said that during showers, SHU staff searched every cell. He explained that all of the SHU cells should have been searched on Friday, August 9 because it was a shower day. He said SHU staff should also conduct cell searches when inmates go to the recreation area or for attorney visits. According to the Day Watch SHU Officer in Charge, Epstein's cell should have been searched because both Epstein and Inmate 3 left the cell on the morning of August 9. He further stated that he believed that the majority of cells in the SHU were searched although, as noted above, the SHU staff logged only one cell search in TRUSCOPE on August 9 and the search was not of Epstein's cell.

---

[47] As noted previously, Epstein's cell contained an excessive amount of linens, some of which had been ripped into thin strips and tied like a noose. Figure 6.5 depicts one such noose, which is illustrative of the types of linens found in Epstein's cell; the noose depicted is not the ligature Epstein used to kill himself.

[48] TRUSCOPE is a BOP database that provides institution staff with detailed inmate and institution security-related information and provides unit officers an electronic event log.

Figure 5.6

Photograph of Epstein's Cell After His Death

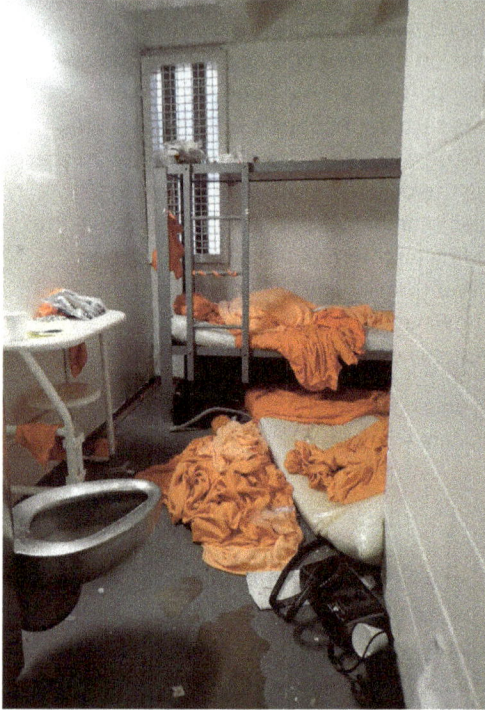

Source: Office of the Chief Medical Examiner, City of New York

The Day Watch SHU Officer in Charge told the OIG that in August 2019, each inmate would have been authorized to have two sheets and one blanket. He said that in the winter, inmates are allowed to have an additional blanket. When interviewed by the OIG, the Day Watch SHU Officer in Charge reviewed a picture of Epstein's cell from August 10, 2019, after Epstein had been removed from the cell. The Day Watch SHU Officer in Charge said there appeared to be an excess number of linens and blankets in the cell, which he believed were for both Epstein and Inmate 3, and that there were possibly a couple of extra sheets as well. He noted that there were two mattresses in the cell and deduced that Inmate 3's assigned items had not yet been removed even though he had departed MCC New York earlier that day. According to the Day Watch SHU Officer in Charge, Inmate 3's items should have been removed as soon as the SHU staff knew Inmate 3 was not returning. He told the OIG that any extra linens or blankets should be removed when the inmates take showers and their cells are searched. He told the OIG that he believed the purpose of limiting the linens provided to the inmates was to ensure there was enough to go around and that it was more of an administrative matter rather than a security matter.

The Captain also reviewed the picture of Epstein's cell from August 10, 2019, when interviewed by the OIG. He said Epstein had too many linens, t-shirts, and blankets in his cell. The Captain said the SHU staff were responsible for removing those items because they did not want to hear the other inmates complain that they were not issued the same number of items. The Captain stated that it is also a security issue because it "gives the inmates the materials to be able to make homemade fashioned and improvised nooses" or "use it as escape paraphernalia," such as a rope that inmates had used to escape from another facility in Chicago.

Inmate 3 told the OIG that Epstein was allowed to sleep on the floor, which he said was unusual for the SHU where that was not normally allowed. Inmate 3 said Epstein also had two extra blankets, which no other inmate had, as well as two pens, which inmates were not allowed to have. Epstein would ask for things, and if the COs said no, Epstein would tell them he was writing down their name and providing the information to his lawyer. According to Inmate 3, the COs were on "eggshells" around Epstein. Inmate 3 said that when he left the SHU on August 9, 2019, there was an orange cloth twisted around the ladder, strings on the side of the ladder, and a string tied across the bed. Inmate 3 explained that the string tied across the bed served as a clothesline, and that the strings were part of a sheet they had ripped. According to Inmate 3, one night he woke up, saw Epstein fidgeting with the clothesline, and asked Epstein what he was doing. Epstein said he was trying to fix the clothesline, but Inmate 3 told him no and flushed the clothesline down the toilet. As discussed in Chapter 4, when Inmate 3 and Epstein first became cellmates upon Epstein's return to the SHU following suicide watch and psychological observation, Inmate 3 asked Epstein not to kill himself while Inmate 3 was his cellmate because Inmate 3 had a chance to go home soon. In response, Epstein told Inmate 3 not to worry and that he was not going to cause him any trouble.

When Inmate 3 left on August 9, he told Epstein that he would leave the clothesline in the cell so that Epstein could wash his clothes. Inmate 3 did not say anything about a noose having been in the cell, but he said there were five blankets in their cell when he left.

C.   Autopsy Results

On August 11, 2019, the Office of the Chief Medical Examiner, City of New York, performed an autopsy on Epstein and determined that the cause of death was hanging and the manner of death a suicide. One of the office's Medical Examiners performed the autopsy, and the autopsy report was reviewed by the First Deputy Chief Medical Examiner. In connection with this investigation, the OIG interviewed the Medical Examiner who performed the Epstein autopsy (hereinafter the "Medical Examiner"). The Medical Examiner told the OIG that the pattern of Epstein's neck bone fractures was consistent with a hanging. The Medical Examiner explained that a different fracture pattern is present if there has been a manual compression of the neck versus a sustained pressure like in a hanging, and the pattern of Epstein's neck fractures was that of a hanging. The Medical Examiner also said Epstein had petechial hemorrhages, which are pinpoint bleeds in skin, on his face and mouth. These hemorrhages are caused when the blood flow is obstructed and the small skin capillaries burst. The Medical Examiner additionally identified plethora, which is purple discoloration of the skin, and stated that both petechial hemorrhages and plethora are consistent with suicide by hanging. The Medical Examiner stated that Epstein's petechia and plethora were identified from his neck up. In homicidal strangulations, according to the Medical Examiner, these conditions are normally found only in the eyes and mouth, and in a different pattern. Epstein also had, the Medical Examiner explained, a marked and obvious ligature furrow that peaked upward which is consistent with suicide as opposed to a ligature strangulation.

The Medical Examiner further stated that there was no evidence of defensive wounds consistent with what is seen in victims of strangulation. The Medical Examiner told the OIG that in strangulation cases there is invariably some signs of a struggle, even if the victim is impaired. The Medical Examiner noted that the autopsy did not identify any signs of a struggle. Epstein did not have any marks on his hands (no broken fingernails, no debris under the fingernails, no contusions to his knuckles) that would have evidenced a fight, and, other than an abrasion on his arm likely due to convulsing from hanging, no bruising on his body. We also were told by the Medical Examiner that Epstein did not have strap muscle hemorrhages of the neck, which is bleeding in the lung muscles in the front of the neck. Nor did he have, the Medical Examiner told the OIG, hemorrhaging in the muscles in the back of his neck. The Medical Examiner explained that you would expect to see that hemorrhaging when there has been an incomplete compression as opposed to a sustained compression like a hanging.

In addition, the Medical Examiner determined that the cloth material of the ligature (noose) found in Epstein's cell could have caused the fractures and superficial injuries the Medical Examiner identified during the autopsy. The Medical Examiner also told the OIG that the ligature furrow was too broad to have been caused by the electrical cord of the medical device in Epstein's cell. The Medical Examiner said blood toxicology tests were conducted and no medications or illegal substances were identified in Epstein's system. The Medical Examiner stated that the ruling of Epstein's death a suicide was the Medical Examiner's independent medical judgment and that the Medical Examiner was not pressured or otherwise subjected to any attempt to influence her ruling.

Chapter 6: The Availability of Limited Recorded Video Evidence Due to the Security Camera Recording System Failure

In August 2019, the Metropolitan Correctional Center located in New York, New York (MCC New York) had approximately 150 video security cameras (no audio) placed throughout the institution. The Office of the Inspector General (OIG) found that approximately 11 cameras were located in and around the Special Housing Unit (SHU) where Epstein was confined at the time of his death on August 10, 2019, including one at the end of the L Tier where Epstein was housed that showed any movement in or out of inmate cells and in the Tier's hallway. In addition to broadcasting live video, MCC New York had a system that recorded the live video feeds. Following Epstein's death, MCC New York officials and Federal Bureau of Investigation (FBI) investigators attempted to review video recordings related to the incident and discovered that, although the security cameras were working and transmitting live video, recorded video from most of the cameras in the SHU area was not available due to a malfunction of the video recording system that had occurred on July 29, 2019, including video from the camera at the end of the L Tier. As a result, while the L Tier video camera was transmitting a live video feed on the night of August 9, 2019, and morning of August 10, 2019, the video was not being recorded. One of the cameras that had available recordings from August 9 and 10 was a camera located outside a housing unit adjacent to the SHU. That camera captured video of a large part of the common area of the SHU, including the SHU Officers' Station and portions of the stairways leading to the different SHU tiers, including the L Tier. Thus, anyone entering or attempting to enter the L Tier from the common area of the SHU, including on August 9 and 10, would have been picked up by the video recorded by that camera. In addition, the recordings showed the SHU Officers' Station where the two SHU staff were seated at a desk immediately outside the entrance to the L Tier and diagonally across from Epstein's cell, which was the first cell on the righthand side of the L Tier.

I. Background on the Security Camera System at MCC New York

All video surveillance from MCC New York's cameras was connected to a Digital Video Recorder (DVR) system. The DVR system had two data storage systems that were labeled "DVR 1" and "DVR 2," and each consisted of 16 hard drives used for storing digital recordings. Roughly half of MCC New York's security cameras were assigned to record to DVR 1, and the other half were assigned to record to DVR 2. Cameras assigned to DVR 1 only recorded to the DVR 1 hard drives, and cameras assigned to DVR 2 only recorded to the DVR 2 hard drives. Therefore, if DVR 2 crashed, no video from the DVR 2-assigned cameras could be retrieved from DVR 1, and vice versa.

The OIG's investigation revealed a history of camera problems at MCC New York. In August 2019, the Electronics Technician was the only such technician at MCC New York. The Electronics Technician told the OIG that when he began work at MCC New York in 2016, he found that the facility's security camera system needed to be upgraded. According to the Electronics Technician, the system had not been properly maintained prior to his arrival, the hard drives in the DVRs frequently malfunctioned and needed to be replaced, and the overall system was outdated, in part because the cameras were analog and not digital.

The Electronics Technician told the OIG that, throughout his tenure at MCC New York, the camera system was subject to frequently recurring failures, particularly with respect to the DVR hard drives.[49]

The Warden, who assumed his responsibilities at MCC New York in May 2018, told the OIG he was generally aware that there were problems with the security camera system throughout the institution. He further stated that efforts were undertaken to determine which cameras were working and which needed to be fixed, and that MCC New York officials intended to ultimately seek funding to replace the entire system. Federal Bureau of Prisons' (BOP) records reflect that on September 6, 2018, the Warden submitted a memorandum to the BOP's Northeast Regional Director to request $800,000 in funding to replace the entire camera system. The memorandum identified an estimated project start date of December 1, 2018, and an estimated completion date of February 9, 2019. The BOP approved the funding request, and on September 21, 2018, a contract in the amount of $698,108.99 was awarded to Company 1 to provide various equipment for the project and associated labor. On September 24, 2018, a separate contract in the amount of $34,089.28 was awarded to Company 2 to provide assorted networking equipment and wiring needed to install the camera system.

As the camera upgrade project was beginning, BOP officials recognized that MCC New York's mechanical, electrical, and plumbing systems were also in need of major repairs. MCC New York did not have enough qualified technicians on staff to complete both the camera installation and other repairs needed at the facility, so beginning the week of March 17, 2019, the BOP's Northeast Regional Office arranged for technicians from other BOP institutions to conduct temporary duty (TDY) assignments at MCC New York to perform the work. During the course of the TDY rotations, work was not consistently conducted on the camera upgrade because sometimes TDY staff assigned to the project were used to cover shortages at MCC New York's custody posts, and sometimes there were not enough TDY volunteers who possessed the skills required to do the camera work.

At the time of Epstein's death on August 10, 2019, the camera system upgrade had not been completed. Immediately following Epstein's death, Company 1 officials arrived at MCC New York and installed the new recording system within a couple of days, and recording functionality was restored using the existing cameras. The majority of the new cameras did not arrive at the facility until October 2019, and they were installed in stages as the wiring work was conducted. According to the Electronics Technician, as of August 2021, when the MCC closed, the wiring work had still not been fully completed.

II. Discovery of Security Camera System Recording Issues in August 2019

A. Discovery on August 8 of the DVR 2 Failure that Occurred on July 29

According to forensic analysis conducted by the FBI after Epstein's death, disk failures occurred in MCC New York's DVR 2 system on July 29, 2019, which resulted in the system being unable to record. According to BOP records and OIG interviews, the BOP did not learn about the failure until August 8, 2019, when the Special Investigative Services (SIS) Lieutenant and Associate Warden 1 attempted to review recorded surveillance video for a matter unrelated to Epstein. The SIS Lieutenant told the OIG she discovered that no

---

[49] The Electronics Technician provided the OIG with copies of email messages and work orders that documented nine instances between June 2017 and July 2019, in which actions were taken to address a problem with either the MCC New York's cameras or the hard drives used to record video from the cameras.

recorded video was available for several of the institution's cameras, so she reported the matter to the Communications Office, and the Electronics Technician arrived to assess the problem sometime before his shift was scheduled to end. The Electronics Technician told the OIG that he found that roughly half of the institution's approximately 150 cameras, which were assigned to record to DVR 2, were displaying a live video feed but were not recording.

The Electronics Technician told the OIG that, before Epstein's death, no one was specifically tasked with ensuring that video from the cameras was being recorded. The Electronics Technician said he therefore did not perform any daily checks to ensure that video was being recorded. The Warden indicated that SIS staff are usually responsible for checking the system for recording functionality and reporting any problems to the Communications Office. However, the SIS Lieutenant told the OIG that it was her belief that the Electronics Technician should have been checking the system daily to ensure it was recording. The OIG found that there are no BOP policies that specifically state that institutional staff must perform periodic checks to ensure the camera system is fully functional or that security camera systems have the capacity to record.[50] The Facility Manager told the OIG that since Epstein's death, he now checks to ensure that all cameras and the recording system are working on a daily basis, and he subsequently provides a report about the status of the system to the facility's executive staff, the SIS, and the electronics technicians.

B. Response on August 8 and 9 to Discovery of the Recording Failure

On August 8, following discovery of the recording failure, Company 1 service request records reflect that the Electronics Technician contacted a Company 1 technical support representative, who ultimately determined that two hard drives within DVR 2 had failed. According to the Electronics Technician and the Company 1 service request record, the Company 1 representative informed the Electronics Technician that the two drives needed to be replaced and DVR 2 needed to be rebuilt in order for the cameras to record again. The Electronics Technician told the OIG that he informed a Company 1 Technician that he had to obtain the drives from MCC New York's Computer Services Manager. The Electronics Technician further stated that he left the institution at the end of his shift and did not obtain the hard drives and did not continue to work on the matter. The Electronics Technician told the OIG he had "no idea" why he did not stay at the facility to resolve the problem that day, but he noted for the OIG that he had not historically been required to stay after his shift ended to work on such matters, and even if he had begun working on the DVR that day, he would not have completed the work on August 8 due to the time the rebuilding process takes.[51]

The OIG found that the Electronics Technician's immediate supervisor, the Facility Manager, was on leave that week and therefore was not told on August 8 about the DVR recording failure. The Facility Manager confirmed that he did not learn about the camera problem until days after Epstein's death. The Electronics Technician told the OIG that he did not report the problem to the Lock and Security Supervisor, who was the Acting Facility Manager in the Facility Manager's absence. The SIS Lieutenant told the OIG that after the Electronics Technician had examined the system on August 8, the Electronics Technician informed her that cameras were not recording and said, "I'm going to stay and do overtime tonight." Based on his comment,

---

[50] For example, BOP Program Statement 5500.15, Correctional Services Manual, states generally that the Warden must establish a security inspection system that involves all departments but does not specifically address security camera systems. This program statement is a restricted policy that is not released to the public in its entirety.

[51] According to open source information on digital data storage system rebuilds, the rebuilding process can take up to several days to complete depending on the number of hard drives that were damaged and the storage capacity of each.

the SIS Lieutenant assumed that the Electronics Technician would remain at the institution after his shift ended that day to correct the issue. The Electronics Technician told the OIG there must have been some miscommunication because he did not say he was going to work overtime and resolve the problem that same evening since he knew the problem could not be fixed in one evening. The Electronics Technician told the OIG that, in hindsight, he should have stayed at the institution to begin work on the problem that same day.

The SIS Lieutenant told the OIG that she verbally informed the Captain on August 8 that the cameras were down, but BOP records reflect that the Captain left the institution before the malfunction was discovered. The Captain told the OIG that he did not learn about the DVR recording issue until after Epstein's death on August 10 when he asked to see video related to the Epstein incident. Associate Warden 1 confirmed she was with the SIS Lieutenant on August 8 when the camera problem was discovered, but she told the OIG she only knew video could not be replayed. She did not know the recording system for certain cameras was down. She could see live video from the cameras on that date, and therefore assumed they were recording.

According to the Electronics Technician, after he reported to work on August 9, 2019, and attended to other matters throughout the day, the Electronics Technician obtained the replacement hard drives and attempted to perform the repair sometime late in the day. However, the Electronics Technician told the OIG that no SIS staff were present at that time to give him access to the room in which the DVR room was located, so he requested access from the only other individual who had a key to the space, Correctional Officer (CO) 4.[52] According to the Electronics Technician, CO 4 denied him access to the room because CO 4's shift was ending at 4 p.m., and CO 4 was unable to stay and accompany him in the space while the Electronics Technician performed the work. According to the Electronics Technician, CO 4 said he would be at the institution the following day to provide the Electronics Technician access to the room, so the Electronics Technician decided to postpone the repair until the following day. The Electronics Technician said his decision was influenced by the fact that he had historically been told by MCC New York supervisors that such matters did not have to be attended to until the following day, and even if he had replaced the hard drives that day, the rebuilding process would have taken 24 hours to complete and would therefore not have finished until the following day anyway.

C.   SHU Camera Locations and Operational Status on August 10

The Electronics Technician arrived at the institution around 6 a.m. on August 10, 2019, and shortly thereafter, before he could begin working on the DVR system, he heard the staff body alarm sound and he reported to the SHU to assist. Later that day he was asked to pull potential video from cameras located in and around the SHU. The Electronics Technician eventually determined that most of the cameras in the SHU area were assigned to record to DVR 2. While the cameras assigned to DVR 2 were providing live video streams on August 9 and 10, 2019, no recordings from those cameras were available due to the DVR 2 hard drive issue, which the FBI later determined had occurred on July 29, 2019. Among the cameras whose video was not recorded was the camera at the end of L Tier, the SHU tier in which Epstein was housed.

---

[52] The DVR system was located in a locked room, and access to the room was limited to the institution's SIS unit, staff assigned to inmate phone monitoring, and the Electronics Technicians.

Only two cameras in the vicinity of the SHU area were recording to DVR 1 at the time of Epstein's death.[53] One camera was located on the upper-level entrance to the 10 South Unit, a housing unit adjacent to the SHU, near the door MCC New York staff referred to as the "46 door." That camera captured video of a large part of the common area of the SHU, including the SHU Officers' Station and portions of the stairways leading to the different SHU tiers, including the tier containing Epstein's cell. Thus, anyone entering or attempting to enter the L Tier from the common area of the SHU on August 9 and 10 would have been picked up by the video recorded by that camera. Epstein's cell door, however, was not in that camera's field of view. The other camera that was recording was located in one of the ninth floor's two elevator bays and provided video of the ninth-floor fire exit and two of the floor's four elevators.

The available video showed that at approximately 7:49 p.m. on August 9, Epstein was escorted toward the L Tier stairway by an individual believed to be the Evening Watch SHU Officer in Charge.[54] At approximately 10:39 p.m., an unidentified CO appeared to walk up the L Tier stairway, and then reappeared within view of the camera at 10:41 p.m. This is believed to be the last time anyone entered L Tier before approximately 6:30 a.m. on August 10. Between approximately 10:40 p.m. on August 9 and just before 6:30 a.m. on August 10, the OIG did not observe on the recorded video any CO or other individual enter any of the SHU tiers, which is consistent with CO Tova Noel and Material Handler Michael Thomas's admissions to the OIG that the SHU rounds and counts were not conducted during that time frame. At approximately 6:28 a.m., an unidentified officer was observed on the L Tier stairway, presumably to deliver breakfast food trays. Between 6:28 a.m. and 6:32 a.m., an unidentified officer, believed to be Noel, moved back and forth several times between the L Tier stairway and the SHU Officers' Station. At approximately 6:33 a.m., additional officers entered the SHU and ascended the L Tier stairway, presumably after Noel activated her body alarm when Epstein was discovered hanged in his cell.

As noted above, the camera at the end of the L Tier was providing a live video feed at the time of Epstein's death but the video was not being recorded. The Electronics Technician told the OIG that certain MCC New York personnel, including the Control Center, SIS personnel, the Warden, most Lieutenants, and the Electronics Technician, had access to the live video feed of the institution's security cameras. He explained that to view the live feed of a particular camera an employee with access would need to key in the specific camera into the security camera system to call up the live feed. The Correctional Systems Officer, who was working in the Control Center on August 10 from 12 a.m. to 8 a.m., and the Morning Watch Operations Lieutenant both told the OIG that the only live feed from the SHU on their screens was video from the camera showing the SHU common area, and they did not perceive a need to take the necessary steps to see the live feed from the SHU L Tier from either of their duty stations on the evening Epstein died.

---

[53] One additional camera located at the 10 South Officers' Station was recording on August 10, 2019. That camera is not depicted in Figure 4.12 because neither the SHU nor the SHU entrances were within the field of view of that camera.

[54] The OIG found the video captured by the camera at the entrance to the 10 South Unit to be of low quality. Due to the video's low quality and the distance between the camera and the SHU common area, the OIG was able to observe movement of individuals within the SHU but was not always able to conclusively identify the individuals. The OIG was also not always able to determine the specific destinations of the individuals seen in the video given that the camera only captured partial views of the stairways to the various SHU tiers. The OIG found that movements captured on the video were generally consistent with employee actions described by multiple witnesses and certain actions documented in BOP records.

Figure 6.1

SHU Camera Locations and Recording Status on August 10, 2019

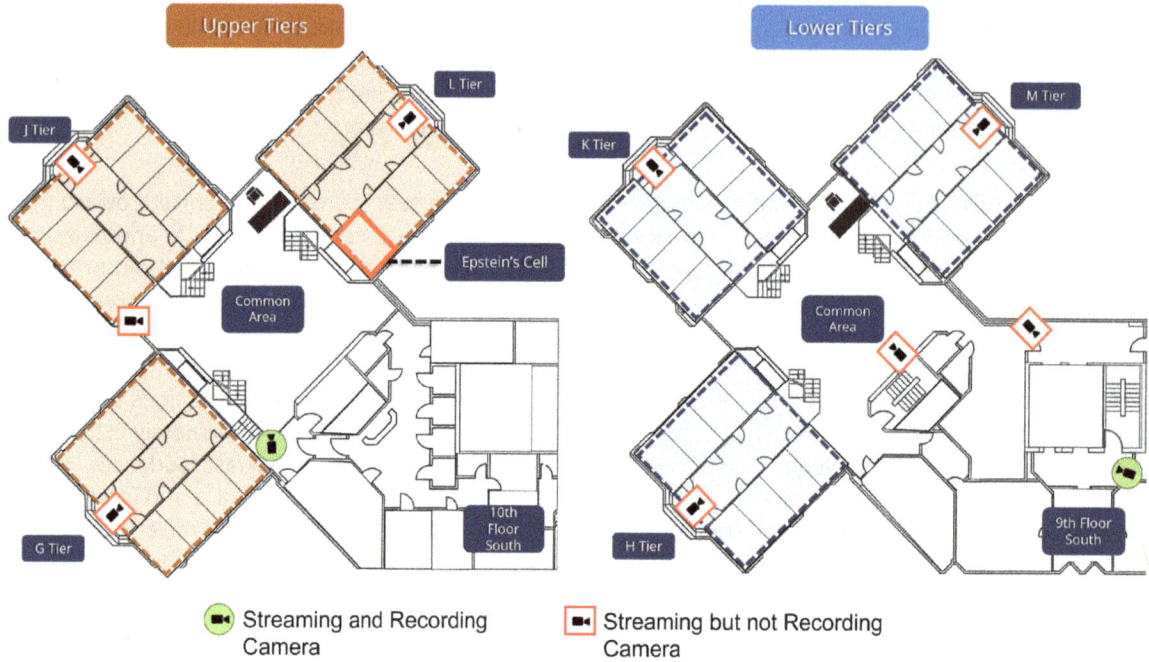

Source: DOJ OIG schematic drawing depicting the MCC New York SHU

Figure 6.2

Location of Recording SHU Camera at 10th Floor-South entrance

Note: The photograph has been modified for privacy reasons.

Source: DOJ OIG photograph and DOJ OIG schematic drawing depicting the MCC New York SHU

Figure 6.3

Field of View of the SHU Camera at 10th Floor-South Entrance

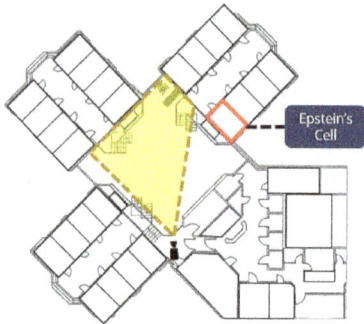

Source: DOJ OIG schematic drawing depicting the MCC New York SHU and the BOP

Figure 6.4

Partial View of L Tier Stairway, from the SHU Camera at 10th Floor-South Entrance

Source: DOJ OIG and the BOP

Figure 6.5

View of SHU Officers' Station from the SHU Camera at 10th Floor-South Entrance

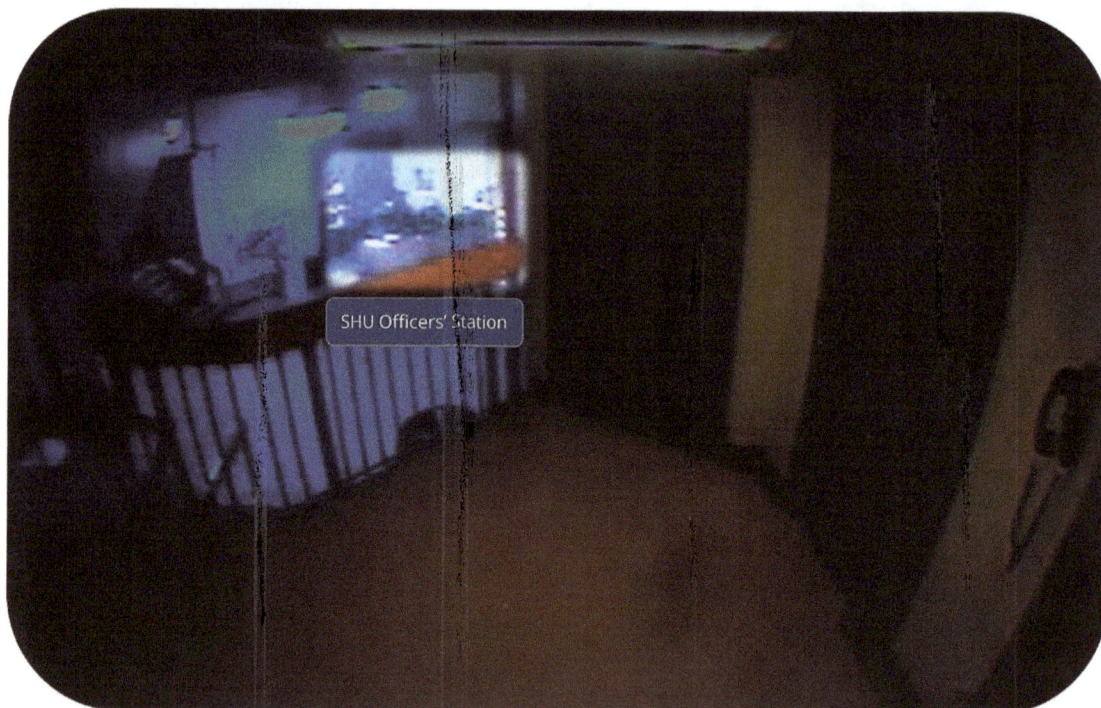

SHU Officers' Station

Source: DOJ OIG and the BOP

Figure 6.6

Field of View of the Recording 9th Floor Elevator Bay Camera

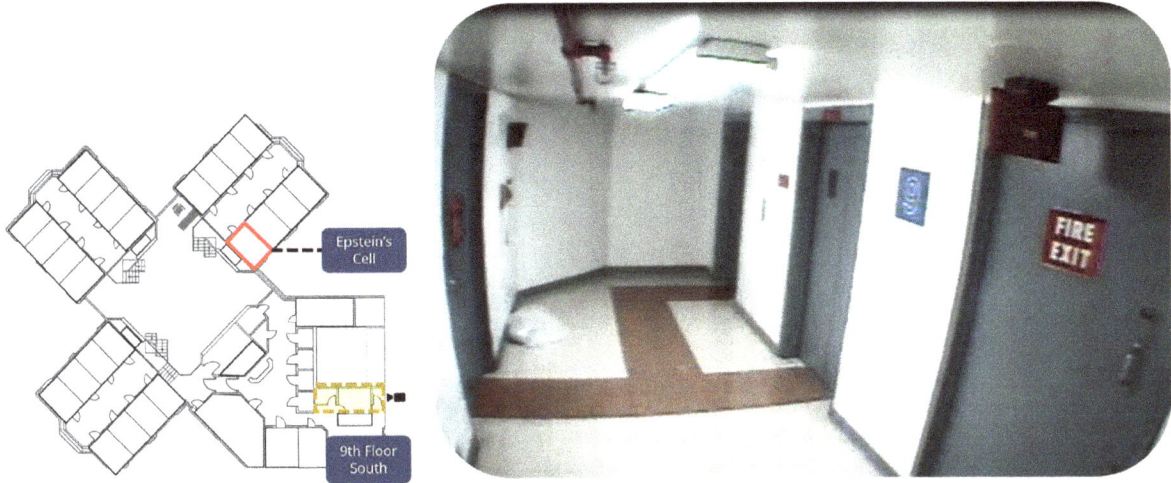

Source: DOJ OIG schematic drawing depicting the MCC New York SHU and the BOP

Figure 6.7

Location of Non-Recording Camera in the L Tier of the SHU

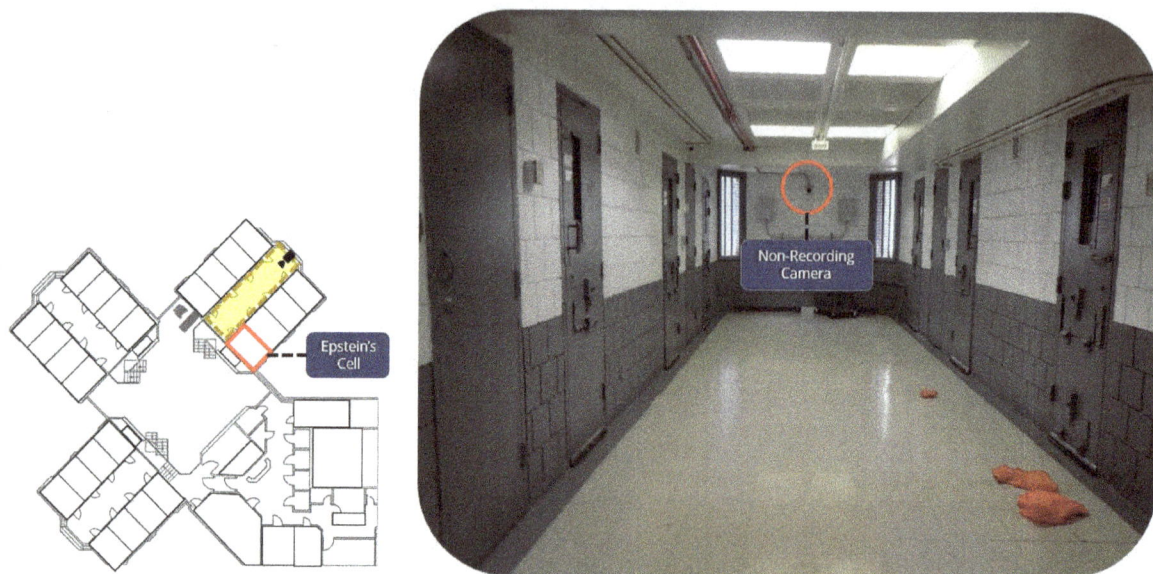

Source: DOJ OIG schematic drawing depicting the MCC New York SHU and the Office of the Chief Medical Examiner, City of New York

The Warden, who was not scheduled to work on August 10, 2019, arrived at the institution later that morning after being notified of Epstein's death and was informed that most of the cameras in the SHU were not recording. He told the OIG that when the SIS Lieutenant arrived at the facility that morning, he informed her that the SHU cameras had not been recording, and the SIS Lieutenant explained that the hard drive issue had been detected on August 8. He told the OIG that prior to August 10, he was unaware that the DVR 2 issue had been detected on August 8, and that approximately half of the facility's cameras, and in particular the cameras in the SHU, were found to not be recording on that date.

The Electronics Technician told the OIG that the Warden had instructed Electronics Technician to try and recover any potential SHU video that may have been recorded by the cameras assigned to the malfunctioning DVR 2 system, but the Electronics Technician was unable to find anything. The Electronics Technician further said that the Warden wanted to have all the facility's cameras recording again as soon as possible, so he instructed the Electronics Technician to begin repairing DVR 2.

D. FBI Forensic Analysis of the DVR System

FBI evidence documents revealed that on August 10, 2019, the FBI seized all hard drives contained within the DVR 2 system. On August 14, 2019, the FBI returned to MCC New York and seized additional DVR 2 components. On August 15, 2019, the FBI seized the entire DVR 1 system.

The FBI's Digital Forensics Analysis Unit in Quantico, Virginia, received MCC New York's DVR system on August 16, 2019, and began to conduct a forensic analysis of the system. According to FBI forensic reports, DVR 2 did not start successfully. The Digital Forensics Analysis Unit found that the system contained three faulty hard drives. The FBI forensic reports state that the three drives were repaired by an FBI Advanced Data Recovery Specialist, but the DVR was never able to be assembled successfully. The forensic reports further state that an FBI computer scientist and the Company 1 Technician reviewed the DVR 2 controller logs and found that there had previously been "catastrophic disk failures" and no recordings would have been available after July 29, 2019.

When the OIG asked the Electronics Technician about this finding by the FBI, he told the OIG he was unaware that cameras were not recording to DVR 2 between July 29 and August 8, 2019. Neither the Warden nor the SIS Lieutenant was aware the cameras assigned to DVR 2 had not been recording since July 29, 2019. The Company 1 Technician could not recall working with the Electronics Technician on any DVR issues prior to August 8, 2019, but he said that if the entire DVR 2 server went down on July 29, 2019, no video would have been able to have been retrieved from that point forward from any of the cameras recording to DVR 2.

Chapter 7: Conclusions and Recommendations

I.   Conclusions

Our investigation and review of the Federal Bureau of Prisons' (BOP) custody, care, and supervision of Jeffrey Epstein identified numerous and serious failures by employees of the Metropolitan Correctional Center located in New York, New York (MCC New York), including falsifying BOP records relating to inmate counts and rounds and multiple violations of MCC New York and BOP policies and procedures, which compromised Epstein's safety, the safety of other inmates, and the security of the institution. Specifically, we found that MCC New York staff failed to undertake required measures designed to make sure that, among other things, Epstein and other inmates were accounted for and safe, such as conducting inmate counts and 30-minute rounds, searching inmate cells, and ensuring adequate supervision of the Special Housing Unit (SHU) and the functionality of MCC New York's security camera system.

We further found that multiple BOP employees submitted false documents claiming that they had performed the required counts and rounds and that several MCC New York staff members lacked candor when questioned by the Office of the Inspector General (OIG) about their actions. Two MCC New York employees, Tova Noel and Michael Thomas, were charged criminally with falsifying BOP records relating to their conducting inmate counts and rounds. The U.S. Attorney's Office for the Southern District of New York subsequently entered into deferred prosecution agreements with Noel and Thomas and the court dismissed all charges against them after Noel and Thomas successfully fulfilled the terms of their agreements. Prosecution was declined by the U.S. Attorney's Office for the Southern District of New York for other MCC New York employees assigned to the SHU on August 9–10, 2019, who the OIG found also created, certified, and submitted false documentation regarding inmate counts and rounds on the day before and the day of Epstein's death.

The OIG also found that the MCC New York staff failed to carry out the Psychology Department's directive that Epstein be assigned a cellmate and that an MCC New York supervisor allowed Epstein to make an unmonitored telephone call the evening before his death.

The OIG determined that the combination of these and other failures led to Epstein being alone and unmonitored in his cell, with an excessive amount of bed linens, from approximately 10:40 p.m. on August 9, until he was discovered hanged in his cell at approximately 6:30 a.m. the following day. Additionally, the OIG found that staffing shortages, a persistent issue for the BOP, compromised the ability of MCC New York staff to adequately supervise inmates. As detailed below, we make a number of recommendations to the BOP to address the serious issues we identified during our investigation and review.

While the OIG determined that MCC New York staff committed significant violations of BOP and MCC New York policies and falsified records relating to their conducting inmate counts and rounds, the OIG did not uncover evidence that contradicted the Federal Bureau of Investigation's (FBI) determination regarding the absence of criminality in connection with how Epstein died. All MCC New York staff members who were interviewed by the OIG said they did not know of any information suggesting that Epstein's cause of death was something other than suicide. Likewise, none of the interviewed inmates provided any credible information that Epstein's cause of death was something other than suicide.

As detailed in Chapter 4 of this report, the SHU was a housing unit within MCC New York where inmates were securely separated from the general inmate population and kept locked in their cells for approximately 23 hours a day, to ensure their own safety as well as the safety of staff and other inmates. Access to the SHU was controlled by multiple locked doors. The primary entrance to the SHU (Main Exterior Entry Door) was opened remotely by a staff member in MCC New York's centralized Control Center. Additionally, there was a second locked door at the main entrance (Main Interior Entry Door), which could be opened only with a key held by a limited number of Correctional Officers (CO) while on duty.[55] Within the SHU, the entrance to each tier could be accessed only via a single locked door at the top or bottom of the staircase leading to the individual tier. Keys to open the locked tier doors were available only to a limited number of COs while on duty. Each tier had eight cells, each of which could house either one or two inmates. Each individual cell, which was made of cement and metal, could be accessed only through a single locked door, to which only a limited number of COs had keys while on duty. The SHU cell doors were made of solid metal with a small glass window and small locked slots that correctional staff used to handcuff inmates and provide food and toiletries to inmates. As a further security measure, during each shift a limited number of the COs had keys while on duty.

BOP policy and practice require that all SHU inmates be locked in their cells overnight. The OIG found no evidence indicating that the door to Epstein's cell or any other cell in the SHU tier in which Epstein was housed was unlocked on the evening of August 9–10, 2019, after SHU staff locked Epstein in his cell at approximately 8 p.m. SHU staff told the OIG that at approximately 8 p.m. on August 9, all SHU inmates were locked in their cells for the evening and that there was no indication that any of the other inmates could have gotten out of their cells. Epstein did not have a cellmate after Inmate 3 was transferred out of MCC New York on August 9, and therefore Epstein was alone in his cell the evening of August 9–10. The door to Epstein's cell was visible from the SHU Officers' Station, and CO Tova Noel and Material Handler Michael Thomas told the OIG that no one entered or exited Epstein's cell during their shift on August 10. Both of them further described delivering breakfast to the L Tier at about 6:30 a.m. on August 10, and how Noel unlocked the door to the L Tier, Thomas entered the L Tier and called for Epstein, and then Thomas unlocked his cell door when Epstein failed to respond. Additionally, the three inmates who were housed in the same SHU tier as Epstein on August 9 and 10, and who had a direct line of sight to the door of Epstein's cell from their cells, stated that no one entered or exited Epstein's cell after the SHU staff returned Epstein to his cell on the evening of August 9, which is consistent with the security measures in place within the MCC New York SHU.

Further, the OIG analyzed the available recorded video of the SHU, which was limited to the common area of the SHU, including the SHU Officers' Station, due to the MCC New York security camera system's video recording issues that we detailed in Chapter 6. The OIG's analysis of the recorded video did not identify any COs (other than those assigned to the SHU during that timeframe or had a specific reason for visiting the SHU) or other individuals present in the common area of the SHU approach any of the SHU tiers, including the L Tier where Epstein was housed, between approximately 10:40 p.m. on August 9 and approximately 6:30 a.m. on August 10. In sum, the OIG's investigation did not find any evidence that anyone was present in

---

[55] The primary entrance doors to the MCC New York SHU are shown in Figure 4.1. Access to the secondary entrance to the SHU, which was adjacent to the elevator bay on the south side of the floor, was also controlled by an exterior entry door opened by the Control Center and an interior door opened only with a key held by one of the COs assigned to the SHU while on duty. The secondary entrance doors to the SHU are shown in Figure 4.2.

the L Tier during that timeframe other than the inmates who were locked in their assigned cells on that tier of the SHU.

We also noted that the surveillance camera in the L Tier, as shown in the photograph in Figure 6.7, was in plain view of the inmates and therefore inmates would have been aware that any hallway movements, including into or out of Epstein's cell, were being live streamed and could be monitored, even if, unbeknownst to them, the Digital Video Recorder (DVR) system was not recording the live stream at that time. As the OIG has noted in numerous prior reports regarding the BOP's camera system, BOP staff and inmates are aware of where prison cameras are located and often engage in wrongdoing in locations where they know cameras are not located.[56] Additionally, the OIG did not observe on the recorded video of the SHU common area that Noel and Thomas, who were seated at the desk at the SHU Officers' Station immediately outside the L tier during that time period, at any time rose from their seats or approached the L Tier. We additionally found that Thomas's and Noel's reaction on the morning of August 10 upon finding Epstein hanging in his cell, as described to us by Thomas, Noel, the responding Lieutenant, and inmates, was consistent with their being unaware of any potential harm to Epstein prior to Thomas entering Epstein's cell at about 6:30 a.m. on August 10.

We further noted that Epstein had previously been placed on suicide watch and psychological observation due to the events of July 23, 2019; that numerous nooses made from prison bed sheets were found in his cell on the morning of August 10; and that he had signed a new Last Will and Testament on August 8, 2 days before he died. No weapons were recovered from Epstein's cell after his death. Additionally, the inmates who were interviewed consistently reported that on the evening Epstein died the SHU staff did not systematically conduct the required rounds and counts, which was one of the primary mechanisms for the SHU staff to ensure the safety and security of inmates housed in the SHU. As a result, Epstein was unmonitored and locked alone in his cell for hours with an excess amount of linens, which provided an opportunity for him to commit suicide.

Finally, the Medical Examiner who performed the autopsy detailed for the OIG why Epstein's injuries were more consistent with, and indicative of, a suicide by hanging rather than a homicide by strangulation. The Medical Examiner also told the OIG that the ligature furrow was too broad to have been caused by the electrical cord of the medical device in Epstein's cell and that blood toxicology tests revealed no medications or illegal substances were in Epstein's system. The Medical Examiner also noted the absence of debris under Epstein's fingernails, marks on his hands, contusions to his knuckles, or bruises on his body that would have indicated Epstein had been a struggle, which would be expected if Epstein's death had been a homicide by strangulation.

This is not the first time that the OIG has found significant job performance and management failures on the part of BOP personnel and widespread disregard of BOP policies that are designed to ensure that inmates are safe, secure, and in good health. For instance, the OIG's December 2022 investigation and review of the BOP's handling of the transfer of James "Whitey" Bulger identified serious job performance and

---

[56] U.S. Department of Justice (DOJ) OIG, *Notification of Needed Upgrades to the Federal Bureau of Prisons' Security Camera System*, Management Advisory Memorandum 22-001 (October 2021); U.S. DOJ OIG, *Audit of the Federal Bureau of Prisons' Management and Oversight of its Chaplaincy Services Program*, 21-091 (July 2021); U.S. DOJ OIG, *Review of the Federal Bureau of Prisons' Contraband Interdiction Efforts*, Evaluation and Inspections Report 16-05 (June 2016).

management failures at multiple levels within the BOP.[57] Similar to the Bulger report, the numerous and serious transgressions that occurred in this matter came to light largely because they involved a high-profile inmate. The fact that serious deficiencies occurred in connection with high-profile inmates like Epstein and Bulger is especially concerning given that the BOP would presumably take particular care in handling the custody and care of such inmates.

Regrettably, the OIG has encountered similar issues on many other occasions. For example, the OIG has investigated numerous allegations related to the falsification of official BOP documentation concerning inmate counts and rounds, several of which have resulted in criminal prosecution. The OIG currently has two open investigations into allegations of falsified inmate count and round documentation, each involving an inmate death (by suicide and homicide) or escape from a BOP facility.

This investigation and review also revealed the direct impact of insufficient staffing levels on inmate safety. Witnesses repeatedly told the OIG that counts, rounds, cell searches, and other methods of inmate accountability were not undertaken because correctional staff were working multiple shifts—including one staff member who worked 24-hours straight—and were tired and overwhelmed with other duties. As discussed in greater detail in our recommendations, the OIG has repeatedly found the need for BOP to address staffing shortages. Most recently, in March 2023, the OIG found that the coronavirus disease 2019 (COVID-19) pandemic exacerbated the effects of preexisting BOP medical and nonmedical staffing shortages, an issue the OIG has identified as a concern for the BOP since at least 2015.[58]

Further, the OIG has repeatedly found that BOP personnel have not consistently been attentive to the needs of inmates at risk for suicide. In this investigation, that inattention manifested in the failure of MCC New York staff and supervisors to ensure that Epstein was assigned a cellmate as required by the MCC New York Psychology Department directive issued after the July 23, 2019 incident in which Epstein was discovered in his cell with an orange cloth around his neck. In a March 2023 report, the OIG found that BOP psychology staff did not assess the suitability of single-cell assignments for five of the seven inmates who died by suicide while in COVID-19 quarantine units between March 2020 and April 2021.[59] The OIG's 2017 report on the BOP's use of restrictive housing for inmates with mental illness also noted that single-celling may present risks to inmate mental health, and both of the recommendations from that report regarding the use and oversight of single-celling remain open as of March 2023.[60]

Lastly, as discussed in greater detail in the conclusions and recommendations that follow, the persistent deficiencies of the BOP's security camera systems are well documented and long-standing.

---

[57] U.S. DOJ OIG, *Investigation and Review of the Federal Bureau of Prisons' Handling of the Transfer of Inmate James "Whitey" Bulger*, 23-007 (December 2022).

[58] U.S. DOJ OIG, *Capstone Review of the Federal Bureau of Prisons' Response to the Coronavirus Disease 2019 Pandemic*, Evaluation and Inspections Division A-2020-011 (March 2023) (*Capstone Report*).

[59] *Capstone Report.*

[60] U.S. DOJ OIG, *Review of the Federal Bureau of Prisons' Use of Restrictive Housing for Inmates with Mental Illness*, Evaluation and Inspections Report 17-05 (July 2017).

The combination of negligence, misconduct, and outright job performance failures documented in this report all contributed to an environment in which arguably one of the most notorious inmates in BOP's custody was provided with the opportunity to take his own life, resulting in significant questions being asked about the circumstances of his death, how it could have been allowed to have happen, and most importantly, depriving his numerous victims, many of whom were underage girls at the time of the alleged crimes, of their ability to seek justice through the criminal justice process. The fact that these failures have been recurring ones at the BOP does not excuse them and gives additional urgency to the need for Department of Justice (DOJ) and BOP leadership to address the chronic staffing, surveillance, security, and related problems plaguing the BOP.

The OIG has completed its investigation and is providing this report to the BOP for appropriate action.

Unless otherwise noted, the OIG applies the preponderance of the evidence standard in determining whether DOJ personnel have committed misconduct. The U.S. Merit Systems Protection Board applies this same standard when reviewing a federal agency's decision to take adverse action against an employee based on such misconduct. See 5 U.S.C. § 7701(c)(1)(B) and 5 C.F.R. § 1201.56(b)(1)(ii).

A. MCC New York Staff Failed to Ensure that Epstein Had a Cellmate on August 9 as Instructed by the Psychology Department on July 30

On July 30, 2019, the MCC New York Psychology Department sent an email to over 70 BOP staff members stating that Epstein "needs to be housed with an appropriate cellmate." The Psychology Department's directive that Epstein have an appropriate cellmate arose out of the events that occurred on July 23, 2019, when Epstein was found lying on the floor of his cell with a piece of orange cloth around his neck. Epstein's cellmate at the time (Inmate 1) told MCC New York staff that Epstein had tried to hang himself, and another inmate housed on the same SHU tier at the time (Inmate 2) corroborated several aspects of Inmate 1's account. Epstein's accounts of what had occurred varied. Epstein initially told MCC New York staff that he thought his cellmate had tried to kill him, but thereafter he repeatedly said he did not know what had occurred. Epstein later asked two different MCC New York staff members if he could be housed with the same cellmate Epstein initially accused of having tried to harm him.

As a result of this incident, Epstein was placed on suicide watch and then psychological observation. Consistent with the Psychology Department's directive, the Captain and the SHU Lieutenant each told the OIG that they verbally informed SHU staff of Epstein's cellmate requirement. These and other witnesses said staff members regularly assigned to the SHU knew that Epstein needed to have a cellmate. However, despite the Psychology Department's widely disseminated July 30 email instruction and the subsequent verbal direction provided by the Captain and the SHU Lieutenant, Epstein was left without a cellmate on August 9 and, less than 24 hours later, Epstein died by suicide.

1. Failure to Make Required Notifications Regarding the Need to Assign Epstein a New Cellmate

The OIG's investigation and review revealed that on August 9, 2019, MCC New York staff assigned to the SHU failed to notify their superiors that Epstein's cellmate, Inmate 3, had been transferred out of MCC New York and therefore Epstein needed to be assigned a new cellmate. The failure to make these required notifications—and the supervisors' failure to properly supervise the SHU staff, discussed further below—

resulted in Epstein being housed without a cellmate at the time of his death, which was contrary to the Psychology Department's directive issued just 10 days earlier.

BOP standards of conduct require that employees "obey the orders of their superiors at all times."[61] MCC New York Post Orders for the SHU require, among other things, that all SHU officers "maintain a log of pertinent information regarding inmate activity, detailing time, persons involved (if pertinent) and the event, which must be logged into TRUSCOPE."[62] Importantly, the SHU Post Orders clarify that they "are not intended to describe in detail all the officer's responsibilities. Good judgment and common sense are expected in all situations not covered in these post orders."

On August 9, the Day Watch SHU Officer in Charge, the Evening Watch SHU Officer in Charge, and CO Tova Noel were each assigned to the MCC New York SHU as their permanent quarterly assigned post and served as the SHU Officer in Charge during their respective shifts.[63] The OIG investigation found that each of these employees knew that Epstein was required to have a cellmate at all times per the Psychology Department's directive.

The OIG further found that on August 9 the Day Watch SHU Officer in Charge, the Evening Watch SHU Officer in Charge, and Noel each became aware at various times during their respective shifts that Epstein's cellmate, Inmate 3, had been transferred from the institution with all of his belongings, a status known to all MCC New York staff members as meaning the inmate was being permanently transferred out of the institution. Specifically, the OIG investigation found that on the morning of August 9, the Day Watch SHU Officer in Charge and CO 1, who was also assigned to the SHU, reviewed the MCC New York daily call out list, a document that identifies all inmates who were leaving their housing units each day, which listed Inmate 3 as being scheduled to depart MCC New York with all of his belongings. At approximately 8:30 a.m., CO 1 escorted Inmate 3 from the SHU to Receiving and Discharge to be transferred out of the institution, and the Day Watch SHU Officer in Charge escorted Epstein from the SHU to the attorney conference room for his daily meeting with his attorneys.[64] During the escort, the Day Watch SHU Officer in Charge and CO 1 discussed the need to assign Epstein with a new cellmate due to Inmate 3's transfer.[65] The Day Watch SHU Officer in Charge told the OIG, and stated in a memorandum that he prepared following Epstein's death, that he notified his relief, the Evening Watch SHU Officer in Charge, of the need to assign Epstein a new cellmate, and that he likely notified an unspecified Lieutenant. However, the OIG did not credit the Day Watch SHU Officer in Charge's account because no other witnesses or evidence confirmed that he had in fact passed on information regarding Epstein's need for a new cellmate, either to a supervisor or his relief.

---

[61] BOP Program Statement 3420.11.

[62] TRUSCOPE is a BOP database that provides institution staff with detailed inmate and institution security-related information and provides unit officers an electronic event log.

[63] Noel served as the SHU Officer in Charge after the Evening Watch SHU Officer in Charge's shift ended at 10 p.m. on August 9, 2019.

[64] Receiving and Discharge is the area of MCC New York that is responsible for processing inmates who enter or leave the facility.

[65] The OIG did not find that CO 1 failed to make appropriate notifications because his immediate superior in his chain-of-command, the Day Watch SHU Officer in Charge, was aware of the need to assign Epstein a new cellmate.

The OIG investigation also found that during the next shift in the MCC New York SHU, both the Evening Watch SHU Officer in Charge and Noel became aware that Epstein was without a cellmate. The Evening Watch SHU Officer in Charge told the OIG that when he escorted Epstein back to his cell after Epstein's telephone call, he saw that Inmate 3 was not there and then he, Noel, and the Material Handler discussed the need for Epstein to have a new cellmate. The Evening Watch SHU Officer in Charge also told the OIG that he notified an unspecified supervisor. However, other witnesses did not corroborate his account. Noel told the OIG that she was unaware both that Epstein needed to have a cellmate and that Inmate 3 had been removed from the institution. Noel also told the OIG that she went to Epstein's cell at approximately 10 p.m.—a time of day when all inmates were secured in their cells—and may have plugged in Epstein's medical device for him. The OIG did not credit Noel's statements that she did not know that Epstein needed a cellmate or that Inmate 3 had been removed from the SHU based on contradictory witness statements (including her own) regarding SHU staff's knowledge of Epstein's cellmate requirement and Inmate 3's transfer out of the SHU.[66]

The OIG investigation concluded that on August 9, 2019, the Day Watch SHU Officer in Charge, the Evening Watch SHU Officer in Charge, and Noel failed to notify a supervisor as required after Epstein's cellmate was permanently removed from the MCC New York SHU, which constituted a violation of BOP standards of conduct. Additionally, their inaction violated MCC New York SHU Post Orders because none of these individuals documented the fact the Epstein needed a new cellmate as required. Finally, all of these officers failed to exercise good judgment and common sense, as required by the SHU Post Orders, by not immediately undertaking steps through their chain-of-command to ensure that a high-profile inmate who had been released from suicide watch and psychological observation 10 days earlier had an appropriate cellmate.

2. Failure to Adequately Supervise SHU Staff

The OIG also found that MCC New York supervisory personnel failed to effectively perform their duties, which contributed to the fact that Epstein was housed without a cellmate at the time of his death. Rather than passively relying on a notification from subordinates, supervisory personnel also had an obligation under federal regulations to "put forth honest effort in the performance of their duties," which included supervision of SHU personnel.[67] The OIG's investigation revealed that the Captain and the Day Watch Operations Lieutenant, the Day Watch Activities Lieutenant, the Evening Watch Operations Lieutenant, and the Morning Watch Operations Lieutenant, among other MCC New York staff, received an email from the U.S. Marshals Service (USMS) on August 8, 2019, notifying them that Inmate 3 was scheduled to be transferred to another facility the following day. If any of these supervisors had read the email attachment, they would have known of the need to assign Epstein a new cellmate. Instead, many of these individuals told the OIG that they believed that Inmate 3 had gone to court on August 9 and they were unaware that he would not return and Epstein needed a new cellmate. The SHU Lieutenant's shift on August 8 ended over an hour before the USMS sent the email notification and he was not working on August 9. In his absence, the Day Watch Operations Lieutenant, the Day Watch Activities Lieutenant, the Evening Watch Operations Lieutenant, and the Morning Watch Operations Lieutenant had oversight of the SHU during their respective

---

[66] Noel reviewed a draft of the report and we considered her comments but made no changes as a result.

[67] 5 C.F.R. § 2635.101(b)(5); see also 5 C.F.R. § 2635.705(a).

shifts, and the Captain had oversight over all of the Lieutenants.[68] The OIG found that the failure of these individuals to adequately supervise SHU staff and ensure that a high-profile inmate who had recently been on suicide watch and psychological observation had an appropriate cellmate constituted a job performance failure.

3. Failure to Have a Contingency Plan for Assigning Epstein a Cellmate

Additionally, the OIG found that the Warden's failure to have a back-up cellmate assignment for Epstein constituted poor judgment. The Evening Watch SHU Officer in Charge told the OIG that although he knew that Epstein needed to be assigned another cellmate, SHU staff could not just put anyone in the cell with Epstein. The Warden confirmed this in his OIG interview, when he explained that he and BOP executive leadership selected Inmate 3 as Epstein's cellmate following the events of July 23, 2019. The Warden told the OIG that no inmates were pre-vetted to serve as Epstein's cellmate if Inmate 3 left MCC New York. [69] The Northeast Regional Director, the Warden, and the Captain all told the OIG that if Inmate 3 had been removed as Epstein's cellmate, they would have had to review a new list of potential cellmate candidates to ensure that Epstein was housed with an appropriate inmate. This selection process, which involved multiple steps undertaken by high-level BOP management, would be difficult to accomplish in a short period of time and ultimately may have impeded SHU officers' ability to house Epstein with a cellmate on August 9, 2019.

4. Lack of Candor

BOP policy requires that "[d]uring the course of an official investigation, employees are to cooperate fully by providing all pertinent information they may have. Full cooperation requires truthfully responding to questions."[70]

As discussed above, the Day Watch SHU Officer in Charge and the Evening Watch SHU Officer in Charge told the OIG that they notified supervisory personnel regarding the need to assign Epstein a new cellmate. Based on a lack of corroborating evidence for these assertions, the OIG found that they lacked candor in their OIG interviews in violation of BOP policy. Similarly, the OIG found that Noel lacked candor in violation of BOP policy when she said she did not know that Epstein needed a cellmate or that his then-cellmate Inmate 3 had been transferred out of the SHU.

The OIG also found that the Morning Watch Operations Lieutenant lacked candor in her interview with the OIG in violation of BOP policy when she said she was not aware that Epstein was required to be housed with a cellmate. Her statement is contradicted by the fact that she was one of the MCC New York staff members who responded to the July 23, 2019 incident involving Epstein, which resulted in him being placed on suicide watch and psychological observation; she was a recipient of the Psychology Department's July 30, 2019

---

[68] The Senior Officer Specialist who served as the Acting Evening Watch Activities Lieutenant from 4 p.m. to 10 p.m. on August 9, 2019, told the OIG that she was not aware of Epstein's cellmate requirement. The OIG credited her account because she did not ordinarily work in or supervise the SHU and did not receive the Psychology Department's July 30, 2019 email regarding the need for Epstein to have an appropriate cellmate or the USMS August 8, 2019 email notifying that Inmate 3 would be transferred to another facility the following day.

[69] Upon reviewing a draft of this report, the Warden told the OIG that there were no suitable backup cellmates for Epstein.

[70] BOP Program Statement 3420.11.

email identifying the cellmate requirement; and the statements of multiple witnesses who told the OIG that Epstein's cellmate requirement was widely disseminated verbally by MCC New York leadership.

> **B.   MCC New York Staff Failed to Conduct Mandatory Rounds and Inmate Counts Resulting in Epstein Being Unobserved for Hours Before His Death**

The OIG's investigation and review revealed that on August 9 and 10, 2019, MCC New York SHU staff did not conduct the mandatory rounds and inmate counts during their shift in the SHU. The failure to undertake these required measures to account for inmate whereabouts and wellbeing—and the supervisors' failure to properly supervise the SHU staff, as discussed further below—resulted in Epstein being unobserved for hours before his death, which compounded the failure of MCC New York staff to ensure that Epstein had an appropriate cellmate.

1.   Failure to Conduct Rounds and Inmate Counts in the SHU

Federal regulations require that employees "use official time in an honest effort to perform official duties."[71] Additionally, BOP standards of conduct required that employees "[c]onduct themselves in a manner that fosters respect for the Bureau of Prisons, the Department of Justice, and the U.S. Government."[72] Because "[i]nattention to duty in a correctional environment can result in escapes, assaults, and other incidents," BOP standards of conduct also require employees "to remain fully alert and attentive during duty hours." BOP policy also requires "[c]ontinuous inmate accountability," which is accomplished through rounds and inmate counts.[73] Among other things, rounds and inmate counts enable staff to observe inmates and ensure that they are safe and secure in their cells and are in good health.

BOP policy and MCC New York SHU Post Orders set out the requirements for these inmate accountability measures, specifying that correctional staff must conduct rounds on an irregular schedule at least twice each hour, no more than 40 minutes apart. BOP policy and MCC New York SHU Post Orders further specify that at least two MCC New York SHU staff members must conduct inmate counts at 12 a.m., 3 a.m., 5 a.m., 4 p.m., and 10 p.m. daily, and also at 10 a.m. on weekends and federal holidays.

The OIG's investigation and review revealed that an inmate (Inmate 4) was internally transferred from the SHU to Receiving and Discharge at approximately 3:15 p.m. on August 9, 2019; however, this inmate transfer was not documented until approximately 12:35 a.m. on August 10, 2019. Based on this internal transfer, BOP records, and witness statements, the OIG determined that the 4 p.m. and 10 p.m. SHU inmate counts on August 9 were erroneous. In addition, the OIG reviewed the available SHU security camera video, which did not show COs walking up or down the stairs leading to the various SHU tiers during the count times, a process that is necessary to conduct an accurate count of inmates.[74] During their OIG interviews, the Evening Watch SHU Officer in Charge, the Material Handler, CO Tova Noel, and Material Handler Michael Thomas each admitted that they did not conduct all of the mandatory rounds and inmate counts in the SHU

---

[71] 5 C.F.R. § 2635.705(a); see also 5 C.F.R. § 2635.101(b)(5).

[72] BOP Program Statement 3420.11.

[73] BOP Program Statement 5500.14.

[74] As discussed in Chapter 5, the OIG found that the security camera video was of low quality. Therefore, the OIG analyzed the video in conjunction with BOP records and witness statements regarding the personnel in the SHU and their activities.

on the evening of August 9 and the morning of August 10. Noel told the OIG that she conducted the 10 p.m. count on August 9. The OIG did not credit her statement based on: (1) its review of the SHU security camera video, which reflects Noel walking up and down the stairs leading to some, but not all, of the tiers several minutes after the SHU inmate count had been called into the Control Center; (2) the 10 p.m. count slip, which erroneously included the SHU Inmate 4, who had been internally transferred to Receiving and Delivery; (3) other BOP records; and (4) the Material Handler's statement to the OIG that no one conducted the 10 p.m. count because everyone was tired.

Instead of performing the required duties to account for inmate whereabouts and wellbeing, the OIG found that officers assigned to the SHU on August 9 and 10, including the Material Handler, Noel, and Thomas primarily remained seated in the SHU Officers' Station—sometimes without moving for a period of time, suggesting that they were asleep—and conducted a variety of Internet searches on MCC New York computers. Thomas also admitted to the OIG that he "dozed off" for periods of time during his shift. The OIG's analysis of the SHU security camera video revealed that after approximately 10:40 p.m., no CO entered Epstein's tier in the SHU until just before 6:30 a.m. when Noel and Thomas began to serve breakfast to the inmates.

The OIG investigation and review concluded that the Evening Watch SHU Officer in Charge, the Material Handler, Noel, and Thomas failed to conduct the mandatory rounds and inmate counts during their respective shifts in the MCC New York SHU on August 9 and 10, 2019, and that their actions constituted violations of 5 C.F.R. §§ 2635.101(b)(5) and 2635.705(a), BOP Program Statements 3420.11 and 5500.14, and MCC New York SHU Post Orders.

2. False Statements and Lack of Candor

The OIG's investigation and review found that on August 9 and 10, 2019, the Evening Watch SHU Officer in Charge, the Material Handler, Noel, and Thomas made false statements when they falsified BOP records by attesting that they had completed the mandatory rounds and inmate counts when, in fact, they had not.

Federal law provides that "whoever, in any matter within the jurisdiction of the executive...branch of the Government of the United States, knowingly and willfully...makes or uses any false writing or document knowing the same to contain any materially false, fictitious, or fraudulent statement or entry" has violated 18 U.S.C. § 1001(a)(3).

As discussed above, the OIG found that the Evening Watch SHU Officer in Charge, the Material Handler, Noel, and Thomas failed to conduct all of the mandatory rounds and inmate counts. As part of each institutional inmate count, BOP policy and MCC New York SHU Post Orders require two COs to conduct each count and memorialize the number of inmates in the SHU on an official MCC New York form, often called a count slip.[75] On the count slip, both COs are required to fill in the date and time the count had been performed, write the total number of inmates physically present in the unit counted, and then sign the count slip. Once the COs complete and sign the count slips, the count slips are then collected and delivered to the MCC New York Control Center. Officers assigned to the Control Center are responsible for comparing the count slips from each housing unit to the institution's overall inmate count sheet to ensure that each

---

[75] This BOP form is officially entitled "Metropolitan Correctional Center; New York, New York; Official Count Slip."

inmate was accounted for.[76] Only after all the count slips have been collected from each housing unit, and the numbers on the count slips had been matched to the institution's overall inmate count sheet, could the institutional count be deemed "cleared" or completed.

The Evening Watch SHU Officer in Charge, the Material Handler, Noel, and Thomas each prepared and/or signed a false count slip to create the impression that they had fulfilled their inmate accountability responsibilities when, in fact, they had not.[77] These individuals admitted to the OIG that instead of performing their assigned duties, they pre-filled the count slips with the number of inmates they believed were in the SHU based on what officers from the previous shift had told them and signed off on the documents knowing that they falsely attested to having completed the counts. Additionally, Noel admitted to the OIG that she had prefilled the official MCC New York forms documenting the times of the 30-minute rounds, often referred to as round sheets, and falsely attested to having completed the rounds.[78]

Noel and Thomas were indicted by a grand jury for their false certifications of having conducted counts and rounds. Subsequently, each entered into a deferred prosecution agreement with the U.S. Attorney's Office for the Southern District of New York. The U.S. Attorney's Office of the Southern District of New York declined prosecution for the Evening Watch SHU Officer in Charge and the Material Handler.

The OIG investigation has found that the Evening Watch SHU Officer in Charge, the Material Handler, Noel, and Thomas knowingly and willingly falsified BOP records in violation of federal law by attesting that they had completed the mandatory rounds and inmate counts on the evening of August 9, 2019, and morning of August 10, 2019.

Additionally, as noted above, BOP policy requires employees to cooperate fully with an official investigation and truthfully respond to questions. The OIG found that Noel lacked candor when she told the OIG that she had conducted the 10 p.m. count when the weight of evidence indicates that, at most, she may have conducted a round at the time.

3. Poor Judgment Regarding the Use of Overtime

The OIG's investigation and review revealed that on August 9, 2019, MCC New York supervisory staff requested that a staff member fill an overtime position within the SHU, which resulted in that staff member working three shifts back-to-back, that is, 24 hours straight.

The collective bargaining agreement between the BOP and unions representing BOP employees provides that "[o]rdinarily, the minimum time off between shifts will be seven and one-half (7 ½) hours, and the

---

[76] The official name for the document used to record an institutional count is "Bureau of Prisons Count Sheet."

[77] The Evening Watch SHU Officer in Charge and Noel signed the 4 p.m. count slip; Noel and the Material Handler signed the 10 p.m. count slip; and Noel and Thomas signed the 12 a.m., 3 a.m., and 5 a.m. count slips.

[78] This BOP form is officially entitled "MCC New York, Special Housing Unit, 30 Minute Check Sheet."

minimum elapsed time of on 'days off' will be fifty-six (56) hours, except when the employee requests the change."[79]

The Material Handler told the OIG that on August 9 he reported for a voluntary overtime shift from 12 a.m. to 8 a.m. and then worked his regular 8 a.m. to 4 p.m. shift in the warehouse. At some point during the day shift, the Day Watch Operations Lieutenant, a higher ranking official, called and asked the Material Handler if he could work overtime in the SHU and he agreed. The Material Handler told the OIG that he felt pressured to work the third shift, which resulted in him working 24 hours straight, from 12 a.m. on August 9 through 12 a.m. on August 10. As discussed previously, the Material Handler admitted to the OIG that on the evening of August 9, during his third shift which he worked in the SHU, he did not conduct the mandatory inmate counts and rounds because he was too tired.

The OIG investigation and review concluded that the Day Watch Operations Lieutenant exercised poor judgment when he requested that the Material Handler work a third consecutive shift. As the Day Watch Operations Lieutenant, he had access to the staff roster and schedule and therefore he should have known that the Material Handler had already worked 16 straight hours. Additionally, the Day Watch Operations Lieutenant's action was inconsistent with the collective bargaining agreement and did not reflect sound correctional judgment, as it would have been extremely difficult for the Material Handler to have effectively performed his duties during his third shift.

4. Clearing the 10 p.m. Institutional Count Knowing that It Was Inaccurate

The OIG's investigation and review determined that on August 9, 2019, MCC New York staff cleared the 10 p.m. institutional count knowing that the inmate counts from two housing units were inaccurate.

BOP policy and MCC New York SHU Post Orders require that COs conducting an institutional count relay the count verbally to the Control Center, which maintains the master count of all inmates.[80] If a count reported verbally does not match the master count, the Control Center must notify the Operations Lieutenant and the staff members must recount the inmates. MCC New York SHU Post Orders further provide that "[c]ount slips which appear to be altered will not be accepted."

As discussed previously, the OIG determined that an internal transfer of an inmate (Inmate 4) from the SHU to Receiving and Discharge on August 9 was not documented appropriately at the time of the transfer. The failure to document the transfer, along with the SHU staff not conducting the required inmate counts, resulted in the MCC New York Control Center receiving a count slip from the SHU with an incorrect number of inmates identified as being present within the SHU at the 10 p.m. institutional count.

During his OIG interview, Senior Officer Specialist 6, who was assigned to the Control Center, admitted that he amended the 10 p.m. count slips he received from the SHU and Receiving and Discharge in an attempt to reflect the correct number of inmates in the SHU following the internal inmate transfer that resulted in a SHU inmate (Inmate 4) being moved to Receiving and Discharge earlier in the day. Senior Officer Specialist 6 acknowledged that he should have requested a recount from the SHU, but instead he cleared the 10 p.m.

---

[79] BOP and Council of Prison Locals, Master Agreement, July 21, 2014–July 20, 2021 (extended until 2026).

[80] BOP Program Statement 5270.11.

count. Senior Officer Specialist 6 explained that the action he took was known as "ghost counting," something he said he would not have done without authorization from the Operations Lieutenant or someone of a higher rank than himself. The Morning Watch Operations Lieutenant denied having authorized a "ghost count" and we found no evidence to corroborate Senior Officer Specialist 6's claim that the Morning Watch Operations Lieutenant knew of and approved the false count.

The OIG found that Senior Officer Specialist 6 modified the count slips received from the SHU and Receiving and Discharge, failed to request a recount of the SHU inmates, and cleared the 10 p.m. institutional count knowing that it was inaccurate in violation of BOP policy and MCC New York SHU Post Orders.

5. Failure to Adequately Supervise SHU Staff and Conduct Lieutenant Rounds

The OIG also found that MCC New York supervisory personnel failed to effectively perform their duties, which contributed to the fact that Epstein was unobserved for many hours before his death. As discussed above, federal regulations require that MCC New York supervisory personnel "put forth honest effort in the performance of their duties," which includes appropriate supervision of SHU personnel.[81] Additionally, BOP policy requires that a Lieutenant visit the SHU during each shift to ensure that all procedures are being followed.[82]

The OIG's investigation revealed that the Evening Watch Operations Lieutenant and the Morning Watch Operations Lieutenant had oversight of the SHU during their respective shifts.[83] The Evening Watch Operations Lieutenant told the OIG that on August 9, 2019, he did not supervise the 4 p.m. count or conduct any rounds in the SHU. He acknowledged that he signed some of the pages of the 4 p.m. count, but he did not sign all of the pages as he should have. Beginning at 10 p.m. on August 9, the Morning Watch Operations Lieutenant was the sole supervisor overseeing the SHU. The Morning Watch Operations Lieutenant told the OIG that she noticed an error in the 12 a.m. count on August 10, which was due to SHU staff including Inmate 4, who had been internally transferred to Receiving and Discharge, among the inmates in the SHU. According to the Morning Watch Operations Lieutenant, the SHU staff should have conducted another count and submitted a new count slip, but she did not know if they actually did so.

During her shift, the Morning Watch Operations Lieutenant conducted one round in the SHU at approximately 4 a.m. on August 10. The OIG's review of the available SHU security camera video revealed that the Morning Watch Operations Lieutenant was present in the SHU for approximately 7 minutes, during which time she conferred with Noel and Thomas, who were seated at and around the SHU Officers' Station in the common area of the SHU. The Morning Watch Operations Lieutenant told the OIG that she was not required to visit each tier or go to each individual cell during a lieutenant round, but rather the purpose of the Lieutenant round was for her to speak with the officers on duty. This description of a Lieutenant round

---

[81] 5 C.F.R. § 2635.101(b)(5); see also 5 C.F.R. § 2635.705(a).

[82] BOP Program Statement 5270.11.

[83] The Acting Evening Watch Activities Lieutenant also had oversight over the SHU during her overtime shift (4 p.m. to 10 p.m. on August 9, 2019) in an acting capacity. The Evening Watch Operations Lieutenant and the Acting Evening Watch Activities Lieutenant told the OIG that the Acting Evening Watch Activities Lieutenant did not supervise any institutional counts, which was due to the start and end time of her overtime shift. The Acting Evening Watch Activities Lieutenant also told the OIG that she conducted one round in the SHU sometime between 5 p.m. to 8 p.m., during which time she walked down all of the tiers.

is inconsistent with the statements of many other supervisors and BOP Lieutenant training, all of which emphasized the need for Lieutenants to walk down all of the SHU tiers during a round. During their interviews with the OIG, the Northeast Regional Director, the Warden, Associate Warden 1, and the Captain clarified that they expected a Lieutenant conducting a round in the SHU to check in with the officers, walk down each of the tiers in the SHU, speak with inmates, and address inmate concerns. They explained that the Lieutenants did not act responsibly if they did not walk down each of the tiers to check on the inmates in the SHU. As the Acting Evening Watch Activities Lieutenant explained, unlike inmates in general population, SHU inmates cannot approach a supervisor because they are confined within a cell. Further, the BOP Lieutenant training, which the Morning Watch Operations Lieutenant attended in 2011, taught that Operations Lieutenants were required to visit the SHU at least once during each shift and that "[t]his visit will be substantially more than just entering the unit, signing the log book, and talking with staff." Instead, Operations Lieutenants were trained to, among other things, walk through each range (or tier), inspect logs and reports, observe activities, and periodically observe counts within the SHU.

The OIG found that the failure of the Evening Watch Operations Lieutenant and the Morning Watch Operations Lieutenant to adequately supervise SHU staff, and of the Morning Watch Operations Lieutenant to adequately conduct a Lieutenant round in the SHU, which contributed to the SHU staff's failure to conduct mandatory rounds and counts, constituted a job performance failure.

C.   MCC New York Staff Allowed Epstein to Place an Unmonitored Telephone Call on August 9

The OIG's investigation and review revealed that on the night before his death, Epstein placed an unrecorded, unmonitored telephone call using a non-Inmate Telephone System line from 6:58 p.m. to 7:19 p.m. Other than an MCC New York call log, no other BOP records exist regarding this unmonitored call, including the identity of the person Epstein called or a summary of the conversation.

Federal regulations require that the Warden of each BOP institution establish procedures to monitor inmate telephone conversations, which is "done to preserve the security and orderly management of the institution and to protect the public."[84] For safety and security reasons, BOP policy requires that all inmate telephone calls be made through the Inmate Telephone System.[85] BOP policy recognizes that "on rare occasion, in times of crisis," inmates may be permitted to make a telephone call outside of the Inmate Telephone System. In such circumstances, the telephone "must be placed in a secure area (e.g., a locked office), and "must be set to record telephone calls." Additionally, the staff member coordinating the call must notify the BOP's Special Investigative Services via email, providing the inmate's name and register number, the date and time of the call, the number and name of the individual called, and the reason for the call. The Special Investigative Services must enter this information into the telephone recording system within 7 days.

The OIG's investigation determined that on August 9, 2019, Epstein asked to call his mother. The Unit Manager told the OIG that after Epstein's attorney visit had concluded, he agreed to allow Epstein to place a telephone call on an unrecorded legal line. The Unit Manager explained that it was his understanding that Epstein did not have the ability to place a telephone call through the Inmate Telephone System. The OIG's

---

[84] 28 U.S.C. § 540.102.

[85] BOP Program Statement P5264.08.

investigation established both that Epstein's mother was deceased at the time he asked to telephone her and that Epstein had been assigned the necessary documentation that would have allowed him to place calls through the Inmate Telephone System, although he did not take the necessary steps to complete the setup process that would have given him the ability to place calls through that system. The Captain told the OIG that when the Unit Manager was escorting Epstein from his attorney visit back to the SHU and Epstein's requested call was discussed, he told the Unit Manager that Epstein's telephone call had to be monitored and logged.

The Unit Manager told the OIG that he escorted Epstein from his attorney visit to the shower area of the SHU, where he connected a telephone into an unrecorded legal line and dialed the phone number provided by Epstein. The Unit Manager said that when a male answered the call, he handed the telephone to Epstein, and then left MCC New York for the day because his shift had ended. Before leaving the SHU, the Unit Manager said he told the Evening Watch SHU Officer in Charge, the Material Handler, and Noel, who were at the SHU Officers' Station, to make sure Epstein got his 15 minutes on the telephone, but he did not instruct them to monitor the telephone call. The Unit Manager admitted that he did not verify the recipient of the telephone call, and that neither he nor anyone monitored or logged the telephone call as required.

The OIG found that the Unit Manager violated BOP policy by allowing Epstein to make an unrecorded and unmonitored telephone call, and by failing to verify the telephone call recipient, monitor, and log the call. We further found that the Unit Manager exercised poor judgment when he left MCC New York while Epstein was still on the telephone call that the Unit Manager had arranged and failed to instruct the Evening Watch SHU Officer in Charge, the Material Handler, or Noel to monitor the call.

> D. MCC New York Staff Failed to Conduct and Document Cell Searches and Eliminate Safety Hazards in Epstein's Cell on August 9 Leaving Epstein with Excessive Linens in His Cell

The OIG's investigation and review determined that MCC New York staff assigned to the SHU on August 9, 2019, failed to conduct and document searches of Epstein's cell in the SHU. BOP policy requires that BOP staff routinely and irregularly search housing units.[86] MCC New York SHU Post Orders require that SHU staff conduct at least five cell searches each shift during daytime and evening hours (7:45 a.m. to 12 a.m.), in addition to other searches of SHU cells and common areas, and BOP policy and MCC New York SHU Post Orders require written documentation of cell searches. BOP policy explains that the purpose of cell searches is to, among other things, maintain sanitary conditions and eliminate safety hazards. To that end, MCC New York General Housing Unit Post Orders provide that when an inmate is transferred out of a facility, all of the inmate's linens should be taken to Receiving and Discharge.

The OIG reviewed MCC New York SHU TRUSCOPE entries for August 9, and identified only one cell search entered by MCC New York SHU staff for the entire day. During his interview with the OIG, the Day Watch SHU Officer in Charge stated that multiple cell searches were conducted in the MCC New York SHU on August 9; however, the Day Watch SHU Officer in Charge stated that he failed to document the cell searches within the TRUSCOPE system as required because he was too busy with other duties. The Day Watch SHU Officer in Charge further stated that any of the SHU staff could have logged the cell searches into

---

[86] BOP Program Statement 5521.06.

TRUSCOPE, but that it was primarily the SHU Officer in Charge's responsibility to do so. The Evening Watch SHU Officer in Charge told the OIG that he and other staff members did not conduct any cell searches during his shift in the SHU on August 9. Additionally, the OIG determined that there was an excessive amount of bed linen within Epstein's cell. The Captain reviewed photographs of Epstein's cell and told the OIG that the excessive linens were a security issue because they could give inmates materials to fashion an improvised noose or use as escape paraphernalia.

The OIG found that on August 9, 2019, the Day Watch SHU Officer in Charge either failed to conduct the required cell searches or failed to document the cell searches that he conducted in the SHU, and that the Evening Watch SHU Officer in Charge failed to ensure that MCC New York staff assigned to the SHU conducted cell searches and himself failed to log cell searches in violation of BOP policy and MCC New York SHU Post Orders. Additionally, the OIG found that it was a performance failure for the Day Watch SHU Officer in Charge, the Evening Watch SHU Officer in Charge, and Noel, who served as the SHU Officer in Charge during their respective shifts on August 9 and 10, 2019, to have permitted Epstein to have an excessive amount of linens in his cell.

E. MCC New York Staff Failed to Ensure that the Institution's Security Camera System was Fully Functional Resulting in Limited Recorded Video Evidence

This investigation and review revealed longstanding deficiencies with MCC New York's security camera system. These deficiencies resulted in nearly all of the cameras in and around the SHU where Epstein was being housed to not record video starting in late July 2019 and continuing through the date of Epstein's death on August 10, 2019. According to forensic analysis conducted by the FBI after Epstein's death, on July 29, 2019, a disk failure in MCC New York's DVR 2 system caused approximately half of the institution's cameras—including nearly all of the cameras in and around the SHU—to display only a live video feed with no video recording. MCC New York personnel did not learn of this system failure until 11 days later on August 8, 2019. MCC New York personnel determined that the DVR 2 system needed to be rebuilt to restore recording functionality. Despite the lack of recording functionality, this repair was not completed until after Epstein's death.

The Warden told the OIG that he was generally aware that there were problems with the camera system. The Warden sought and received approval from BOP to replace the entire camera system and in September 2018, BOP entered into contracts totaling over $730,000 to purchase new equipment for the camera replacement project. Although MCC New York management procured new DVR components approximately 9 months prior to Epstein's death, the new system was not installed in a timely manner. The new cameras required new conduit and wiring to be installed before the camera installation. Management faced staffing shortages, temporary rotating facility managers, and other competing priorities that did not allow for completion of the installation of the wiring or the new camera system. The OIG determined that as of August 2021—nearly 3 years after MCC New York contracted for replacement camera equipment—the system upgrade still had not been completed.[87]

---

[87] The BOP temporarily closed MCC New York in October 2021 due to substandard conditions that are unrelated to this investigation and review.

MCC New York's failure to ensure that its security camera system was fully functional and make timely repairs is consistent with the OIG's previous observations regarding weaknesses in the BOP's overall system of security cameras. Dating back to at least 2013, the OIG has repeatedly observed inadequacies in the BOP's overall system of security cameras, including inoperable cameras, an insufficient number of cameras, poor video quality, and inadequate video storage. In a 2016 report on the BOP's contraband interdiction efforts, the OIG identified specific deficiencies with the camera system, and recommended that the BOP evaluate the system to determine needed upgrades.[88] In response to the 2016 recommendation, the BOP assessed the camera systems at each institution over the next several years and determined that 45 of its 122 institutions, including MCC New York, required camera system upgrades. The BOP worked to upgrade the systems at those 45 institutions between 2019 and 2021. In June 2021, the BOP reported that it had updated all cameras at the 45 institutions with the latest software and equipment, and that it had installed additional cameras to bolster surveillance. However, as reported in an October 2021 Management Advisory Memorandum issued to the BOP, the OIG analyzed the reported upgrades at the 45 institutions and found that the BOP had addressed some but not all of the deficiencies described in the 2016 OIG report. In its 2021 Management Advisory Memorandum, the OIG recommended that the BOP develop a comprehensive strategic plan for transitioning to a fully digital security camera system. The BOP has provided the OIG with a strategic plan that includes estimated cost projections and timelines for addressing the camera system concerns and completing the system upgrades.[89] As of 2023, the OIG's 2021 recommendation remains open.

The BOP's failure to address the issue of functional security camera systems across the agency and at individual institutions presents an ongoing risk to the safety of BOP staff and inmates and has the potential to impair the investigation of and accountability for staff and inmate misconduct. It is imperative that the BOP prioritize the expeditious expansion and modernization of its security camera system to mitigate security risks.

II. Recommendations

The OIG investigation identified multiple shortcomings in BOP policies that should be further assessed to ensure the BOP can more effectively handle issues that arise in connection with the custody and care of inmates. The recommendations address issues related to and the custody and care of inmates at risk for suicide; measures designed to increase safety, such as staff rounds, inmate counts, and cell searches; and institutional security camera systems and staffing shortages, two longstanding issues for the BOP.

1. **The BOP should implement a process for assigning a cellmate following suicide watch or psychological observation, with criteria for exceptions based on the particular individual or security considerations.**

According to the MCC New York Institution Supplement policy to the Suicide Prevention Program Policy Statement 5324.08, inmates discharged from suicide watch will be assigned a cellmate. The supplemental

---

[88] U.S. DOJ OIG, *Review of the Federal Bureau of Prisons' Contraband Interdiction Efforts*, Evaluation and Inspections Report 16-05 (June 2016).

[89] U.S. DOJ OIG, *Notification of Needed Upgrades to the Federal Bureau of Prisons' Security Camera System*, Management Advisory Memorandum 22-001 (October 2021).

policy does not, however, describe how long the cellmate requirement should last or if any staff must approve the removal of the cellmate requirement. The Suicide Prevention Program Policy Statement 5324.08 does not describe any process or procedure that requires cellmate assignments for inmates coming off of suicide watch. The Warden stated there was no BOP policy mandating that an inmate coming off of suicide watch have a cellmate, but that doing so was "sound correctional judgment."

The OIG's investigation and review revealed that there were knowledge gaps among MCC New York staff regarding Epstein's cellmate requirement, indicating that improved communication with institutional staff would be beneficial. The OIG therefore recommends that the BOP implement a requirement that all inmates coming off of suicide watch or psychological observation to be assigned cellmates with criteria for exceptions based on the particular individual or security considerations, provide guidance for determining when a cellmate is no longer required, and implement a process for approving, documenting, and communicating to institutional staff the assignment and removal of cellmates for these inmates.

2. **The BOP should establish procedures to ensure inmates at high risk for suicide and for whom a cellmate is recommended will continue to have a cellmate until the recommendation is changed or rescinded, including establishing a contingency plan for cellmate re-assignment, with criteria for exceptions based on the particular individual or security considerations.**

The OIG's investigation and review found that there was no contingency plan in place to assign Epstein a new cellmate when his then-cellmate was transferred out of MCC New York. Although the failure to assign a new cellmate was due, in part, to SHU staff failing to make required notifications and supervisory staff failing to adequate supervise SHU staff, the gap in cellmate assignment was also due to the lack of a contingency plan. The Evening Watch SHU Officer in Charge told the OIG that although he knew that Epstein needed a new cellmate, he said that SHU staff did not have the authority to assign a new cellmate, which was consistent with what MCC New York supervisory personnel told the OIG. A contingency plan, such as a list of alternate cellmates, would have increased the likelihood that Epstein would not have been housed alone at the time of his death. The OIG therefore recommends that the BOP develop contingency plans for cellmate assignment for high-risk inmates with criteria for exceptions based on the particular individual or security considerations.

3. **The BOP should evaluate its current process for obtaining and documenting approval for social or legal visits while an inmate is on suicide watch or psychological observation, which allows for institution-specific variations in the process, and provide guidance on standard components that each institution should include in its process to mitigate security issues that can arise when an inmate is on suicide watch or psychological observation.**

According to the BOP's Suicide Prevention Program Policy Statement 5324.08 and the MCC New York Institution Supplement to the suicide prevention policy, inmates on suicide watch must be under constant observation by staff or trained inmate observers. The MCC New York Institution Supplement policy states that only with rare exceptions that are approved by the Captain as well by the Associate Warden of Programs will visitation either social or legal be permitted for inmates on suicide watch. Additionally, the

MCC New York Procedural Memorandum for Psychological Observation states that inmates on psychological observation will be continuously monitored by either an inmate companion or a staff member.

A review of the Suicide Watch Chronological Logs for July 23, 2019, revealed Epstein was allowed to leave the suicide watch room to visit with his attorneys for more than 6 hours. According to the Psychological Reconstruction conducted by the Assistant Director of the Reentry Services Division, during Epstein's psychological observation on July 24 through July 30, 2019, Epstein was also allowed to visit with his attorneys between 8–11 hours each day without direct observation. Although the MCC New York supplemental policy described an approval process for social and legal visits while an inmate is on suicide watch or psychological observation, the OIG found no evidence that Epstein's legal visits were approved by the Captain or an Associate Warden. Additionally, the BOP Suicide Prevention Program Policy Statement 5324.08 does not describe any process or procedures that allows an inmate to have legal or social visits while on suicide watch or psychological observation. The OIG therefore recommends that the BOP evaluate its current process for such visits to be approved and documented.

4. **The BOP should evaluate its methods of accounting for inmate whereabouts and wellbeing and make changes as may be appropriate to improve those methods through policy, training, or other measures.**

The OIG's investigation and review revealed many inmate accountability deficiencies. Most fundamentally, MCC New York staff assigned to the SHU on August 9 and 10, 2019, did not conduct many of the required rounds and inmate counts. Additionally, there was lacking or delayed documentation regarding inmates, including cell assignments and internal inmate transfers. Internal reports, such as the daily call out list and the Lieutenant log, are either not retained or subject to continuous modification, which reduces their utility as accountability tools. Therefore, the OIG recommends that the BOP evaluate its methods of accounting for inmate whereabouts and wellbeing and make changes as appropriate to improve those methods through policy, training, or other measures.

5. **BOP policy should clarify what is required of a Lieutenant when conducting a round.**

The OIG's investigation and review revealed significant gaps in the supervision of MCC New York staff assigned to the SHU. Although BOP policy requires MCC New York Lieutenants to conduct at least one round in the SHU during each shift, what was required of a Lieutenant during the round is not specified. During their interviews with the OIG, experienced MCC New York supervisory personnel described what should be done during a round, which is also reflected in BOP Lieutenant training, but this expectation was not memorialized in any BOP or MCC New York policy or Post Order. The OIG recommends that the BOP develop a policy, either at an agency-wide or institution-specific level, to define what is expected of supervisory personnel during a round in the SHU to better ensure that BOP staff are appropriately supervised.

6.   The BOP should continue to develop and implement plans to address staffing shortages at its prisons.

Since at least 2015, the OIG has repeatedly found the need for BOP to address staffing shortages, including medical staffing shortages.[90] This investigation and review revealed the direct impact of staffing deficiencies on inmate safety. For example, the Material Handler worked three consecutive shifts—24 hours straight—on August 9, 2019, which was certainly a contributory cause to the lack of adequate means of accounting for inmate location and wellbeing in the SHU. The Material Handler told the OIG that no one did the 10 p.m. SHU inmate count because they were tired. Additionally, the OIG's investigation and review found that in connection with MCC New York's upgrade of its security camera system, the BOP's Northeast Regional Office arranged for technicians from other BOP institutions to perform temporary duty (TDY) assignments to MCC New York to perform necessary mechanical, electrical, plumbing, and wiring work. Yet, during the course of the TDY rotations, work was not consistently conducted on the camera upgrade because sometimes TDY staff were used to cover shortages at MCC New York's custody posts. Without adequate staffing, the BOP cannot fulfill its mandate to ensure safe and secure correctional facilities. The OIG therefore recommends that the BOP continue to develop and implement plans to address staffing shortages at its institutions.

7.   The BOP should evaluate its cell search procedures and make changes as may be appropriate to improve those procedures through policy, training, or other measures.

The OIG's investigation and review found that there was an excessive amount of linens in Epstein's cell at the time of his death. BOP policy and MCC New York SHU Post Orders require that SHU cells be searched, but they do not specifically address the issue of excessive bed linens, which the Captain told the OIG present a safety hazard because an inmate can use them to harm themselves or escape from the institution. Therefore, the OIG recommends that the BOP evaluate its cell search procedures and make changes as may be appropriate to improve those procedures through policy, training, or other measures.

---

[90] U.S. DOJ OIG, *Analysis of the Federal Bureau of Prisons' Fiscal Year 2019 Overtime Hours and Costs*, Management Advisory Memorandum 21-011 (December 2020); U.S. DOJ OIG, *Review of the Federal Bureau of Prisons' Use of Restrictive Housing for Inmates with Mental Illness*, Evaluation and Inspections Division Report 17-05 (July 2017); U.S. DOJ OIG, *Audit of the Federal Bureau of Prisons' Contract No. DJBP0616BPA12004 Awarded to Spectrum Services, Inc., Victorville, California*, Audit Division Report 17-20 (March 2017); U.S. DOJ OIG, *Audit of the Federal Bureau of Prisons' Contract with CoreCivic, Inc. to Operate the Adams County Correctional Center in Natchez, Mississippi*, Audit Division Report 17-08 (December 2016); U.S. DOJ OIG, *Review of the Federal Bureau of Prisons' Medical Staffing Challenges*, Evaluation and Inspections Division Report 16-02 (March 2016); U.S. DOJ OIG, *Review of the Impact of an Aging Inmate Population on the Federal Bureau of Prisons*, Evaluation and Inspections Division Report 15-05 (May 2015). Additionally, multiple remote inspections the OIG conducted as part of its pandemic response oversight work revealed that staffing shortages impacted the BOP's ability to respond to inmates' medical needs during the Coronavirus Disease 2019 pandemic. These findings are summarized in the OIG's Capstone report.

8.   **The BOP should enhance existing policies regarding institutional security camera systems to ensure they specifically state that such systems must have the capacity to record video and that BOP institutions must conduct regular security camera system functionality checks.**

As discussed in the Conclusions section of this chapter, the OIG found that, even though the highest levels of leadership knew of the MCC New York security camera system's recurring deficiencies, prior to Epstein's death, no one was tasked with the responsibility of checking the security camera system on a routine basis to ensure that the system was functional. As a result, when on July 29, 2019, video from approximately half of the institution's security cameras was no longer being recorded, the problem went undetected for 11 days. The OIG also found that there are no BOP policies that specifically state that security camera systems must have the capacity to record or that institutional staff must perform periodic checks to ensure the camera system is fully functional. Cameras that are failing to provide good quality or any live video streams put the safety of BOP staff members and inmates at risk, and the lack of video recordings can potentially hinder investigations of wrongdoing by staff and inmates. The OIG therefore recommends that the BOP enhance existing policies and protocols so they specifically state that all institutional security camera systems must have the capacity to record, and that specified staff at each institution must conduct periodic checks of the security camera system to determine its operational status and take corrective action as soon as possible when the system is found to be inoperable. Such routine checks would help ensure that camera system malfunctions are detected and corrective actions are initiated in a timely manner.

Appendix A: The BOP's Response to the Draft Report

U. S. Department of Justice

Federal Bureau of Prisons

Central Office

Office of the Director

Washington, DC 20534

June 22, 2023

MEMORANDUM FOR SARAH E. LAKE
         ASSISTANT INSPECTOR GENERAL
         INVESTIGATIONS DIVISION

FROM: Colette S. Peters, Director

SUBJECT: Response to the Office of Inspector General's (OIG) Draft Report:
         Investigation and Review of the Federal Bureau of Prisons' Custody, Care,
         and Supervision of Jeffrey Epstein at the Metropolitan Correctional Center
         in New York, New York

The Bureau of Prisons (BOP) appreciates the opportunity to formally respond to the Office of the Inspector General's (OIG) above-referenced draft report. BOP values OIG's careful review of the facts and circumstances surrounding the death of Jeffrey Epstein and concurs with the recommendations resulting from this engagement. The lessons learned during the course of this engagement will be applied to the broader BOP correctional landscape.

The facts and circumstances related to those few BOP employees at MCC New York in this report reflect a failure to follow BOP's longstanding policies, regulations, and/or laws. While this misconduct described in this report is troubling, those who took part in it represent a very small percentage of the approximately 35,000 employees across more than 120 institutions who continue to strive for correctional excellence every day.

In the Report, OIG makes recommendations to enhance BOP policies and practices and improve accountability. In response to this and previous OIG and Government Accountability Office (GAO) engagements, BOP has already begun to evaluate nationwide trends and strengthen employee accountability.

In April of this year, BOP's leadership announced its new mission as "corrections professionals who foster a humane and secure environment and ensure public safety by preparing individuals for successful reentry into our communities." BOP's new core values include accountability, integrity, respect, compassion, and correctional excellence. Of note, our core value of accountability requires BOP employees to be responsible and transparent to the public, ourselves, and to those in our care and custody by the standards we establish, the actions we take, and the duties we perform. As reflected in our mission and core values, BOP is committed to providing a safe environment for both employees and adults in our custody.

Recommendation One: The BOP should implement a process for assigning a cellmate following suicide watch or psychological observation, with criteria for exceptions based on the particular individual or security considerations.

BOP's Response: The BOP recognizes the importance of careful monitoring of adults in custody who face mental health challenges and therefore concurs with this recommendation. Our practice is to carefully consider both the well-being and safety of the individual involved and overarching safety and security concerns. In the years since Mr. Epstein's death, the BOP has updated its process related to suicide watch and psychological observation. Under BOP's revised process, upon removal from suicide watch or psychological observation, psychologists make individualized care recommendations about clinical follow-up and other custodial concerns, including housing and cellmates. Mental health, custody, and unit team employees work collaboratively to ensure that each individual removed from suicide watch is housed appropriately.

Recommendation Two: The BOP should establish procedures to ensure inmates at high risk for suicide and for whom a cellmate is recommended will continue to have a cellmate until the recommendation is changed or rescinded, including establishing a contingency plan for cellmate re-assignment, with criteria for exceptions based on the particular individual or security considerations.

BOP's Response: The BOP concurs with this recommendation. As described in its response to Recommendation 1, BOP's current process related to suicide watch and psychological observation applies an individualized approach to the care and custody of adults in custody. Upon removal from suicide watch or psychological observation, individualized care recommendations are made by psychologists, custody, and unit team for each individual. BOP thoroughly evaluates each celling assignment on an individual basis for persons deemed to be at moderate to high risk for suicide.

Recommendation Three: The BOP should evaluate its current process for obtaining and documenting approval for social or legal visits while an inmate is on suicide watch or psychological observation, which allows for institution-specific variations in the process, and provide guidance on standard components that each institution should include in its process to mitigate security issues that can arise when an inmate is on suicide watch or psychological observation.

BOP's Response: The BOP concurs with this recommendation.

Recommendation Four: The BOP should evaluate its methods of accounting for inmate whereabouts and wellbeing and make changes as may be appropriate to improve those methods through policy, training, or other measures.

BOP's Response: The BOP concurs with this recommendation.

Recommendation Five: BOP policy should clarify what is required of a lieutenant when conducting a round.

BOP's Response: The BOP concurs with this recommendation.

Recommendation Six: The BOP should continue to develop and implement plans to address staffing shortages at its prisons.

BOP's Response: The BOP concurs with this recommendation. Hiring and retaining qualified personnel is a key priority and BOP has developed and implemented a multi-pronged approach that involves enhanced recruitment efforts and appropriate incentives. While the issues raised in the OIG's report were the result of employees failing to adhere to their duties, as opposed to a staffing shortage, the BOP welcomes the opportunity to continue the significant work that has already been undertaken and that is ongoing regarding staffing.

Recommendation Seven: The BOP should evaluate its cell search procedures and make changes as may be appropriate to improve those procedures through policy, training, or other measures.

BOP's Response: The BOP concurs with this recommendation.

Recommendation Eight: The BOP should enhance existing policies regarding institutional security camera systems to ensure they specifically state that such systems must have the capacity to record video and that BOP institutions must conduct regular security camera system functionality checks.

BOP's Response: The BOP concurs with this recommendation.

The BOP appreciates OIG's careful attention to this engagement, and its willingness to provide specific, feasible recommendations that address the root causes of issues raised in the incident described. Thank you for the opportunity to comment on this report. We look forward to working with OIG to close these recommendations.

Appendix B: OIG Analysis of the BOP's Response

The Office of the Inspector General (OIG) provided a draft of this report to the Federal Bureau of Prisons (BOP), and the BOP's response is incorporated as Appendix A. The BOP indicated in its response that it agreed with all eight recommendations.

The following provides the OIG's analysis of the BOP's response and a summary of the actions necessary to close the recommendations. The OIG requests that the BOP provide an update on the status of its response to the recommendations within 90 days of the issuance of this report.

Recommendation 1: The BOP should implement a process for assigning a cellmate following suicide watch or psychological observation, with criteria for exceptions based on the particular individual or security considerations.

Status: Resolved.

BOP Response: The BOP reported the following:

> The BOP recognizes the importance of careful monitoring of adults in custody who face mental health challenges and therefore concurs with this recommendation. Our practice is to carefully consider both the well-being and safety of the individual involved and overarching safety and security concerns. In the years since Mr. Epstein's death, the BOP has updated its process related to suicide watch and psychological observation. Under BOP's revised process, upon removal from suicide watch or psychological observation, psychologists make individualized care recommendations about clinical follow-up and other custodial concerns, including housing and cellmates. Mental health, custody, and unit team employees work collaboratively to ensure that each individual removed from suicide watch is housed appropriately.

OIG Analysis: The BOP's response is responsive to this recommendation. The OIG will consider whether to close this recommendation after the BOP (1) provides for the OIG's review a proposed process for assigning a cellmate following suicide watch or psychological observation, with criteria for exceptions based on the particular individual or security considerations, that addresses issues identified in the OIG's report; and (2) implements the process.

Recommendation 2: The BOP should establish procedures to ensure inmates at high risk for suicide and for whom a cellmate is recommended will continue to have a cellmate until the recommendation is changed or rescinded, including establishing a contingency plan for cellmate re-assignment, with criteria for exceptions based on the particular individual or security considerations.

Status: Resolved.

BOP Response: The BOP reported the following:

> The BOP concurs with this recommendation. As described in its response to Recommendation 1. BOP's current process related to suicide watch and psychological observation applies an

118

individualized approach to the care and custody of adults in custody. Upon removal from suicide watch or psychological observation, individualized care recommendations are made by psychologists, custody, and unit team for each individual. BOP thoroughly evaluates each celling assignment on an individual basis for persons deemed to be at moderate to high risk for suicide.

OIG Analysis: The BOP's response is not fully responsive to this recommendation. Recommendation 1 focuses on the process for assigning a cellmate following suicide watch and psychological observation. Recommendation 2, on the other hand, focuses on procedures to ensure that inmates at high risk for suicide and for whom a cellmate is recommended continue to have a cellmate until the recommendation is changed or rescinded. Our investigation and review determined that BOP employees did not take steps to ensure that Jeffrey Epstein continuously had a cellmate in response to Psychology Department personnel having determined that he needed to have an appropriate cellmate, and absent any indication that security or other considerations relating to Epstein warranted his not having a cellmate.

The OIG will consider whether to close this recommendation after the BOP (1) develops the recommended procedures; (2) provides the procedures to the OIG; and (3) implements the procedures.

Recommendation 3: **The BOP should evaluate its current process for obtaining and documenting approval for social or legal visits while an inmate is on suicide watch or psychological observation, which allows for institution-specific variations in the process, and provide guidance on standard components that each institution should include in its process to mitigate security issues that can arise when an inmate is on suicide watch or psychological observation**.

Status: Resolved.

BOP Response: The BOP reported the following:

> The BOP concurs with this recommendation.

OIG Analysis: The BOP concurred with this recommendation but did not provide any additional information. The OIG will consider whether to close this recommendation after the BOP (1) evaluates the current process for obtaining and documenting approval for social or legal visits while an inmate is on suicide watch or psychological observation; (2) provides guidance on standard components that each institution should include it is process; and (3) provides to the OIG documentation of the evaluation and the guidance forwarded to institutions for inclusion in their institution-specific processes.

Recommendation 4: **The BOP should evaluate its methods of accounting for inmate whereabouts and wellbeing and make changes as may be appropriate to improve those methods through policy, training, or other measures**.

Status: Resolved.

BOP Response: The BOP reported the following:

> The BOP concurs with this recommendation.

OIG Analysis: The BOP concurred with this recommendation but did not provide any additional information. The OIG will consider whether to close this recommendation after the BOP (1) evaluates its methods of accounting for inmate whereabouts and wellbeing; (2) makes any appropriate changes to improve those methods through policy, training, or other measures; and (3) provides documentation of evaluation and any appropriate changes to the OIG.

Recommendation 5: **BOP policy should clarify what is required of a Lieutenant when conducting a round.**

Status: Resolved.

BOP Response: The BOP reported the following:

> The BOP concurs with this recommendation.

OIG Analysis: The BOP concurred with this recommendation but did not provide any additional information. The OIG will consider whether to close this recommendation after the BOP (1) updates its policy to clarify what is required of a Lieutenant when conducting a round; (2) communicates the policy update to all relevant BOP employees; and (3) provides documentation of the policy update and communication to the OIG.

Recommendation 6: **The BOP should continue to develop and implement plans to address staffing shortages at its prisons.**

Status: Resolved.

BOP Response: The BOP reported the following:

> The BOP concurs with this recommendation. Hiring and retaining qualified personnel is a key priority and BOP has developed and implemented a multi-pronged approach that involves enhanced recruitment efforts and appropriate incentives. While the issues raised in the OIG's report were the result of employees failing to adhere to their duties, as opposed to a staffing shortage, the BOP welcomes the opportunity to continue the significant work that has already been undertaken and that is ongoing regarding staffing.

OIG Analysis: The BOP's response is responsive to the recommendation. The OIG will consider whether to close this recommendation after the BOP (1) develops and implements plans to address staffing shortages at its prisons and (2) provides documentation of such efforts to the OIG.

Recommendation 7: **The BOP should evaluate its cell search procedures and make changes as may be appropriate to improve those procedures through policy, training, or other measures.**

Status: Resolved.

BOP Response: The BOP reported the following:

> The BOP concurs with this recommendation.

OIG Analysis: The BOP concurred with this recommendation but did not provide any additional information. The OIG will consider whether to close this recommendation after the BOP (1) evaluates its cell search procedures; (2) makes any appropriate changes to those procedures through policy, training, or other measures; and (3) provides documentation of evaluation and any appropriate changes to the OIG.

Recommendation 8: The BOP should enhance existing policies regarding institutional security camera systems to ensure they specifically state that such systems must have the capacity to record video and that BOP institutions must conduct regular security camera system functionality checks.

Status: Resolved.

BOP Response: The BOP reported the following:

>   The BOP concurs with this recommendation.

OIG Analysis: The BOP concurred with this recommendation but did not provide any additional information. The OIG will consider whether to close this recommendation after the BOP (1) enhances existing policies regarding institutional camera systems to include the recommended language update; (2) communicates the policy update to all relevant BOP employees; and (3) provides documentation of the policy update and communication to the OIG.

www.ingramcontent.com/pod-product-compliance
Lightning Source LLC
Chambersburg PA
CBHW080241270326
41926CB00020B/4327